AF699722

How Commerce Became Legal

HOW COMMERCE BECAME LEGAL

Merchants and Market Governance in Nineteenth-Century Egypt

OMAR YOUSSEF CHETA

STANFORD UNIVERSITY PRESS
Stanford, California

Stanford University Press
Stanford, California

© 2025 by Omar Youssef Cheta. All rights reserved.

No part of this book may be reproduced or transmitted in any form or by any means, electronic or mechanical, including photocopying and recording, or in any information storage or retrieval system, without the prior written permission of Stanford University Press.

Library of Congress Cataloging-in-Publication Data

Names: Cheta, Omar Youssef, author.
Title: How commerce became legal : merchants and market governance in nineteenth-century Egypt / Omar Youssef Cheta.
Description: Stanford, California : Stanford University Press, 2025. | Includes bibliographical references and index.
Identifiers: LCCN 2025003574 (print) | LCCN 2025003575 (ebook) | ISBN 9781503643390 (cloth) | ISBN 9781503644083 (ebook)
Subjects: LCSH: Commercial law—Egypt—History—19th century. | Commercial courts—Egypt—History—19th century. | Merchants—Egypt—History—19th century. | Egypt—Commerce—History—19th century.
Classification: LCC KRM920 .C44 2025 (print) | LCC KRM920 (ebook) | DDC 343.6208/09034—dc23/eng/20250305
LC record available at https://lccn.loc.gov/2025003574
LC ebook record available at https://lccn.loc.gov/2025003575

Cover Design: Ann Weinstock
Cover Art: David Roberts, *Cairo, Looking West* (Shutterstock); seal of Tito Figari (Wikimedia); financial and legal documents (The National Archives, UK)
Typeset by Newgen in 10.5/13.9 Baskerville URW

The authorized representative in the EU for product safety and compliance is: Mare Nostrum Group B.V. | Mauritskade 21D | 1091 GC Amsterdam | The Netherlands | Email address: gpsr@mare-nostrum.co.uk | KVK chamber of commerce number: 96249943

For AbdelAziz EzzelArab
Mentor and friend

Contents

Illustrations

Acknowledgments

No historical study is complete without grappling with the question of origins. My interest in history as a discipline began when I studied economics at the American University in Cairo under AbdelAziz EzzelArab. His expansive approach to economic history as a teacher and researcher inspired me to follow the academic path that I did. I am indebted to him for showing me the importance of intellectual independence. It was through AbdelAziz that I also met Khaled Fahmy, who introduced me to the Egyptian National Archives, encouraged me to explore what went on inside nineteenth-century institutions, and reminded me to never reduce Egypt to a mere site for research. He continues to shape my thinking about studying the past with an eye to the future.

At New York University (NYU), I benefited tremendously from Zachary Lockman's impressive grasp of the methods of social history and Leslie Peirce's deep knowledge of Ottoman legal culture. Being in New York gave me the chance to take part in, or at least listen to, intellectually stimulating conversations, both formal and informal, in and around NYU. I learned a great deal from Aaron Jakes, Ahmad Shokr, Amir Moosavi, Ayelet Zoran Rosen, Bhavani Raman, Charles Anderson, Guy Burak, Ibrahim Kalkan, Irfana Hashmi, Jacques Revel, James E. Baldwin, Jane Burbank, Karam Nachar, Lara Harb, Lauren Benton, Leena Dallasheh, Michael Gilsenan, Mostafa Minawi, Nader Sohrabi, Nadim Bawalsa, On Barak, Rohit De, Samuel Dolbee, and Timothy Mitchell. My exposure to their wide-ranging interests and research agendas was intellectually transformative.

I am grateful to the staff of the different libraries and archives that I conducted research in, especially Dar al-Watha'iq al-Qawmiyya in Cairo and The National Archives in London. I am also thankful to Stephen Urgola and Ola Seif at the American University in Cairo's Rare Books and Special Collections Library for giving me access to the Tawil Papers, which form the basis of Chapter Two of this book. Archival research can be lonely and tedious, but luckily in my case, it was the context for building meaningful social and scholarly connections. In various archives and libraries, I am glad to have worked alongside Camille Cole, Hussein Elsayed, Malak Labib, Muhammad Mabruk Qutb, Peter Valenti, Ramazan Hakki Oztan, Rizk Nuri, Shehab Ismail, and Zoe Griffith. My experience of Dar al-Watha'iq in particular would not have been as rich were it not for the knowledge and generosity of Emad Helal and Nady Abdal-Ghaffar. Mohamed Saleh's groundbreaking research on nineteenth-century censuses alerted me to dimensions of Egyptian history that I was completely ignorant of. In Cairo, the daily walk to and from the archives with Matthew Ellis, when we thought about creative solutions to archival problems or laughed at their absurdity, was the highlight of my research journey.

I was lucky to receive a number of fellowships over the course of researching and writing this book. During the early phase of research, support from the Social Science Research Council (SSRC), the Middle Eastern and Islamic Studies Department at NYU, the Mellon Foundation (through the History Department at NYU), and the NYU Center for the Humanities were crucial. Since then, a Summer Stipend from the National Endowment for the Humanities (NEH), a Franklin Research Grant from the American Philosophical Society, and an Appleby-Mosher Grant from Syracuse University's Maxwell School gave me the opportunity to return to old archives and visit new ones. I am especially grateful to Susan Elvin Cooper at Bard College and Jill Ferguson and Sarah Workman at Syracuse University, who helped me identify and apply for these opportunities. I also thank Joumana Kalouch and Jacquelyn Sorci, who helped me read French and Italian-language documents. This book would not have been possible without Kate Wahl's support and the professionalism of the editorial team at Stanford University Press.

I received helpful feedback from colleagues at the annual meetings of the Middle East Studies Association, the American Historical Association, and the American Society for Legal History, as well as at smaller workshops at Bard College, City University of New York, Collège de France, Duke, Harvard, Syracuse, and Yale. I am grateful to the organizers, commentators, and co-panelists, especially Adam Mestyan, Alan Mikhail, Beth Baron, Ceyda Karamursel, Fahad Bishara, Farida Makar, Hussein Omar, Jeff Culang, Johan Mathew, Judith Surkis, Julia Stephens, Junaid Quadri, Kenneth Cuno, Mai Taha, Nada Moumtaz, Sherene Seikaly, Will Hanley, and Will Smiley. One of the most valuable aspects of these meetings was learning about other in-progress research projects. Henny Ziai, Olga Verlato, Pascale Ghazaleh, Samy Ayoub, Shana Minkin, and Terence Walz were all kind enough to answer extensive questions or share their unpublished drafts to help me advance my own work. Stephan Stohler was an ideal writing accountability partner. Bahaa EzzelArab, Laura Goffman, Sarah El-Kazaz, Stefano Giannini, and Waiel Ashry read and commented on draft chapters. Sadly, Kathryn Schwartz, a remarkable friend, scholar, and co-author, with whom I exchanged drafts and research ideas, left our world too soon. Some of her published work is cited here, but her critiques also informed several arguments present throughout the book.

I started writing this book when I was teaching at Bard College and finished it at Syracuse University, where I am currently based. I miss working with Bard's historians, especially Cecile Kuznitz, Christian Crouch, Greg Moynahan, Joel Perlmann, Richard Aldous, Robert Culp, and Tabetha Ewing. I am particularly proud of the unique Middle Eastern Studies program that I built with Beth Holt, Dina Ramadan, Sophia Stamatopoulou-Robbins, Tehseen Thaver, and Ziad Dallal. Outside of these disciplinary bases, my friendship with Rob Cioffi and Lauren Curtis defined my time at Bard. I am grateful to have joined Syracuse's History Department at this stage of my career. The commitment of colleagues to read each other's work and the mutual support among the junior faculty have been particularly inspiring. I thank them for welcoming me into their midst, especially Aaron Luedtke, Albrecht Diem, Amy Kallander, Brian Brege, Denisa Jashari, Junko Takeda, Martin Shanguhyia, Michael Ebner, Norman Kutcher, Osamah Khalil, Radha Kumar, Robert Terrell, Samantha Herrick, Susan Branson, and Tessa Murphy.

My only regret in taking as long as I did to write this book is that my father, Youssef, passed away before reading it. He was an avid reader of history and would have liked to see both our names on a book cover. My mother, Mervat El Azzouni, has been a constant source of love and wisdom. Her own academic career continues to inspire me. I am forever grateful to Lamis Abdelaaty for the life we are building together and, of course, for her limitless understanding during the moments of despair that writing generates every now and then. It takes our son, Mourad, a week to write a book (including illustrations) in second grade. I hope that one day he will understand why it took me longer.

Note on Transliteration

In general, I adopted a simplified version of the *International Journal of Middle East Studies* (IJMES) style guidelines, omitting diacritics except for the ʿayn (ʿ) and the hamza (ʾ).

In the case of transliterating names, however, a certain level of inconsistency in transliteration was unavoidable. The individuals we meet in this book had their names transcribed differently across (mostly legal) documents in multiple languages. For example, the Egyptian merchant "Musa al-ʿAqqad" appeared in British consular records as "Mussa El Akkad" and in Italian journalistic accounts as "Mussa El Accad." In Arabic language court documents, non-Arabic names were transcribed phonetically, with slight differences in spelling occurring occasionally within the same document. In the case of names that recur in the text, I standardized the spelling to avoid confusion, except in direct quotes. However, when a name only appeared once or in relation to a single episode (usually a legal case), I chose what I thought would be the most legible spelling, even if by usual transliteration standards it was irregular, as in the examples of "Yusuf Cohen" and "Ilario al-Hakim."

How Commerce Became Legal

INTRODUCTION

"How Come I Have Never Heard of Them?"

AS A TEACHER, I REMIND my students that, at some point during their research process, they should be ready to acknowledge that what they set out to explore might be a mirage. I emphasize that the subject that they will end up exploring will emerge only toward the end of that process as an answer to a question they had not yet asked. As a researcher, directing that same advice to myself is much harder. I set out to write a history of capitalism in Egypt before the British occupied the country in 1882. In preparing for archival work, I was convinced that my starting point should be the institutions of market of governance for a practical reason: the organization of Egypt's massive national archives, *Dar al-Watha'iq al-Qawmiyya* (DWQ), mirrored that of Egypt's nineteenth-century state bureaucracy. I would therefore begin by reading the archival paper trail of merchant courts, known in Arabic as *majalis al-tujjar*, and see where that would take me. But as soon as I embarked on that research journey, I started wondering if that subject was indeed a mirage.

In a break between conference panels, I struggled to explain my research agenda to a prominent historian of British-ruled Egypt. I described *majalis al-tujjar* as "mixed courts before the Mixed Courts," in reference to the famous institutions that distinguished the Egyptian judicial landscape under the British occupation. I went on to list their features: what rules they applied, who presided over them, what languages they operated in, and so forth. My interlocutor listened patiently and said the expected words of encouragement, but he seemed genuinely confused as we prepared to rejoin the conference. "How come I have never heard of them?" he asked. In the archives, I read volume after volume of merchant court proceedings, case summaries, internal regulations, and incoming and outgoing correspondence. As I got a glimpse of what went on inside these courts, I was thrown off by the abruptness with which certain cases were dismissed. The reasoning that court documents outlined in relation to these dismissals was curious. Merchants who approached the court to complain about a breached contract or an unpaid debt were told that their cases would not be heard because, according to the letter of the law, they were not really merchants. If merchant courts did not consider disputes among merchants, what was the reason for their existence, and what did this voluminous paper trail contain?

This book is my attempt to answer these two questions. Namely, why is a key institution of market governance—the merchant courts—practically unknown even to those who know the most about Egypt's modern history? And how did nineteenth-century legal mechanisms of market governance redefine the field of commerce in ways that survived through the decades of British colonial rule and into the postcolonial moment? To respond to these questions, I started in the institutional sphere of the courts but eventually departed from them to trace the trajectories of merchants and their agents into various social contexts. I completed my answer by defining the conceptual legal boundaries of the commercial sphere on the eve of British rule.

It is common for historians of the modern period to expect traces of the past to persist into the present. Their objects of study would have metamorphosed over a period of two centuries, but they could still draw a connecting line to the present, however faint, between institutions, ideas, urban planning, and the like. This contemporary relevance serves as a justification for their research agenda. For better or worse, this is not the case with *majalis al-tujjar* (sing. *majlis*), which left very weak and sporadic traces in the contemporary academic historical literature and, more strikingly, seems to have been little known even to state officials in the last two decades of the nineteenth century. Nationalist lawyers and British colonial administrators alike had a hazy idea about what they deemed the legal chaos of the mid-nineteenth century, which they agreed was not worth remembering. They thought of themselves as constituting a complete break with that past anyway. One century later, there was very little scholarship on this topic; most importantly was Jan Goldberg's authoritative article "On the Origins of *Majalis al-Tujjar* in Mid-Nineteenth Century Egypt."[1] That treatment of the question of origins aside, there were incidental references to the *majalis* but no systematic treatment of their inner workings or trajectory.

My initial interest in this one institution soon gave way to a broader engagement with the themes of law and capitalism in the decades preceding the British occupation of Egypt in 1882. To be specific, *How Commerce Became Legal* is a study of merchants and law practitioners and how they influenced and navigated a legally constituted realm of commerce in the years between the 1840s and 1870s. The book considers two levels of analysis: one structural, concentrating on ideas, state regulations, and institutions; the other social, reconstructing the life trajectories of individuals and the ways in which they engaged with or avoided these structures. The primary geographical focus in the following chapters is on Alexandria and Cairo. This choice reflects the scope of the archival evidence since these cities were where the merchant courts existed for the longest time, most litigants with access to them came from, and where the merchants and law practitioners I studied resided. However, because commerce is essentially about the circulation of commodities and money, other cities in Egypt, Sudan, Syria, and England are taken into account in relation to specific points of analysis. For example, Khartoum is mentioned quite a few times in relation to commercial disputes that were later litigated in Cairo, and Liverpool in relation to cotton prices affecting Alexandrian cotton exporters. The Egyptian countryside is always in the background of the study since it was also the site of exchange processes and the source of important commodities such as cotton. However, its secondary status in this book is the result of the mid-nineteenth century legal definition of commerce as an urban activity that is separate from rural-based exchanges, including, for example, those centered on agricultural land and crops.

It is difficult to categorize the historical individuals who feature in this study into one group based on a single economic activity. Some were wealthy merchants who were a part of long-distance trade networks.

Others worked on a small scale, trying to preserve a portion of an inheritance or to claim a commission for a service they performed. A common experience that tied them together was their belonging to the law-defined realm of commerce. For example, this realm encompassed those city-based merchants who positioned themselves as intermediaries, buying agricultural crops to sell them on the market and keeping their business ledgers in a particular order. It excluded wealthy landowners who made money through selling agricultural crops. Throughout the book, the reader will encounter diverse individuals whose presence within the realm of commerce serves as an illustration of its boundaries and inner workings. In addition to this prosopographical approach, three of the book's five chapters reconstruct in some detail the social and career trajectories of a Syrian-Alexandrian merchant, Butrus Tawil; a father and son who presided over Cairo's *majlis al-tujjar*, Musa and Hasan al-'Aqqad; and an Italian-Cairene law practitioner, Tito Figari.

No study of modern Egypt can overlook the far-reaching modern state-building project that was launched during the reign of Mehmed Ali (r. 1805–1848). There is a general agreement over the radical change in modes of government and social life that materialized during his reign. Yet the origins of his project are complex. Some historians highlighted reforms of his government that were applications of late eighteenth-century Ottoman policies. Others emphasized the role of the short-lived French occupation of Egypt (1798–1801) as the original source of political inspiration. A third group characterized some of his plans as an intensification of early modern developments that preceded the French occupation and were independent of Ottoman politics.[2] This book's focus on the realm of commerce, its legal constitution, and the experiences of individuals navigating it brings into sharp relief the interaction of the multiple origins of the nineteenth-century state in Egypt.

To begin with, we need to consider Egypt's place within the Ottoman world. The Ottoman conquest of Egypt in 1517 was a transformative moment in the empire's history. Hereafter, the Ottomans eliminated the rival Mamluk Empire, came to rule over a majority of Muslim subjects, expanded their power in the Mediterranean, dominated the Red Sea, claimed religious supremacy through ruling over

Islam's oldest centers of learning and holiest sites (they had defeated the Shi'i Safavids a few years before), and set the stage for their own "age of exploration" in the Indian Ocean.[3] The former seat of the Mamluk Empire, Cairo became an Ottoman city. Cairo's Ottoman governor was responsible for ensuring the continued flow of grain from the Egyptian countryside to Constantinople, a guarantee of political stability for early modern states. He was also given the responsibility of foreseeing the governance of the Hijaz and Yemen.[4]

The city's importance in Ottoman politics was proportionate to the sense of danger that it could engender. Several times during the seventeenth century, janissaries based in Cairo rebelled against and deposed the Ottoman governors of Egypt.[5] In the eighteenth century, military households, most famously the Qazdaglis, reinvented themselves as local notables and governed Egypt as equals, not subordinates, of the Ottoman sultan.[6] To understand Egypt's precarious position within the Ottoman Empire throughout these three centuries, from the sixteenth to the eighteenth, one has to keep in mind the character of early modern empires at large. From that angle, the shakiness of Constantinople's political grip over Cairo is not entirely surprising. The specificities of this relationship aside, rebel soldiers and governors were familiar figures in the early modern world, and they typically did not cross certain political lines. They would seize control of a province and promote alternative policies to the ones dictated from the imperial center. At the same time, they would abide by the existing imperial legal regime. For example, while a power struggle might play out in Cairo over whether to apply certain imperial administrative and fiscal policies, the authority of the Ottoman law code of Egypt *(Kanunname-i Misr)* was never in question.[7] Meanwhile, to enable the supply of provisions to the Ottoman center from Egypt, the imperial government relied on private merchants to serve as intermediaries following market imperatives.[8]

This was the situation that the French colonizers of Egypt in 1798 tried to dismantle. For a short three-year period, they struggled to co-opt local elites and to introduce new technologies and institutions of government. Among those was their establishment of a merchant court to be presided over by a group of Muslim and non-Muslim merchants. After all, in his proclamation to the Egyptian people, General Bonaparte had stated that his armies invaded because Egypt's practically autonomous rulers had "persecuted [French] merchants with all manner of extortion and violence."[9] In doing so, the French occupation undermined the existing mechanisms of dispute resolution in the commercial sphere. It also established a political connection with powerful local merchants, who, in addition to enabling the readjustment of the jurisdictional map, served as intermediaries between the colonial administration on one hand and the urban population (including the merchant class) and the governor of Hijaz on the other. As Pascale Ghazaleh has explained, the French reliance on "the merchants' connections and influence to secure their position" was a continuation of an Ottoman practice. However, this political connection was realized through novel institutions, and it came at the cost of eroding the independence of the merchants. For example, "[i]t seems plausible that Napoleon introduced the practice of confirming the head merchant's authority, a practice that continued after the expedition's departure."[10] It would become a hallmark of Mehmed Ali's reign and the modern state that became his legacy.

Before being identified with modern state building, we can think of Mehmed Ali as an early modern Ottoman rebel. He arrived in Egypt as an irregular soldier in a largely heterogeneous Ottoman military force that was itself a part of an Anglo-Ottoman joint force. Constantinople reluctantly agreed to appoint him as Egypt's governor (1805) after he had already seized power and became the *de facto* ruler of Cairo (1804) in the violent and chaotic aftermath of the French withdrawal (1801). Khaled Fahmy has famously argued that throughout his reign of over 40 years, Mehmed Ali was worried about the Ottomans removing him from the governorship of Egypt and that despite his ultimate military defeat and staggering territorial losses to Constantinople in 1840, he considered the Ottoman edict granting his descendants the hereditary governorship of Egypt as his crowning political achievement.[11] In the context of thinking of Mehmed Ali as an Ottoman governor, it should not be surprising that the modern state-building projects launched from Cairo and Constantinople during the nineteenth century resembled each other. A good example is the elimination of the older military elites: the "Massacre of the Mamluks" of 1811 and the "Auspicious Event" of 1826. It is not difficult to see why these moments of violence opened the way for building a new institution so central to the existence of the modern state, whether in Cairo or Constantinople: an army that is based on universal conscription. But what about more ordinary moments that expanded or redefined certain departments within the government? Could we assume that modern state building in Cairo and Constantinople was always closely related?

One way in which these questions were answered in the past was through attempts to identify the elite. For example, when and how did the Turkophone elite that surrounded Mehmed Ali assimilate into Egyptian society? When did Arabic take over Turkish as the language of the bureaucracy?[12] This book's approach differs in that it shifts the focus from these attempts to infer the self-image and *mentalité* of the elites—even if through a material explanation à la Ibrahim Abu-Lughod—toward an empirical study of institutional practices. To clarify, consider the challenge of situating an institution like the merchant courts of the mid-nineteenth century into its historical and imperial contexts. We know that there is a line of state-enacted institutions by the same name, *majlis al-tujjar*, that existed in Egypt's urban centers since the French occupation of 1798–1801 and during the 1820s. They all followed the same organizational principle, which was the "mixing" of merchants of different ethno-religious identities (e.g., Muslims and Christians or Egyptians and Turks). As we will see in more detail in Chapter One, the mid-1840s brought about a new kind of merchant court under the same name. Within a few years, these courts would adopt the newly issued Ottoman Code of Commerce as a source of legal authority. At the same time, many Ottoman cities hosted institutions with the same or very similar names.[13] In the absence of a systematic study of this plethora of merchant courts, a comparison is not possible.

Yet, given our current state of knowledge, it is reasonable to assume that in its mid-nineteenth-century iteration, Egypt's merchant courts were part of a broader Ottoman legal culture, even if they were not identical to merchant courts in other Ottoman cities. Through that lens, *How Commerce Became Legal* concretizes assumptions about the existence of a modern state in Egypt during the so-called "Khedival period," its attachment to the Ottoman Empire, and its position within capitalist trade networks. It does so beneath the surface of political competition that pit successive Ottoman sultans against Mehmed Ali and his successors, the Khedives, at different moments in the nineteenth century. In 1851, 'Abbas Pasha (r. 1848–1854) sent a diplomatic mission to Constantinople to negotiate, for over a year, the suspension of the newly instituted rule "requiring the Sultan's sanction for the execution of death sentences in Egypt."[14] Meanwhile, as we will see in the coming pages, merchant court officials, who were cognizant of the capitulations—and the coexistence of multiple jurisdictions that the capitulations entailed—used the terms "subjects of the sublime government" and "subjects of the local government" interchangeably. According to Will Hanley, the "persistence of Egyptians' Ottoman status" will continue not only under the Khedives but "well into the twentieth century."[15]

Beyond the question of Ottoman-ness, this book constitutes an engagement with two dynamic research areas within the historiography of the modern Middle East: law and capitalism. It is indebted to the breakthrough in the study of modern law that resulted from archival discoveries in the 1990s. Rudolph Peters spearheaded this research trend with studies of "Mehmed Ali's first Criminal Legislation," the codification of Islamic law, and new methods of investigating and punishing homicide.[16] In 1999, he published an influential article on "The Development of a Secular Judiciary in Egypt, 1842–1871," in which he offered a blueprint of the nineteenth-century state's judiciary, including the place of *shari'a* courts within it.[17] As described by Peters, the institution at the pinnacle of this multi-tiered judiciary since 1849 was *Majlis al-Ahkam* (Council of Ordinances), which served as the highest appellate court. Hence, the archives of *Majlis al-Ahkam* did not only contain short summaries of disputes and their legal resolution but extensive descriptions of disputes (and disputants) as they made their way through the judiciary, exposing methods of investigation, the interaction of Islamic and state-enacted laws, the possibility of appealing a court decision, and the sanctioning of punishment. This wealth of archival information became the basis of new studies like 'Imad Hilal's exploration of social life in the countryside[18] and Khaled Fahmy's reinterpretation of the place of *shari'a* in Egypt's modern legal regime.[19] These studies established the continued relevance of Islamic legal concepts to consecutive cycles of judicial reorganization. Parallel studies of the Ottoman center, such as Avi Rubin's examination of the Ottoman *Nizamiye* Courts[20] and Samy Ayoub's study of "Ottoman Imperial Authority and Late Hanafi Jurisprudence,"[21] offer important insights on the Ottoman legal regime as it existed in the imperial center. In this scholarship too, we see the survival of *shari'a* as an active element of legal reform programs. However, while these works focused on legislation and criminal and civil law, *How Commerce Became Legal* re-introduces commercial law and its site of application, the merchant courts, into the scholarly map of the Khedival, and by extension Ottoman, legal regimes.

The scholarly interest in extraterritoriality has often been the link between legal and economic histories of the Middle East. The capitulations are understood to have started as a benign, even useful, diplomatic arrangement between Middle Eastern and European states in the pre-modern period and to have gradually transformed into an insurmountable obstacle to the sovereignty of the Ottoman Empire in the nineteenth century. The existence of multiple jurisdictions for European subjects and protégés, and the economic privileges and legal immunity that came with it, hindered imperial programs for modernization. The Ottomans could neither consolidate the legal regime, which was necessary for building a centralized state, nor could their own subject merchants compete in trade. The result was a deficient sovereignty and "European economic penetration" of the Middle East.[22] In this account of the capitulations, Egypt features not simply as one part of the Ottoman Empire that was affected by this overarching politics but as the site where the capitulations were exploited the most.[23] *How Commerce Became Legal* engages with this dominant understanding from the standpoint of daily business and legal practices.

Yet, without necessarily challenging the fundamentals of this narrative, it is important to note two dimensions of extraterritoriality that will be particularly useful in understanding how the topic features in the following chapters. First, the capitulations should be understood as "part of the logic of the so-called *millet* system" whereby Europeans—merchants, in this case—"were a minority given substantial responsibilities of self-regulation in the Ottoman world."[24] Second, from an analytical perspective, reducing the historical significance of the capitulations to their exploitative effect on local economies is insufficient. For example, a recent study of nineteenth-century Egyptian censuses argued that local non-Muslims acquiring extraterritorial privileges through European consulates had a specific, practical motive: to achieve more certainty "about which law would apply to any contractual relationship in an environment where multiple legal systems co-existed."[25] As will be shown, the merchant courts of the mid-nineteenth century foreshadowed the Mixed Courts of 1875, in that they represented an attempt to overcome the issue of multiple jurisdictions in the realm of commerce without undermining the capitulatory regime.

In 1969, Roger Owen wrote in the introduction to his pathbreaking study of *Cotton and the Egyptian Economy* that "it would not be too much of an exaggeration to say that the economic history of Egypt during the nineteenth century was almost wholly shaped by cotton."[26] Evidence of that observation is present throughout the book. To remain focused on the book's main subject, which is the delineation of a law-defined sphere of commerce and how merchants were a part of that process, there is a particular juncture in that cotton-dominated economic history that deserves emphasis: the breakdown of the monopolies. Cotton was introduced as a cash crop in Egypt in 1821 and became, under a state monopoly, the economic engine of Mehmed Ali's state-building project. Almost two decades later, following Mehmed Ali's military defeat and as a part of his reintegration into the Ottoman fold as Egypt's governor and dynastic ruler, an Anglo-Ottoman treaty abolished monopolies. What ensued was the re-opening of Egypt's markets to private capital and the redefinition of state authority in the economy as a regulator (through the law), not a participant. The years following the end of the monopolies witnessed the legal defining of a new realm of commerce and the establishment of a commercial-legal infrastructure to facilitate dispute resolutions among merchants, both local and foreign. These developments created the space for the rise of the merchants (and their aides) whose trajectories are reconstructed in the following pages.

Despite its centrality to Egypt's modern history, the abolishment of the monopolies in 1841 does not typically feature as a starting (or turning) point in the most influential studies of state building. The standard starting point in these studies is 1882, in which the land regime generally, and the cotton economy specifically, became spheres of competition and/or cooperation between British imperialists, European capitalists, and Egyptian landowners. For example, in historicizing property law, Timothy Mitchell showed that the regime of private property of the late 1800s was created not only to regulate the ownership of agricultural land but, more importantly, to manage those who farmed that land.[27] In a more recent study, Aaron Jakes uncovered the economistic logic of the British colonial rule of Egypt. Specifically, he argued that the British aimed at creating the structural conditions that would enable the ruled classes to fulfill their narrow material interests while shutting down any space for politics or participation in government. The process for realizing this vision included new laws, institutions, and creating channels for European financial capital to flow into Egypt.[28] Both Mitchell and Jakes offer compelling explanations of the mechanisms of modern state-building in Egypt that focus on the period of direct British rule (1882 onward) and on the land regime. In other words, in these studies, state formation is an extension or a manifestation of land-related politics. In this book, I aim to introduce a dimension that is missing from these works—namely, commerce—to highlight the varied origins of state formation in modern Egypt. As I will show in Chapter Five, one of the tenets of the legal constitution of commerce in the mid-nineteenth century was separating the legal spheres of commerce and land.

Those who are familiar with the arch of Egyptian history in the long nineteenth century are likely to summarize it as beginning with the demise of merchants, the early modern social elites *par excellence*, and ending with their replacement by landowners. In between the beginning and the end, a modern state was built on the ruins of the old commercial class and inherited by the new landowning class. In *Fortunes urbaines et stratégies sociales*, Pascale Ghazaleh has documented in great detail how the wealthiest Cairene merchants tried to preserve and pass on their property during the establishment of Mehmed Ali's state while their political influence was being erased.[29] In a later article, she offered a cogent explanation for the change in merchants' influence by the end of Mehmed Ali's reign. At that point, they had lost their autonomy and could no longer wield wide political influence, but they "occup[ied] a new sphere: that of trade, narrowly defined."[30] A main goal of *How Commerce Became Legal* is to unpack this last observation through substantiating the "narrowly defined sphere," which I refer to as the "law-defined realm of commerce." Another objective of the book is to uncover the extent of merchants' influence, not through diplomacy but through their participation in maintaining the commercial-legal infrastructure, such as their role in interpreting Ottoman commercial law.

Instead of taking the claim regarding the state's co-optation of the merchants as an end point, *How Commerce Became Legal* offers a fairly detailed account of the life trajectories of three merchants and one law practitioner who focused on commercial litigation. Aware of the diminished political influence of these merchants compared to their early modern predecessors, this choice is influenced by recent historiographical trends that took shape after the economic crisis of 2008.[31] As intuitive as it is, William Sewell Jr.'s definition of the history of economic life is especially useful in this regard: "I simply mean the history of human participation in the production, exchange, and consumption of goods."[32] However, in engaging with it, the book's emphasis is not only to historicize "economic life" but also to explore the social context in which it is embedded and the experience of individuals who inhabited it. Therefore, the four figures who the reader will encounter in the next chapters—Butrus Tawil, Musa al-'Aqqad, Hasan Musa al-'Aqqad, and Tito Figari —are presented as individuals whose lives intersected with the law-defined realm of commerce and who had access to the commercial-legal infrastructure (both defined below). However, neither alone could account for their entire experience, which also included non-commercial interests, political affinities, and communal responsibilities. Capturing the complexity and expansiveness of their life trajectories helps us put the power of the modern state, and the reach of its institutions, in perspective.

The foundation of *How Commerce Became Legal* is empirical archival research. This is most evident in the sections that explain institutional structures and follow actual individuals who populated them in order to realize material goals, such as the fulfillment of a financial obligation. To clarify the framework of this study, there are two concepts used throughout it that should be highlighted. The first is the *commercial-legal infrastructure*, by which I mean the totality of all the rules and institutions that were created by the Khedival state to regulate commercial activities through state-sanctioned laws.[33] This *infrastructure* then included commercial legal codes, such as the Ottoman Code of Commerce. It also encompassed the institutions that were established to enact the rules such as merchant courts and debtor prisons. Accessing the commercial-legal infrastructure required abiding by certain norms (e.g., recordkeeping and the writing of contracts) and could be done through a particular form of legal representation. It did not encompass everyone who exchanged goods and money in a marketplace, nor was it a site where every instance of market exchange gone wrong could be settled. These exclusions, which may initially seem counterintuitive, constituted by default new boundaries for the realm of commercial activity. Of course, the term "*tijara*," simply translated as "trade" or "commerce," continued to be used widely as a seemingly self-evident term referring to any market exchange. However, in effect, there was now a second overlapping—but not identical—way in which the term "*tijara*" was used: to refer to the commercial exchanges that fell within the purview of the commercial-legal infrastructure. It is in reference to "*tijara*" in that sense that I use the term *law-defined realm of commerce.*

Using the term "market governance" to refer to the overall focus of the book is also significant. While this is a historical study that is based on extensive archival research, its core idea about the legal constitution of a sphere of material exchange (i.e., commerce) is influenced by Michel Foucault's writings on the concept of "government." In his words, "To govern . . . is to structure the possible field of action of others."[34] In the context of mid-nineteenth-century Egypt, the end of economic monopolies and the subsequent influx of private merchants to assume market-related activities that either did not exist previously or were not open to them overlapped with the establishment of state-enacted institutions that defined which exchanges were commercial (as opposed to "civil" or "familial") and therefore would be regulated through specialized commercial laws. The usefulness of this Foucauldian lens in studying a comparable setting can be seen in Ritu Birla's *Stages of Capital.*[35] Although focusing on a different geography and slightly later period (1870–1930), Birla's book shows that a primary effect of modern/colonial governance was to create a legal boundary between the market (i.e., the economy) and the family (i.e., indigenous culture). This demarcation evokes developments that were taking shape in Egypt before the British occupation.[36]

Another challenge pertaining to language is the translation of the name of the institution "*majlis al-tujjar.*" The norm among contemporary legal historians of Egypt is to translate the term "*majlis*" as "council." This is both linguistically accurate and serves an important analytical purpose, which is to preserve the difference between established *shari'a* courts, referred to in archival documents as "*mahakim al-shari'a,*" and modern state-organized judicial bodies, referred to as "*majalis al-siyasa.*" The latter were originally established as an extension of the government's administrative apparatus and were presided over by bureaucrats who applied state-issued laws but were not legally trained judges. According to this norm, conflating the terms "*mahkama*"/"court" and "*majlis*"/"council" obfuscates a historical reality. Despite its persuasive power, this line of thinking is more appropriate for histories of criminal and civil legal developments. It is less useful when applied to the realm of commerce for two reasons. First, while Islamic jurisprudence has historically served as an important legal field for the regulation of commerce, there was not a separate class of *shari'a* courts that specialized only in adjudicating commercial matters. Referring to "*majalis al-tujjar*" as merchant courts highlights their function while not interfering with the historiographical space reserved for *shari'a* courts. Second, the French occupation created the initial versions of the merchant court, and the Ottoman Code of Commerce was largely a translation of its French counterpart. Paris's eighteenth-century "tribunal de commerce" was very similar to Alexandria and Cairo's "*majlis al-tujjar*" in terms of its constitution, formalism, and, crucially, the fact that it was presided over by merchants. Hence, referring to the latter as "merchant courts" maintains the possibility for a global comparative approach to studying the practice of commercial law. Instead of stressing the idiosyncrasy of Khedival—or, for that matter, Ottoman—legal reforms, this translation choice enables their integration into a comparative scholarly field.

The first iteration of the DWQ as a repository of historical knowledge that is available for scholarly research dates to the interwar period. Modern Egypt's first sovereign ruler, Fu'ad I (r. 1917–1936), sponsored the writing of a national history centered on the achievements of Mehmed Ali's dynasty to which he belonged.[37] Today, one of the first discoveries that researchers make when they enter the DWQ is that its organization of documents corresponds to the bureaucratic design of the nineteenth-century state. To examine any topic, the researcher needs to conjecture the bureaucratic departments that most likely oversaw or overlapped with this topic and therefore generated a paper trail about it. But research work is not all intellectual. In his memoir-cum-ethnography of the DWQ, *My Egypt Archive*, Alan Mikhail offered an astute account of the challenges (and promise) of conducting historical research in Egypt in the past two decades. A leading and prolific historian of late Ottoman Egypt, he captured the difficulty of gaining permission to enter and use the archive and of convincing the staff that certain documents are relevant to one's approved (by state security officers) topic of research.[38] Frustration with missed chances and work under restrictive conditions aside, the path to writing an archivally based history of modern Egypt, even a social one, usually has to pass through a study of its bureaucratic institutions.

The archival sources at the center of this book are records of the Cairo Merchant Court (*majlis tujjar misr*). The court that was established in 1846 and functioned until 1876 had an interdependent relationship with its sister court in Alexandria, which was established one year earlier in 1845. The two merchant courts followed the same set of procedures and laws, and each served as a court of appeals for the other's decisions. Therefore, studying either of these merchant courts is a window into commercial and legal activities in both cities. The Cairo Merchant Court's proceedings offer details of merchant disputes that allow us to understand the norms of market exchange, contracting, and moneylending. In addition, this rare view of what unfolded inside the courthouse reveals the law in action. For example, we see the merchants presiding over the court disagree over the interpretation of commercial law and hear the voices of law practitioners bringing up procedural points from Ottoman and French legal codes in their attempt to prevail over their rivals. The merchant courts' correspondence with the European consulates and the higher departments of the Khedival bureaucracy brings to life how sovereignty was practiced on the ground. In other words, it allows us to look beyond the academic clichés of "European economic penetration" and the "abuse of the capitulations" toward an understanding of the day-to-day operation of merchants in what Lauren Benton termed "spaces of uneven sovereignty."[39]

Complementary to the merchant court archives, the book also draws on research in consular archives in The National Archives of the United Kingdom (TNA) and a collection of private business letters held by the American University in Cairo's Rare Books and Special Collections Library. British consular records were helpful in more than one way. As will be explained in more detail in Chapter One, the operation of the commercial-legal infrastructure depended on the cooperation of the European consulates with the Khedival state. Because market operations brought subjects of the Ottoman Empire with merchants who enjoyed extraterritorial privileges, understanding how their disputes were understood and processed from the consular side was equally important to what went on in the Khedival state-organized merchant courts. Reliance on the British records in particular is based on the assumption that, generally speaking, the European consulates interacted with the merchant courts in similar ways. The British consular archives have also preserved the original rulings that were issued to British subjects by the merchant courts of Cairo and Alexandria. Therefore, in addition to offering a view from the institution responsible for upholding extraterritorial privileges, it supplied a category of merchant court documents that were inaccessible in the DWQ. Finally, the private papers of Butrus Tawil, an Alexandria-based merchant, became the basis for another view that lay outside of local (governmental) and foreign institutions (consulates). The contents of this private archive are discussed in Chapter Two, which touches on how a merchant can belong in the law-defined realm of commerce but avoid using the commercial-legal infrastructure.

Before introducing the outline of the book, it is important to alert the reader to the way in which social identities are presented through it. The focus of this work is on the mechanisms of conducting commercial business and the related pursuit of litigation. An individual's religious, ethnic, or gender identities are highlighted only when they seem to further our understanding of these mechanisms. Hence, the reader will encounter the names of numerous individuals, of which some will be discussed in detail and others only presented briefly. For example, Chapter Two discusses the trajectory of one person: Butrus Tawil. It places him within Alexandria's resident Syrian community and, specifically, to its Greek Catholic denomination because these facts clarify his social world and decision to reside in Egypt as opposed to North or South America. However, in following Butrus, the reader will encounter many Syrian names such Mashaqah, Shumayyil, and Samnah. The chapter does not dwell on the precise communal significance of these connections beyond the fact that they existed. Similarly, when citing examples from merchant court cases, I prioritized their demonstrative potential in relation to certain processes such as the declaration of bankruptcy or the admissibility of evidence. Because the commercial-legal infrastructure was designed to facilitate dispute resolutions between locals (Egyptians and/or Ottomans) and foreigners (subjects and protégés of European states), I consistently clarified these identities. That those involved were Muslims, Christians, or Jews, or whether they were men or women, is in most cases clear from the naming patterns but is not pursued further. In other words, these discernible facts do not constitute the basis of a claim about how religious and gender identities interacted in the law-defined realm of commerce. They could, however, be a starting point for future research that brings identity-based questions to bear on our understanding of commerce and law in the nineteenth century.

The organization of the book reflects the interrelation of institutional structures and individual trajectories and experiences. Two chapters focusing on the structures of, and practices within, institutions serve as bookends. The three chapters in between revolve around individuals who engaged with these structures and practices. There are two reasons behind this design. First, it constitutes a practical demonstration of one of the book's main points: namely, that neither level of analysis should take priority over the other. If the arch of the book started with mapping out the relevant institutions and laws that defined the commercial realm and then moved to discuss the trajectories of individuals navigating them, it would create an incorrect impression that an all-powerful modern state apparatus created sound plans that were later populated by individuals. Alternatively, if the book started with individual trajectories, the implication would be that merchant strategies were conceived and realized irrespective of institutional constraints. The second reason is simpler: readability. The chapters discussing institutions and legal concepts were written with an eye to state-initiated top-down decisions and the totality of relevant individual actions. The latter is deduced mostly from snapshots of merchant disputes, for which the known context of each single case is often incomplete. In that sense, individual experiences are incidental to these chapters—collectively, they serve a methodological purpose, but individually they may appear to be of little importance. The chapters that focus on individual trajectories follow a more narrative style, which at times can stray away from the legal and economic focus as these individuals seamlessly entered and exited the law-defined realm of commerce.

Chapter One documents the layout of the commercial-legal infrastructure of mid-nineteenth-century Egypt. Historically, the idea of a judicial domain that is dedicated exclusively to commercial litigation may be understood as an extension of arbitration within early modern merchant guilds. It also has roots in the short-lived tribunals, known as *majalis al-tujjar*, that were created under direct state supervision during the French occupation of Egypt at the turn of the nineteenth century. The functioning of these dispute resolution mechanisms took into account either vocational—in the case of guilds—or ethno-religious—in the case of the French experiment—identities. The merchant courts, also known as *majalis al-tujjar*, that were at the center of Egypt's commercial-legal infrastructure starting in the 1840s were established with an eye to another kind of identity that was particularly relevant to the existing political reality: how to resolve disputes between local and foreign merchants in light of the existence of a regime of extraterritorial privileges. In addition to piecing together the chronology and highlighting the political logic and sources of legal authority underlying the merchant courts, the chapter discusses the groups that were well positioned to take advantage of them. Ultimately, what emerges is a multi-layered blueprint of the commercial-legal infrastructure that applied a hierarchy of laws—Khedival, Ottoman, and French—and that was a site of contestation and/or cooperation between local and foreign merchants, as well as Khedival state officials.

The ways through which merchants engaged this commercial legal infrastructure, however, were not straightforward. Some avoided litigation altogether (Chapter Two). Others engaged it from varying positions of power or technical expertise (Chapters Three and Four).

To put into perspective the strategy for seeking the resolution of commercial disputes outside of the purview of the state, Chapter Two reconstructs the life of a Syrian merchant who was based in Alexandria from at least the late 1850s and into the twentieth century. Butrus Yusuf Tawil—also known as Pierre Joseph Tawil—was engaged in a wide array of commercial activities, most importantly the cotton trade. Relying on agents and business associates, Butrus's business constituted a node in the network that tied cotton cultivators in the Egyptian countryside to the cotton factories of England. What stands out about Butrus's economic life is not his participation in the lucrative business of exporting Egyptian cotton, which is well documented in historical studies. Rather, it is his meticulous recordkeeping practices, which shed light on the daily operation of his commercial enterprise and raises questions about how he engaged with the nascent, law-defined realm of commerce. The chapter primarily utilizes Butrus's extensive business letters to demonstrate how he financed his commercial dealings, communicated with associates, supervised the movement of goods, and kept abreast of local and international markets. It also raises a question about Butrus's engagement with commercial law. His emphasis on keeping his business records in such a way that mirrored modern bureaucratic norms, residing in a major urban center, being acquainted with law practitioners, and enjoying the protection of a European consulate all point to his preparedness to benefit from the existing commercial-legal infrastructure. Yet he consistently avoided litigation.

For others, the merchant courts operated as sites of conflict resolution among merchant disputants. Chapter Three reconstructs the experiences of Musa al-'Aqqad and his son, Hasan Musa al-'Aqqad, as they navigated the law-defined realm of commerce. Unlike Butrus Tawil, who was careful to resolve his disputes outside of the courts, Musa and Hasan were among the merchants who presided over the Cairo Merchant Court. This leading position that they took turns assuming was hitherto undocumented, although both father and son are relatively known figures in the historiography of modern Egypt. Musa al-'Aqqad was a wealthy merchant and, later, landowner, with interests in Sudan and connections to the Khedive. His son, Hasan, is best known for his somewhat enigmatic role in the 'Urabi revolt, which the British defeated in 1882. This chapter offers a more nuanced account of their trajectories, not just as members of the Egyptian elite but, more importantly, as merchants who navigated the law-defined realm of commerce of the second half of the nineteenth century. A slave trader whose commercial activity was part of the southern expansion of the Khedival state, Musa al-'Aqqad first appeared in the Cairo Merchant Court as a litigant in the 1850s. Later, he sat on the same court alongside a small group of local and foreign merchants. Soon after he died, his heir, Hasan, occupied the same position but went further in simultaneously suing debtors and business-partners-turned-rivals before the same court. This chapter shows how a powerful clique of local merchants used the commercial-legal infrastructure to promote their own interests.

Over time, it became more common for powerful figures, like the al-'Aqqads, and ordinary merchants alike to access the commercial-legal infrastructure with the help of technical legal expertise. Hence is the relevance of the protagonist of the fourth chapter, Tito Figari "*al-avukatu*" (It. *avvocato*). A Damascus-born Italian, he studied law in France as part of a Khedival state-sponsored education mission in the 1850s. Upon his return, he did not join the Khedival government like other newly-minted lawyers but rather opted for private practice. His career choice poses an interesting question that cannot be answered if the existing historiography of the Egyptian legal profession is to be believed. If legal representation and professionalization were only introduced with the creation of the Mixed Courts in 1876, how did Tito Figari *al-avukatu* exist almost two decades earlier? As this chapter demonstrates, Tito was among the first generation of modern law practitioners who came to dominate the proceedings of the merchant courts starting in the 1860s. Like his peers, at first, Tito avoided referring to himself as an "*avukatu*" while pursuing his commercial law practice. As soon as the Mixed Courts opened, partially replacing the merchant courts, Tito seamlessly assumed the professional title and joined the newly-formed professional association of lawyers. This biographical account of Tito Figari follows him inside Cairo's merchant court as he made arguments that reflected his legal training and outside of it as he assumed leadership positions within Cairo's significant resident Italian community, established relations with Italian colonial explorers who passed through Egypt, crossed paths with Ahmad 'Urabi on the eve of his defeat, and represented Hasan Musa al-'Aqqad (discussed in the previous chapter) in court.

The complexities of Butrus Tawil, Musa and Hasan al-'Aqqad, and Tito Figari being merchants, merchant court officials, and law practitioners beg the question of what constituted commerce legally. The commercial-legal infrastructure consisted of a network of merchant courts, a hierarchy of laws, a set of procedures, and a group of powerful merchants. These features, which are described and animated throughout the book, capture the inner workings of this infrastructure and, in the case of Butrus, what happened on its margins. The final chapter deals with the question of boundaries, specifically who had access to the commercial-legal infrastructure and under which conditions. Relatedly, to what extent did the boundaries of the commercial-legal infrastructure and its effects constitute a break from *shari'a*, which was the source of laws governing commerce up until that point in the nineteenth century? At the center of the chapter are cases that the Cairo Merchant Court refused to hear on the grounds that they lay outside of its jurisdiction or, as the court documents put it, they were "not matters of commerce." These exclusions are noteworthy because they all concerned what seemed to be market exchanges. Scrutinizing the court's rationale, it becomes clear that these initially undetectable jurisdictional boundaries were meant to separate a law-defined realm of commerce from the land regime, inheritance arrangements, and civil—as opposed to commercial—debt. It was also tied to a related definition of which buyer/seller legally qualified as a merchant. In parallel to exploring these legal developments, the chapter explores their consistency with existing *shari'a* norms.

In lieu of a conclusion, the book ends with an epilogue that focuses on the afterlife of this moment of commercial legislation and practice. The period from the mid-1840s to the mid-1870s gave way to what Will Hanley refers to as "a 'settlement' that emerged in Egypt between 1875 and 1885."[40] During that decade, Egypt's legal map changed rapidly, all branches of government were gradually taken over by the British colonial administration, and the three decades of commercial and legal vibrancy that preceded—the subject of this book—were widely forgotten. Yet, as the epilogue shows, essential features of the mid-century law-defined commercial sphere persisted, such as the definition of commerce itself in new jurisprudential studies of commercial law, which were written by professional lawyers.

ONE

Institutions

THE COMMERCIAL-LEGAL INFRASTRUCTURE

IN 1853, THE DIRECTOR OF the military supplies wanted to establish the price of a particular kind of wood. Lacking the means to do so independently, he sent his request, along with a sample of the wood, to the Cairo Merchant Court. The panel of merchants, including Europeans, that presided over the court were used to this kind of request but did not have a ready answer. None of them, it seems, traded in wood, but they were all merchants and they followed a protocol. They enlisted the help of two experts in wood (*ahl khibrat sinf al-khashab*), *al-mu'allim* Almas Hanna and 'Ali, in order to calculate the common price of this particular kind of wood during the previous month. When the experts provided their opinion, a court clerk wrote it down and, in proper bureaucratic fashion, sent it along with the wood sample in a package sealed with red wax to the director of military supplies.[1] Three years later, the tax department (Ar. *Diwan al-Wirku*)[2] contacted the same merchant court to help with assessing the price of a certain woolen shawl "according to the ongoing norms" (*tatminaha bi-ma'rifatihim hasb al-usul al-jariya*). Accordingly, the court summoned a guild leader who, after examining the shawl, explained, "this shawl is worth nine *qurush* because it is not sewn (*ghayr mukhayyata*). A sewn [shawl] is worth eleven *qurush* because the sewing costs two *qurush*."[3]

These mundane anecdotes from the Khedival bureaucracy are symptomatic of a new state structure and a novel mode of market governance. The 1850s witnessed the reconfiguration of the Khedival state in the years following the death of Mehmed Ali Pasha. The expansive military confrontations of the 1830s had given way to a small army of 18,000 men and a long peace. Unlike his predecessors of a previous generation who would have been focused on providing for active-duty personnel engaged in combat in Syria, Anatolia, or the Peloponnese, the director of the military supplies in 1853 was probably in his office in Cairo preparing a budget for peacetime construction work. During the same period, the apparatus of tax collection and management had become more sophisticated. Under 'Abbas Pasha (r. 1848–1854) in particular, predictable tax revenues combined with reduced state expenditures (including a smaller army) sufficed to produce balanced state budgets.[4] The state's debts would start building up over the next two decades under the pressures of costly infrastructural projects, such as the Suez Canal, and financial speculation.

On the surface, these anecdotes about wood and wool show us that the Khedival state, the core of which was a massive modern bureaucracy, supported a military force and collected taxes during peacetime. They also harbor a less visible dynamic that could alter our understanding of Egypt, the model centralized province of the nineteenth-century Ottoman world.[5] What they show us, in effect, is that the inner workings of state institutions were facilitated by the expertise of private merchants. The latter presided over state-organized merchant courts and, in that capacity, oversaw the resolution of commercial disputes that included both local and foreign merchants. The European consulates cooperated with these merchant courts, and the Khedival state integrated them within its growing network of judicial councils (*majalis al-siyasa*) and enforced their rulings.[6] In this chapter, I trace the creation of the merchant courts in the context of the state's economic reorientation away from the monopolies of the 1820s–30s toward a free market from the 1840s onward. To explain how bureaucrats and merchants, including foreigners who enjoyed extraterritorial privileges under the capitulations, interacted, I also reconstruct the commercial-legal infrastructure—the totality of institutions, laws, and practices that regulated the domain of commerce. In other words, this chapter provides a practical demonstration of the blueprint of market governance during the middle decades of the nineteenth century.

Analytical Chronology

Residents of Cairo in the long nineteenth century would have certainly observed political ruptures: the French invasion, the power vacuum and civil war that followed, the gradual creation of a centralized state structure, and the ultimate co-optation of that state by the British occupation. They would have also experienced fluctuating prices and occasional food shortages. Yet it is unlikely that most people would have noticed the momentous changes underlying the regulation of the commercial economy. After all, the terms referring to merchants (*tujjar*, sing. *tajir*) and their multiple associations (*ta'ifa*, *jam'iyya*, *majlis*), as well as those denoting commercial activities (e.g., *tijara*, *bay' wa-shira'*, *akhth wa-'ata'*, *iflas*, *dayn*, *sharika*, *mudaraba*) and documents (e.g., *'aqd*, *sanad*, *waraqa*) had all remained seemingly unchanged. This was the language of commerce not only in the Arabic-speaking world but also wherever Islamic law was influential.[7] Linguistic stability, however, belied legislative and conceptual shifts that were initially only visible to government officials and, eventually, to an increasingly well-defined community of merchants. A systematic examination of the constitution of the Khedival state's legal infrastructure in relation to commerce reveals that a new mode of market governance was introduced in the mid-1840s and refined in the subsequent decades and that certain merchant groups, although with a drastically reduced autonomy compared to their status at the turn of the century, played a leading role in "governing" the market.

Up until the 1840s, documentary evidence of commercial activity could be found in various forums, namely, *shari'a* courts, guilds, consular courts, state-organized mixed tribunals, and *diwans*.[8] There were differences between these institutions but also significant potential overlap, especially in the absence of systematic and enforceable state coordination. Although equipped with a large Islamic legal tradition that focused on commerce, *shari'a* courts functioned frequently as a public registry, where merchants deposited contracts and agreements.[9] Merchants commonly attempted to resolve their disputes among themselves, either through soliciting the intervention of the chief merchant, the *shahbandar*, or within a guild structure.[10] Cairo's *shahbandar* was holding "judgment sessions" in his home to arbitrate merchant disputes as late as 1819.[11] The practical functions of these venues of dispute resolution were complementary. Whereas the *shari'a* court, an extension of the state apparatus, served as a repository of private commercial agreements, the guild *shaykh* and the *shahbandar*, who were largely independent of the state, enforced resolutions without leaving an extensive paper trail. Within the ensuing eighteen years, however, that arrangement would be reconstituted into a state-owned operation. In 1827, the *shahbandar* of Alexandria was judging merchant disputes but only with authorization from the governor Mehmed Ali, and starting in 1835, no longer in his capacity as *shahbandar* but as Mehmed Ali's appointed president of a state-organized commercial court.

The evidence of the state co-opting leading merchants is only known to us in broad outline. Within the first year of the brief French occupation of Egypt (1798–1801), Napoleon introduced commercial tribunals that were presided over by an equal number of Muslim and non-Muslim local merchants, who were in turn supervised by the French colonial administrators. The tribunals existed in three urban centers: the capital city of Cairo, which was also the location of Egypt's busiest riverine port, and the Mediterranean port towns of Dumyat and Rashid.[12] The actual operation of these tribunals has not been ascertained because they left no paper trail and are only known to us from narrative sources. Yet the logic behind their particular organization could be deduced from the general context. With the support of an invading army, the French colonial administration needed to bring the fragmented late-eighteenth-century provincial government under its control.[13] It also aimed to expand the domain of government at the expense of zones of elite autonomy. Therefore, the French targeted wealthy local merchants who held considerable power in the cities. They may have, for example, "introduced the practice of confirming the head merchant's authority," who had hitherto derived his authority from his election by private merchants.[14] They also organized tribunals that would bring merchant disputes that otherwise would have been handled within the merchant community into the view of the state. This process of co-optation had an identitarian character. Armed with orientalist knowledge about Muslims and their laws and anticipating an alliance with the Coptic community, the French organized the tribunals along confessional lines, as opposed to, for example, by guild or trade.[15]

By the end of the first decade of the nineteenth century, Mehmed Ali had established himself as the most powerful man in Egypt. He had received an investiture from the Ottoman sultan recognizing him as governor, and even though his astounding achievements of the 1820s and 1830s could not be predicted, he was already surrounding himself with a corps of loyal elites and consolidating power through a nascent but growing state apparatus. Accordingly, he continued the eighteenth-century trend, prominent in the Ottoman and French colonial administrations, to co-opt the merchants and, thus, reconstituted merchant tribunals, albeit along different lines. In the 1820s, he reportedly formed a merchant court in Rashid, a location that the French had supposedly also chosen for a merchant tribunal at the turn of the century.[16] In 1837, the *Siyasatname*, Mehmed Ali's outline of Egypt's centralized bureaucracy, listed three existing merchant courts. Two were located in Cairo, with one dedicated to local merchants and the other to European merchants (*Majlis al-Tujjar wa Majlis Tujjar Uruba*). Alexandria had the third court, which, beyond its location, is not described.[17] With little empirical evidence, it is unknown whether the court of local merchants followed the confessional logic that was introduced by the French or if locals or Europeans presided over the court in Alexandria. A later British consular record refers to the existence of "mixed tribunal[s]" that settled "commercial questions between British and Ottoman subjects" in Alexandria and Cairo "until the early part of 1843."[18] The information about these tribunals is brief and scattered. There may be, for example, a distinction between a merchant court dedicated to disputes that include *any* European merchant and a mixed tribunal that only hears cases between "British and Ottoman subjects." It is still reasonable to assume that if these were not parts of a continuously operating network of merchant tribunals, the references must be to judicial forums that were being formed and re-formed in quick succession to deal with similar kinds of questions.

Taken together, the discrete references to the discontinuous but recurring existence of some forum for commercial litigation that accommodated European interests in the 1790s, 1820s, 30s, and 40s are noteworthy. They reflect a growing interest within the state apparatus to administer private commercial disputes, including ones that involved European interests or individuals. One important factor to consider when thinking about the scope of these courts is Mehmed Ali's growing monopoly over the trade of agricultural crops, initially with grain in 1811 and significantly with the introduction of long-staple cotton in 1821. Under those monopolies, local merchants could survive only through conducting business with Mehmed Ali's government, while those who engaged in foreign trade needed the protection of European consuls.[19] In other words, the commercial dealings that would have led private merchants to a merchant court were probably quite sparse.

Consistent with the existence of an expansive state monopoly over trade, as well as other areas of economic activity, the operation of these courts must have been overshadowed by a more pressing concern and one that was different from regulating inter-merchant relations, namely, the interactions between merchants and state agents.[20] Therefore, by contrast to the brief information it included about the courts, the *Siyasatname* outlined detailed rules for the bureaucrats who were tasked with facilitating state commercial dealings with independent merchants. The regulations explained to the bureaucrats how to select merchants for commercial business with the government, defined what would be considered as unacceptable preferential treatment, and included instructions on how to collect outstanding debts owed by private merchants to the government.[21] The latter ranged from the confiscation of an insolvent merchant's possessions to rescheduling debts over a maximum period of fifteen years and offering partial debt forgiveness.[22] The *Siyasatname* also threatened the bureaucrats with punitive measures if they failed to carry out those regulations. Imprisonment would be the fate of the bureaucrats who would enable insolvent debtors to trade in government-owned goods (*al-ashya al-miriyya*). The harsh punishment was meant to ensure that bureaucrats would thoroughly investigate the financial history, solvency, and reputation of the chosen merchants.[23]

The application of the *Siyasatname*'s regulations, however, could not have been a straightforward matter. The bureaucrats who were put in charge of carrying out these government policies soon discovered that they had to rely on the merchants whom they were supposed to hold sway over. On the one hand, merchants who wanted to buy from the government had first to obtain the relevant bureaucratic permission. On the other hand, the "leaders of the European and Arab [*sic*] merchants" (*'umad al-tujjar al-ifrank w-al-'arab*) were expected to compile comprehensive lists of merchants' names and provide them to the bureaucrats in order to facilitate and standardize the process of locating suppliers of goods to the government.[24] This practical attempt to enumerate all potential merchants in Egypt meant that "[i]f a passerby (*'abir tariq*) wanted to buy something [from the government], nothing should be sold to him unless he brought an authorization . . . ."[25] The efforts to differentiate between *bona fide* merchants and occasional or opportunistic buyers or sellers that became established bureaucratic practices in the late 1830s will become a major bone of contention for the jurisdiction of the merchant courts from the 1840s onward, as will be discussed in detail in Chapter Five.

European merchants were explicitly mentioned in the *Siyasatname* as a separate group but with no indication in the text of that document that the government would treat them differently. Yet narrative sources and European consular reports are filled with evidence to the contrary. In the late eighteenth century, ahead of Napoleon's invasion, it appears that European merchants residing in Egypt had become increasingly restricted in their ability to conduct business or even to move around Cairo, to the extent that some, like the Levant Company, closed its offices altogether, while others relocated out of Egypt, leaving their business affairs in the hands of Levantine deputies.[26] This state of affairs had material and political repercussions. It served, for instance, as a part of Napoleon's pretext for invading Egypt, as he specified in his proclamation to the people of Cairo.[27] A community of foreign merchants started to re-form somewhat surprisingly in the context of Mehmed Ali's monopolies.[28] European consuls also extended protection to local merchants active in the trans-Mediterranean import and export businesses. It was probably the case that, until the early 1840s, the intervention of the European consuls, and the cooperation between the chief European merchants and the government in the context of the abovementioned *Majlis Tujjar Uruba* (in existence in 1837) or the mixed tribunals open to British subjects (in existence until early 1843), sufficed. However, the survival of that model was conditional upon the existence of a limited sphere of private business activity.

These conditions changed radically with the formal abolition of the monopoly system in 1841 and the subsequent expansion of a free market that was inhabited by local and European merchants. The economic changes paralleled Mehmed Ali's most extensive organization of the judiciary in 1842, which was centered on establishing *al-Jam'iyya al-Haqqaniyya*, the first state-organized body, located outside of (and above) the existing courts, to specialize exclusively in legal matters "such as the investigation of the legality of sentences, settling administrative disputes and trying high officials in the first instance."[29] The concurrent creation of a free market and a state-organized legal infrastructure formed the context for reviving the concept of a court that would be dedicated solely to resolving merchant disputes. The rapid rise in private commercial activity and the practical absence of a commercial-legal infrastructure in the late 1830s and early 1840s must have presented merchants with great opportunities and risks. From the standpoint of the consuls, this situation was untenable. Their subjects, who, under the capitulations, enjoyed tax benefits and immunity from many local laws, were facing an unexpected problem. Their extraterritorial privileges seemed hollow now that they were conducting business more extensively with local merchants—there was no clear forum for resolving commercial disputes, and there was no effective mechanism for collecting outstanding debts. The scale and geographic range (now spanning rural Egypt) of "mixed" commercial transactions exceeded the capacities of the state-organized legal infrastructure and of the consulates. The latter were equipped to handle straightforward cases, such as the transfer of estates in the case of death, but were now finding it increasingly difficult to even determine which individuals were indeed subjects or protégés of their respective governments.[30]

The first documented effort to establish an effective merchant court was in May 1845, when the consuls of France, Britain, Austria, Prussia, and Russia met in Alexandria to discuss the matter and coordinate action. Next, they contacted Artin Bey, the director of Commerce and Foreign Affairs, to criticize the inability of the existing merchant courts (probably those mentioned in the *Siyasatname* of 1837) to resolve commercial disputes that ensued between local and European merchants. They proposed the reconstitution of these courts as "mixed" courts, with an equal number of European and local merchants presiding over them and a written statute serving as an authoritative legal reference.[31] The general outline of their suggestion was consistent with Mehmed Ali's state's ongoing effort to expand and refine the legal infrastructure. Within three months, a committee formed by Artin Bey issued the statute of the reformed merchant courts (*Tartib Majalis al-Tujjar*).[32] It consisted of nineteen articles detailing the courts' staff job descriptions, court procedures, and a number of substantive instructions regarding debt-related disputes. According to this statute, the merchant court in Alexandria would be the first court to operate according to the new rules under the presidency of a certain Ali Bey, a senior government official.[33] A court in Cairo would follow soon afterward.

Hence, the term "*majlis al-tujjar*," already in circulation for decades to refer to merchant-operated councils or ad hoc tribunals, came to signify an institutionalized merchant court with a stable and defined position within the state's legal infrastructure, exclusive jurisdiction over a subarea within the law, as well as a written statute enumerating its internal procedures. After a short number of years, it would be linked to Ottoman and French commercial legal codes. While the term "*mahkama*" was reserved, at least in theory, for *shari'a* courts that were presided over by a Muslim magistrate (Ar. *qadi*), bureaucratic documents on occasion have referred to the newly reconstituted merchant courts by that term—a tendency that could be observed in both Egypt and the Ottoman center. Before turning to the structure of the merchant courts, how it changed over time, and what it can tell us about the creation of a new mode of market governance, we should consider two features of the merchant courts that pertain to their position in relation to contemporaneous Ottoman imperial policy and the interests of the courts' main constituencies in Egypt.

Jan Goldberg launched a successful "archeological attempt" to accurately reconstruct when and how the merchant courts were created. He concluded that the courts were not Ottoman but Egyptian in origin. Specifically, he argued that the reconstitution of the merchant courts in 1845 was the result of the convergence of official and commercial European and Egyptian desires and capabilities, independently of Ottoman imperial policy, which only turned its attention to the creation of a vast network of merchant courts several years later in 1848. This empirically-grounded claim, which was made regarding the moment of the creation of the courts, does not discount the hypothesis that legal innovations existed within a broader Ottoman legal culture. The fact that an imperial province may precede the center in instituting a particular kind of practice or bureaucratic department was not unheard of. While the development of the mechanisms and legal thought that animated market governance in Cairo and Istanbul were not fully synchronized, they tended to converge over time.

Because of their "mixed" constitution, which included European and local merchants, the creation of new merchant courts in the mid-1840s in the context of the capitulations raises the question of who these courts were expected to benefit. Yet, rather than imposing a binary lens of "local versus European," it would be more useful to think of the opportunities and limitations that the existence of the merchant courts afforded to the consulates and their subjects, Egypt's autonomous provincial government, and powerful local merchants. For the European consulates, the existence of an effective merchant court with significant European representation solved two problems. It ensured that their subjects who engaged in commerce would be able to carry out business and accumulate wealth and that the bureaucratic burden of sustaining this juridical operation would fall on the government of Egypt. Yet, at the same time, the consulates could no longer shield their subjects completely from Ottoman or Egyptian laws. The Khedival government gained the ability to monitor small-scale merchant activity, which otherwise would have occurred outside of its purview. Additionally, it expanded its legal control of commercial activity by setting the rules for litigation and even defining what constituted commerce (discussed in detail in Chapter Five). Finally, the merchants, having seen their power dwindle over several decades, managed to institutionalize their position within the government as the interpreters of commercial law and the potential beneficiaries of the courts.

In the following section, I explain how these relationships played out within the commercial-legal infrastructure.

Positioning

The merchant courts under study existed continuously for three decades. They were established in the mid-1840s through the reconstitution of previous, disconnected merchant tribunal experiments, and they were terminated at the moment of the creation of the Mixed Courts in the mid-1870s. During these thirty years, the merchant courts were a permanent feature of Egypt's legal map. Bureaucrats on the payroll of the Khedival government were appointed to the merchant courts. Correspondence between them, on the one hand, and other bureaucratic departments and European consulates on the other flowed continuously. The paper trail produced by the courts reflected the same features of legal formalism that are to be found in (near) contemporaneous court documents in Khedival Egypt and the Ottoman Empire more broadly.[34] This permanence, however, is not to be mistaken for stagnation. Between 1845 and 1876, the statutes governing the inner workings of the merchant courts were revised multiple times to allow for the incorporation of new procedures, such as legal representation, and of the courts themselves into the Ottoman legal regime through ascertaining the authority of the Ottoman Code of Commerce. Geographically, the merchant court network, which was originally to be found in the main port city of Alexandria and the capital city of Cairo, expanded in 1856 to another Mediterranean port city, Dumyat, and eventually to Asyut in upper Egypt. The Khedival government issued further regulations to allow for the litigation of small-scale commercial disputes in the countryside, in rural town police departments, and in provincial councils, thus effectively enabling the merchant courts to focus on disputes over substantial commercial value. In parallel, the government shifted the merchant courts' administrative place within the bureaucracy from their respective local governorates to Egypt's highest court, *Majlis al-Ahkam*.[35] At that point, the merchant courts would also allow for two degrees of litigation.

As established components of the bureaucracy, albeit ones that were being reconfigured and moved around, the merchant courts resembled other nineteenth-century judicial councils in that they were legal forums that were concerned with a particular category of social activity, namely commerce, rather than with the religious affiliation of the litigants. Still, certain structural features set them apart from other forums. The merchant courts reserved a primary role for leading merchants to resolve commercial disputes. Thus, they extended the long-held practice of merchants soliciting the mediation of a *shahbandar* or seeking the justice of their peers within guilds, ad hoc tribunals, or arbitration sessions.[36] The structure of the merchant courts also adhered to the extraterritorial privileges granted by the capitulations. As such, the courts did not summon European merchants as defendants. Moreover, the courts would be presided over by a combination of local and European merchants. As a judicial forum that was embedded within the Khedival bureaucracy, each merchant court was officially headed by a senior bureaucrat, who oversaw the deliberations of the merchants presiding over the court and served as a tie-breaker whenever they reached a deadlock. In the overwhelming majority of cases consulted in this book, local and foreign merchants issued unanimous decisions. On fewer occasions, they reached majority decisions, and only rarely did they split evenly and create the condition for the bureaucrat president to determine the outcome of a case. In the unusual situations where local and foreign merchants reached an impasse after voting as unified blocs, the president did not vote consistently with either party.

Thus emerges an empirically-based representation of the merchant courts as integral to the Khedival bureaucracy while, at the same time, possessing structural features that make them consistent with, and supportive of, the capitulatory regime. What follows is an attempt to answer a question that emerges from this representation: Did nineteenth-century historical actors, both merchants and state officials, actually think of the merchant courts as state-organized judicial forums? Or, alternatively, did they consider them to be state-sponsored institutions in the service of European interests?

My answer revolves around three interconnected observations: the ubiquity of a bureaucratic discourse on mediation, the ambiguity surrounding the localness or foreignness of the merchant courts, and the attempt to level representation among the ranks of those presiding over these courts. To keep this answer empirically grounded, I will refer to British merchants—metropolitan citizens as well as colonial subjects—in particular as examples of the larger and more diverse community of European merchants operating in Egypt in the mid-nineteenth century.

Archival records show that the British consulate facilitated and recorded the contacts between British merchants and the merchant courts or the Khedival bureaucracy more generally. Those British merchants who appeared in the merchant courts, either in person or through legal representatives, had to go through consular channels first. In parallel with the increased awareness about the existence of functional merchant courts, British merchants were turning to their consulates not with requests to directly adjudicate disputes with Ottoman merchants but to petition the consul to bring their cases to the merchant courts. After the court ruled on the matter, those merchants would often return to the consulate to report that a favorable decision was not carried out or to complain about what they deemed to be an unfair court ruling. In the case of the latter, the merchants had to appeal the decision before a different merchant court, again, with the consulate's approval. Once a case was finally closed, the merchant court would send its final decision to the consulate, where the plaintiff would collect his or her copy. Interestingly, the range of actions available to the Khedival government in relation to local merchants who wanted to sue their British counterparts before the consular courts was very similar. Whenever the British consular court needed to summon a local or Ottoman merchant, those referred to in the archival record as "subjects of the local government" or "subjects of the sublime state," it submitted a request to the police department, which would notify the person in question. On one occasion at least, the police department helped an Ottoman subject locate a legal practitioner to represent him before the British consulate.[37]

British consular and Khedival government officials thought of their roles as intermediaries (Ar. *wasit*). The widespread governmental mediation that occurred on both ends of commercial litigation influenced the process of possessing and circulating private commercial capital. Yet, despite the apparent resemblance between the consular and Khedival state self-definitions, they were positioned to influence the process of commercial litigation slightly differently. The British consulate, like other European consulates, could disrupt the operation of the multi-jurisdictional legal system by not cooperating with the Khedival government. Merchant court records include numerous examples of European merchants who defied a court's summons in spite of repeated requests to their respective consulates.[38] The merchant courts were powerless in the face of this lack of cooperation. The motives behind such non-action are unascertainable. They could have been employed strategically to protect a British subject from being bound by an impending unfavorable court decision or simply resulted from the incapacity of the European consulates to locate, not to mention persuade, some of their subjects who resided in Egypt to go to the merchant court.

While European consulates often did not respond, the Khedival government always answered queries, petitions, and other correspondence. Government-issued correspondence arrived in the British consulate on a daily basis, where it was annotated and archived. However, these frequent communications did not always contain positive responses to the British consulates' requests. The various branches of the Khedival government often explained their refusal to cooperate with the consulates in terms of bureaucratic or legal specialization. In a telling example, the British consulate requested that the police department sequester Muhammad Sha'rawi's property for failing to pay a debt he owed to a British subject. The police department did not grant the request. It explained its decision by asserting that it was "only an executive government agency that carries out the rulings it receives from administrative and commercial councils (*ma hiyya illa hukuma ijra'iyya lima yasdur laha min ahkam al-majalis al-siyasiyya w-al-tijariyya*)."[39] The answer could point in several directions: a sign of the administrative autonomy of the merchant courts, an attempt on the part of the police department to shield a local subject, a narrow bureaucratic concern about following procedure, or even a manifestation of the boundary between executive and judicial powers.

To summarize the argument so far, the ability to suspend cooperation between the consulates and the government was an essential feature of the multi-jurisdictional legal system of nineteenth-century Egypt. The Khedival government and the British consulates acted within a framework of reciprocity. As mediators between British and Ottoman subjects, they cooperated and often succeeded in bringing mixed disputes to successful resolutions. Yet, because their cooperation was necessary, they were also capable of bringing the operation of this legal system to a halt. In such cases, the consulates dismissed governmental requests for cooperation, and government agencies stressed their administrative autonomy at the expense of the imagined ideal of a unified governmental actor.

A consulate's decision to cooperate with the Khedival government and serve as a mediator between its own subjects and the merchant court network may have relied on characterizing the merchant courts as "mixed" or "native." The courts were mixed because they were presided over jointly by local and European merchants, with the latter chosen collectively by the European consuls. At the same time, the courts were situated in the Khedival state bureaucracy, which provided them with the physical space they occupied, the registers in which they recorded their operations, and the salaries of their staff. A merchant court could be called upon to advise the government on commercial questions, and a government-appointed bureaucrat always served as its president. The ambiguous character of the merchant courts was cause for confusion among the European consuls during the buildup to the establishment of the new merchant courts of the mid-1840s.

Around the time that the European consuls were negotiating with the Khedival government to introduce new, better-functioning merchant courts to Alexandria and Cairo, the British consul in Cairo wrote to the Foreign Office in London at length about his uncertainty over whether British subjects should appear before mixed merchant courts because he regarded them as native courts.[40] He reported that in February 1844, a Tuscan merchant was summoned before the merchant tribunal in Alexandria.[41] "[H]is consul objected to [the court]'s competence contending that the defendant was amenable only to his own consular authority." This incident instigated a conversation between the consuls of Austria, France, and Britain over the acceptability of such summons. The Austrian consul asserted that the consulate "had never sent a subject of its flag before a *native* tribunal but had constantly judged itself all civil and commercial suits of an Ottoman plaintiff against an Austrian defendant." In doing so, it never encountered any objection from local authorities. The French consul adopted a more rigid position. Regardless of whether a French subject would be a plaintiff or a defendant, the consul "believed the *mixed* tribunals to be illegal for us, in as much as they are unrecognised by treaties; and . . . considered arbitration the proper course to follow where the defendant happened to be under French protection." In his report, the British consul cited inconclusively from the text of the relevant capitulations treaty. In the end, he asked for instructions from the Foreign Office.[42] This disagreement over whether to allow European subjects and protégés to appear before mixed merchant courts at all, or when they were suing local merchants, was settled with the opening of the newly reconstituted merchant courts in Alexandria in 1845 and Cairo in 1846. There, European merchants showed up only to sue local merchants.

However, by the mid-1840s, an increasing number of European merchants were establishing businesses outside of the largest urban centers. For these European subjects, consular representation in their new business locations was uneven or altogether absent. The patchiness of consular support in the Nile Delta and upper Egypt coincided with the expansion of the Khedival state-organized network of judicial councils. As the latter became an option in provincial towns in areas far from Alexandria and Cairo,[43] the consuls' initial reservations about the appearance of European merchants before state-organized tribunals lost their practical significance. An example from upper Egypt that involved a British and a local merchant shed light on this quandary. On October 13, 1853, Mustafa Agha traveled from Luxor, where he was based, about 40 miles north to Qina. There, he signed a contract with *khawaja* Dimitri Tumbaku, a Greek merchant enjoying British protection. Mustafa received the substantial amount of 37,500 *qurush*. In exchange, he promised to deliver 500 *ardebs* of wheat to Dimitri in Alexandria, from where the wheat was most probably to be exported overseas. When

Mustafa failed to deliver by the agreed-on date, Dimitri decided to sue for breach of contract and to demand compensation for his losses. The identity of the defendant—in this case, Mustafa—would determine the appropriate forum before which he would be sued. Until recently, Mustafa, like Dimitri, had enjoyed British protection because he worked as an agent for the "Consulate of England in Luxor." If Dimitri had decided to sue him earlier, they would have both been obligated to seek the judgment of a British consulate. At that point though, Mustafa was legally a local.

Since the commercial deal in question was reached in upper Egypt, far from the established merchant courts, Mustafa insisted that only the local *shari'a* court enjoyed jurisdiction over him. Dimitri objected, approaching instead the General Directorate of Qina and Isna, the provincial branch of the central government, which declined to hear the case because it included a larger monetary value than it was authorized to consider. Dimitri was at a loss. It was his right, according to the laws of Khedival Egypt, to have his case resolved "according to the norms of commerce" (*yasir fasl al-qadiyya bi-tariqat al-tijara*), but that was impossible because the nearest merchant court that could administer justice was in Cairo, 350 miles north of where the contract was signed. The hands of the General Director of Qina and Isna were tied. If traveling to Cairo to sue Mustafa was not an option, he saw no options for Dimitri other than voluntarily going to the local *shari'a* court or agreeing to resolve the dispute according to the norms of commerce outside of the government, potentially through arbitration. Dimitri wrote to seek the advice of the British consulate and eventually decided to travel to Cairo. His case against Mustafa was scheduled for a hearing at the Cairo Merchant Court on October 30, but to his disappointment, when the day arrived the court was running behind and postponed the hearing. Dimitri soon grew tired of waiting. Ultimately, he contacted the British consulate asking it to withdraw the case from the merchant court and to hand it to arbitrators.[44] The archival paper trail ends here, but despite its inconclusiveness, the case is telling. The extraterritorial privileges enjoyed by European merchants, and the intransigence of their consuls, could very well lose their significance in the case of relatively large commercial deals that were conducted outside the largest urban centers.

Thus far, we have considered the discourse on mediation and the ambiguity of the merchant courts' local identity in an attempt to answer the question of whether the merchant courts represented the Khedival state's effort to accommodate European commercial interests. The third component of the answer to this question concerns the repeated attempts to create parity among the Europeans and locals presiding over the courts.

Coordinated pressure from European consuls in the summer of 1845 was an immediate cause behind creating the merchant courts. It was not the only one, since there were other historical processes at work such as the Ottoman and Khedival plans for legal consolidation and the changing economic situation with the end of the monopolies. Yet the visibility of the European diplomatic pressure, the prominence of the capitulations, and, later, Egypt's bankruptcy and the British occupation led historians to reduce the merchant court experiment to a ruse meant to solidify European economic dominance. These assumptions and projections do not hold when considered in relation to the actual distribution of authority among those merchants who presided over the court at the moment of its inception in 1845. Then, it was decided that the first merchant court in Alexandria would be presided over by eight merchants, of which five would be locals and three Europeans.[45] Quorum was set at five merchants, and two-thirds of their votes were needed to issue a ruling. As a result, the court could operate even if all European members boycotted a session. If only one European member was absent, the local merchants could decide on cases exclusively among themselves. This calculus institutionalized European representation in merchant courts not on equal footing with the local merchants but as a minority with a veto power—if they all attended, and voted as a bloc, they could block a ruling, but they had a very slim chance of actively deciding the outcome of a dispute.[46] It was only eleven years later, in 1856, that the merchant courts' procedures mandated equal representation between local and European merchants presiding over the court. Court membership would now be set at six merchants (down from eight), which were to be evenly split between locals and Europeans. Quorum was reset to four members (instead of five), which had to be evenly divided into two locals and two Europeans. In other words, if one European merchant failed to show up to a court session, one of the local merchants had to withdraw in order for the court to maintain equal representation for both groups.[47] Furthermore, court decisions would now pass by a simple majority of 50 percent plus one vote. From 1856 onward, if local and European members decided to vote as unified groups, they would reach a stalemate, which in turn would trigger the intervention of the court's president, a Khedival state official, to break the tie.

The broader political context may contain a hint about why this change toward stronger European representation took place. 'Abbas Pasha assumed power in 1848, not long after the merchant courts were opened in Alexandria and Cairo. He would be the subject of resentment within European diplomatic circles for his unresponsiveness to their requests and suggestions. His successor, Sa'id Pasha (1854–1863), had the exact opposite reputation of an impressionable ruler who was always eager to accommodate European interests.[48] The title of the 1856 revision of the merchant courts' statute, "The Consuls' Provisions . . . Regarding the Merchant Court and the Court of Appeals" (*Tartib al-Qanasil . . . al-Mukhtass bi-Majlis al-Tujjar wa Majlis al-Abillu*),[49] points to the consuls' leading role in reshaping the court. Another addendum to the merchant courts' statute under Sa'id Pasha, issued in August 1861, refers to an "agreement between the [Khedival] government and the General [European] Consuls." It was the first time that the rules under which the courts operated were referred to as the result of a binding agreement between governments, rather than as a Khedival decision that was intended to protect commercial interests.[50]

Broad characterizations of the governors' sentiments toward European influence aside, shifts within the more deeply ingrained distribution of power inside the merchant court network should also be considered. At its inception, the five local members of the courts belonged to certain guilds (*ta'ifa*) and were replaced every six months with members of those same guilds.[51] In other words, a fixed group of local merchants monopolized court membership, affected who accessed the courts, and shaped the courts' decisions. In 1861, the rules were rewritten to enable more direct governmental intervention, whereby the governors of Alexandria and Cairo would convene an assembly of "notable" merchants, who would elect the local merchants to preside over the merchant courts. On the European side, the consuls were originally responsible for selecting the European members of the court, but it was only in 1861 that they agreed to follow a standardized and transparent procedure for this selection. The longest-serving European consul general would form a general assembly of the different consuls who would decide based on lists of all the "notable" merchants belonging to the different consulates.[52] In other words, during the first half of the courts' existence, the Khedival government and the European consulates gradually came to monitor and administer the process of selecting the merchants who presided over the court—a process that coincided with the institution of equal representation between local and European merchants.

The Court in Action

Having outlined a chronology of how the merchant courts came into existence and explored the question of whether they primarily served local or foreign interests, I now turn to the inner mechanisms of the courts' operation. These mechanisms were not immediately apparent even to contemporaries of the merchant courts not only because of their mundane bureaucratic character but also because the discourse surrounding the courts' existence in government and journalistic circles revolved around them being mixed judicial forums that were particularly sensitive to foreign commercial interests. For government officials, oversight over the merchant courts' operations, not least among them the faithful application of mandated legal procedures, was conducted through routine inspections that were led jointly by government and consular representatives. The courts were also required to publish certain information—such as the names of the members of the court and their deputies, the time and location of the court sessions, as well as a French translation of court decisions—in commercial newspapers or communiques (*jara'id al-tijara*). This evident concern to render the merchant courts transparent and therefore viable in the eyes of European officials and merchants does not fully capture how this judicial forum actually worked.

It would be inaccurate to reduce the constitution of the merchant courts to its presiding merchants whose selection was an act of political expediency. Consular and Khedival state officials chose merchants with an eye on balancing out various commercial and political interests. The appointment of a senior bureaucrat as president of the court was meant to ensure the continued collaboration of those potentially rivalrous merchants. The presiding merchants, as well as the court's president, often missed hearings, likely to attend to their private businesses in the case of the former or parallel government responsibilities in the case of the latter. When that happened, the merchants' deputies, themselves independent merchants, and the court's vice president, himself a senior bureaucrat, would take charge of the court temporarily.[53] As an additional measure of flexibility, established quorum rules mandated that the court can operate even in the absence of some of its presiding members and their deputies. In light of this movement, the work of the lower-rank bureaucrats who went to the courthouse every day of the week to carry out its administrative functions was essential to the uninterrupted operation of the merchant courts.

At their inception, each merchant court appointed two full-time clerks (*kuttab*, sing. *katib*). They prepared case summaries for the benefit of the voting members of the court, who only met twice a week. They also recorded the proceedings for all the sessions, handled incoming and outgoing correspondence, and archived all case-related documents. Given their wide range of responsibilities, the clerks were supposed to have specific qualifications. The head clerk (*bashkatib*) had to be proficient in both Arabic and Italian. His language skills would enable him to prepare case summaries for local and European members of the court without recourse to a translator.[54] The other clerk needed only to know Arabic but was expected to have sufficient experience in accounting.[55] While at their desk jobs, they were aided by several "servants" (*khadamat al-majlis*), like a coffeemaker and a porter. When they were required to leave the courthouse to inventory a merchant storehouse or oversee a court-sanctioned auction for the benefit of a creditor, they relied on a court guard (*qawwas*). This division of labor would remain more or less the same throughout the courts' existence.[56]

This level of administrative support ensured the functionality of the merchant courts. Yet the courts' overall bureaucratic structure was more sophisticated. The presiding merchants assumed their judicial authority under novel provisions that were meant to limit conflicts of interest—after all, every litigant was a potential business competitor or partner to a member of the court. Therefore, starting in 1857, litigants were entitled to object to the involvement of certain members of a merchant court when their cases were being heard and decided on.

> [F]irst, [if] he [the court member] was related to one of the litigants through blood or marriage (*qaraba aw nasab*); second, if there was a [legal] case between him and one of the litigants; third, if, in the context of the [ongoing] case, he was proven to have provided advice related

> to the dispute, served as an attorney or wrote something related to it; fourth, if he had testified in relation to the case; fifth, if he was proven to have accepted gifts from one of the litigants after the case was opened.

These stipulations were limited to ascertainable personal or commercial connections that would likely undermine the integrity of a court decision. That they were not concerned with subjective considerations, such as judicial bias more broadly, is intrinsically linked to the courts' enforcement capacity and its access to necessary expertise—two crucial tools that bolstered the courts' efficacy and enabled the presiding merchants to interfere in the commercial circles to which they belonged.

Commercial litigation was not only about the restitution of lost money and goods but, more importantly, about the speedy resolution of debt obligations. Ideally, the courts would resolve these disputes quickly enough to ensure the ability of merchants, who were constantly imbedded within circles of credit, to continue to circulate money and goods. Therefore, the presiding merchants were obliged to hear cases within eight days of receiving them and to accept appeals only if submitted within three months of their decision.[57] Meanwhile, the president of the court was authorized to immediately undertake temporary measures, such as the sequestration of assets (*al-wasayit al-tahaffuziyya*), until the court convened and issued a final decision.[58] The Khedival government committed to enforcing all decisions. To resolve disputes within a short timeframe, the merchant courts expanded what counted as admissible evidence over time. At their inception in the 1840s, the courts only considered cases that were referred to them by the state bureaucracy (*Diwan al-Khidiwi*) rather than through the direct application of litigants. They decided on commercial disputes exclusively through written documents, such as contracts. By the 1860s, the courts allowed for oral witness testimonies, legal representation, and repeatedly sought the help of auditors (*al-mumayyizun*), and the knowledge of experts (*ahl al-khibra*).[59]

For example, it was not uncommon for the courts to seek outside experts to determine the legal designation of a partnership. This was precisely the case when four Mansura-based merchants disagreed among themselves over the nature of their company in the context of terminating a business partnership with the British-owned Robert Corkling and Company Limited. The head of the Mansura-based company, Awadayn al-Alfi, claimed that the company was a "*quliqtif*" (Fr. *collectif*) in which "all partners, collectively and individually, were responsible for the company's debt." His partners—Mustafa Sallam, Ibrahim Sallam, and Rifa'i Abul-Nasr—insisted that it was a "*kumandit*" (Fr. *commandite*), in which they were limited partners who were not individually responsible for its debts. Faced with this disagreement and keen on helping the British-owned company reclaim any outstanding debts, the Cairo Merchant Court forwarded the partnership's papers to experts in the hope that their opinions would set the court up for a prompt decision.[60]

The outsourcing of such tasks, and the ultimate integration of outside opinions into court operations, points to assumptions about the coherence of the commercial sphere. The merchant court, in other words, must have been fairly certain that the solicited opinions would be compatible with the substantive laws that it had to follow. The 1857 statute of the merchant courts outlined a clear hierarchy of legal authority that considered prevalent commercial practices to be the first frame of reference in adjudicating commercial disputes. Therefore, the presiding merchants, as well as those independent auditors and experts whom they relied on and who must have been often connected to their own business circles, were in a position to define the law. If they could not agree or, as we will see in later chapters, were challenged seriously by the litigants, they were obligated to turn to Ottoman law, Khedival state regulations, and, ultimately, to French law.

Article 40

> The merchant courts must rule on cases according to the current norms of these lands (*al-'awayid al-jariya fi hathihi al-diyar*) . . . the stipulations of the Ottoman Commercial Law (*al-ahkam al-muqarrara bi-qanun al-tijara al-'uthmani*) and . . . what is mentioned in this law [i.e., statute].

Article 41

> If it was agreed that the aforementioned [Ottoman] commercial law does not include rulings relevant to some cases or if the state-enacted laws (*al-qawanin al-mulkiyya*) hinder a commercial operation, members of the court must follow the relevant articles of the French Law (*al-qanun al-faransawi*) [*sic*] as long as these articles do not contradict the articles of this statute.

Prevalent norms aside, the hierarchy of the codified laws and regulations is indicative of certain political and legal lineages that were dominant in Khedival Egypt in the decades prior to the British occupation. The elevation of Ottoman law is significant because it marks a larger move within the Khedival government to formally adopt Ottoman legislation.[61] Direct Ottoman political authority in Egypt was weak, and the statutes of the merchant courts were not dictated from Istanbul. Yet, evidently, Egypt was still very much a part of the Ottoman legal sphere, and the set of policy tools and ideas available to officials in Cairo and in Istanbul was similar. The Ottoman Code of Commerce was itself "a partial replica of the French Code de Commerce of 1807."[62] In that sense, it should not be surprising that French law would be included as the ultimate reference. In a way, the Khedival and Ottoman legal regimes were united in part by this connection to French law.

The presence of this hierarchy of laws created a context whereby specialized legal practitioners could spar over the interpretation of Ottoman and French laws before a panel of merchants who were well acclimated to commercial norms but possessed no technical legal knowledge. A dispute between a British and a local merchant, Joe Zaghlah and Mustafa al-Maghribi, in Mina al-Basal in Alexandria in 1872 sheds light on how this scenario often played out. A broker by the name of Ibrahim introduced the two merchants and wrote up a "note (*nuta*)" that specified the details of a commercial deal between them, in which Mustafa would supply Joe with 124 bales of cotton. No money was exchanged, and no cotton was delivered. Yet both Joe and Mustafa hired counsel and engaged in a lawsuit. Joe demanded the promised cotton and compensation for its delay, and Mustafa stated that while an agreement was made initially and a note written, he never signed it, which rendered the note void. In other words, the business deal was never finalized in the first place. The exchange that followed revolved around how each legal counsel understood the relationship of prevalent customs to legal codes. Joe's attorney argued that note-based sales were common, and that the notes, often unsigned, were enforced as a matter of "common custom (*'ada jariya*)." He presented the court with a certificate signed by a number of merchants stating that they all recognized the prevalence of note-based sales. He even added that Mustafa himself had concluded business deals based on unsigned notes. Finally, he warned the court that its decision on the validity of this practice so common in Egypt (*al-qutr al-misri*) was consequential. It "could lead to the ruin or the preservation of commercial houses (*bi-sababiha yumkin kharab wa islah mahallat tijariyya*)." Mustafa's rebuttal, also articulated through his legal counsel, followed a more formalistic approach. His argument rested on the status of Ibrahim, who had brokered the deal. If Ibrahim was unauthorized (*ghayr shar'i*) to engage in such activity—because, for example, he was not a member of the brokers' guild (*ta'ifat al-samasira*)—then the note, signed or not, would be of no value. Negating the weight of common commercial custom, he argued that "current customs are not considered legitimate unless they were consistent with the law (*mutabiqa lil-qawanin*)." Furthermore, he turned the argument about the importance of customs to the integrity of the commercial economy on its head, issuing his own warning to the court: "Many from rural areas (*ahali al-aqalim*) come to Mina al-Basal to sell their cotton in person. If, as the plaintiff says, current custom applies to them, merchants and brokers could collaborate and buy their goods at cheap prices without even searching for their signature on a sales contract or a [broker's] note." This deflation of prices, he implied, is what would destroy the commercial economy. Ultimately, the court decided in favor of Mustafa, but in doing so it maintained a delicate balance between recognizing the prominence of prevalent custom as an authoritative legal reference and rejecting its applicability to this case in particular. In the final ruling, the court stated that its decision did not rest on elevating codified law over custom but rather on the fact that no money or goods were actually exchanged.[63]

The increased level of technicality that is apparent in both the attorneys' arguments and the court's decision coincided with two novel features of the Khedival legal regime. The merchant courts were the first among all nineteenth-century judicial councils to allow for some sort of legal representation. From the beginning, the merchant courts must have admitted written statements authored by petition writers (*'ardhalji*), a practice that was common and historically ingrained in the Islamic world and beyond. Departing from this tradition, by the mid-1860s legal practitioners had become a common feature of merchant court sessions, with consequences to the character of commercial litigation.[64] Similarly, petitioning the sovereign in relation to unfavorable court rulings was a historically continuous and well-known practice. The merchant courts' version of this model initially involved *Diwan al-Khidiwi*, which, when prompted, reconsidered decisions that pertained to "grave claims (*al-da'awa al-jasima*)." It did so indirectly by employing "an assembly of merchants (*jam'iyyat tujjar*) that is constituted of individuals other than those [serving as members] in the merchant court."[65] Around the time that legal representation was being introduced, the merchant courts' were also reconstituted as a two-tier court system, with the courts of Alexandria and Cairo serving as courts of second instance for each other. Instead of petitioning the sovereign, merchant litigants became entitled to appeal a court's decision before a different court. These changes, which often captured the attention of historians for being heralds of modernity, deepened the divide between wealthier urban merchants on the one hand and poorer rural-based ones on the other.

If only for their location, the merchant courts were more accessible to urban merchants. In particular, wealthy city merchants in Alexandria and Cairo from the mid-1840s, and at least a decade later in Dumyat and Asyut, were the best positioned to attend court sessions in person, to hire legal counsel when the option became available, and to withstand the financial burden of a prolonged, two-stage legal suit that spanned two cities. European merchants, and their Ottoman and colonial protégés, held the additional advantage of consular support. Local urban merchants who were less well-off had direct access to merchant courts but did not always have the means to hire legal support or to pursue a second round of litigation. Until the early 1860s, rural merchants, depending on their wealth and mobility, relied on their connections in the cities that housed the merchant courts in order to participate in commercial litigation. To varying degrees, they all dealt with the difficult question of whether leaving their business and traveling to a city to present their case in the first place was financially feasible.

Khedival state officials were aware of this persistent question and articulated a practical, if incomprehensive, answer to it. Given the ongoing expansion of bureaucratic departments outside of Alexandria and Cairo—and in time, within smaller rural locales—these officials authorized the resolution of small-scale commercial disputes within local government offices. The first significant step in this direction materialized in 1862 with the establishment of provincial councils (*Majalis al-Aqalim*) in Tanta, fifty miles to the north of Cairo, and Assiut, 200 miles to its south. Created by *Majlis al-Ahkam*, the provincial councils were primarily tasked with adjudicating criminal and administrative offenses that took place outside of Cairo and Alexandria. As a secondary assignment, the provincial councils were instructed to rule on commercial cases that were brought to it only through the agreement of all parties to the dispute. Since state-appointed bureaucrats and not merchants presided over these councils, they were provided with copies of the Ottoman Code of Commerce and ordered to follow its stipulations when relevant.[66] The litigants, who had to consent to abide by the decisions of the provincial councils, had to also forfeit the chance to appeal the decision, a condition that they were unlikely to have accepted if they were based in Cairo or Alexandria (see Figure 1.1).[67]

A change in the political ruling structure of the Khedival state led to a noteworthy elaboration on this path to commercial dispute resolution in the countryside. Egypt's first Consultative Assembly (*Majlis Shura al-Nuwwab*), five years after its establishment in 1866, recommended to Khedive Isma'il the creation of new judicial councils on the level of villages (*al-bilad*) and small towns (*al-marakiz*). Landed elites dominated the assembly, and they saw the extension of the network of judicial councils deeper into the countryside to be a means to fight rural crime and administrative corruption and promote the rural economy where their wealth was concentrated.[68] Isma'il acted upon the assembly's recommendation, empowering local elites (*'umad wa mashayikh*) to run these state institutions alongside Cairo-appointed bureaucrats and revising the rules that governed commercial litigation in the countryside along the way. From 1871 onward, governorates (al-Mudiriyya)

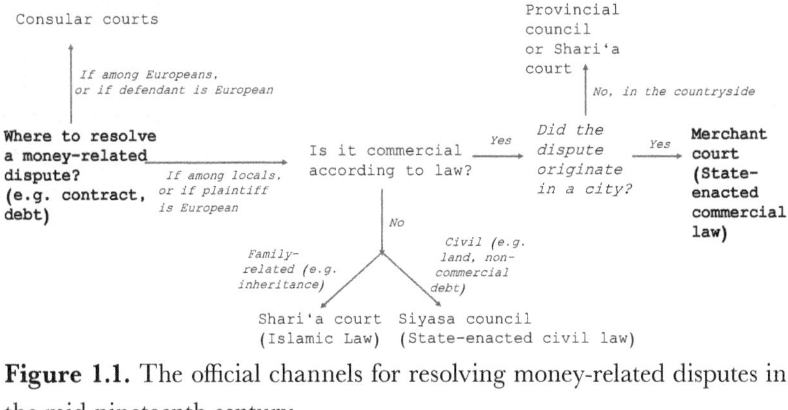

Figure 1.1. The official channels for resolving money-related disputes in the mid-nineteenth century.

rather than provincial councils would hear commercial cases as long as the disputant parties consented. Dispute resolution would become the subject of arbitration by a bureaucrat, with no explicit references to merchant court statutes or the Ottoman Code of Commerce. Yet, in a significant reversal of the status quo, litigants enjoyed the right to appeal the result of arbitration before one of the established merchant courts, now a network comprising of at least three courts, including in Dumyat and, potentially, Asyut.[69]

Simultaneous to the efforts to extend a mode of commercial litigation that was compatible with the merchant courts into the countryside, the courts became involved in adjudicating transnational commercial disputes. This possibility was not explicitly addressed in the merchant court statutes, but archival records contain evidence of Egypt-based merchants who were sued by European businesses for their alleged violation of exportation contracts. The number of such cases constituted a small percentage of the total presented to the merchant courts. Still, qualitative examples show that European consulates were active in bringing such lawsuits to the merchant courts, which considered and applied to them its own corpus of legal references, including Ottoman and French laws.

In the early 1860s, for example, an Ottoman merchant by the name of *khawaja* Jurji Shammas traveled to England from Egypt to find buyers for his wool. He concluded a deal, through public auction, with the Liverpool-based Huth and Company, which, in turn, sold it to a buyer in Heckmondwike, a town outside of Leeds. Soon afterward, this process by which wool was exported from Egypt to a major center of woolen cloth manufacturing in England became the subject of a legal dispute. Upon receiving the wool, the ultimate buyer claimed that it was counterfeit (*maghshush*) and requested a refund from Huth and Company, which complied but asserted its status as a brokerage firm that never formally owned the wool at any stage of the process. The Liverpool-based firm contacted the British consulate in Egypt, emphasizing that it had only mediated the sale of the wool in exchange for a commission and demanded that the consulate help it reclaim from *khawaja* Jurji the amount that it had refunded to the final buyer. Thus, a manufacturer in Yorkshire's Heavy Woolen District triggered a legal process through which *khawaja* Jurji was summoned to the merchant court in Cairo. In court, *khawaja* Jurji's defense rested on two points.

The first, a procedural one related to the statute of limitations, was rather straightforward: the return was initiated later than the cutoff date specified in the contract. The second point was more complex. Citing "article 1998 of the French Civil Law," he argued that a broker was only permitted to act within the mandate set to him by his client and that he (i.e., *khawaja* Jurji) had never authorized the refund. He then added an explanation that the merchant court was familiar with in the Egyptian context: Huth and Company did not only disregard the contract; "it also acted contrary to the established conditions of selling wool in Liverpool (*tasarrafu bi-didd al-shurut al-muqarrara li-mabi' sinf al-suf fi lifirbul*)." *Khawaja* Jurji's defense convinced the court.[70] This and similar cases shed light on the geographical reach of the Khedival state's commercial-legal infrastructure.[71]

Concluding Remarks

As the first step toward explaining what market governance was and how it operated in the decades preceding the British occupation, this chapter zoomed in on the key institution that adjudicated merchant disputes, both local/Ottoman and foreign/European in the mid-nineteenth century. Despite its three decades of existence, the merchant courts have been rendered invisible or dismissed as dysfunctional by most historians of modern Egypt. The dismissive attitude of the scholarship follows from the following line of questioning: If the economic history of nineteenth-century Egypt is often told as one of state co-optation of merchants and of European domination over locals, what is there to say about the contribution of the co-opted and dominated local merchants? If the middle decades of that century were defined by the gradual loss of sovereignty that culminated in the British occupation, why would the cooperation of Khedival and European consular officials to manage the capitulatory regime be taken as anything other than an act of surrender? And, if the judicial institutions of the mid-century were only a transitory phase that preceded the more permanent and better-defined courts of the late century—the National Courts of 1883 are still operational today—why investigate ultimately failed experiments?

In this chapter, I have shown how the merchant courts occupied a vital position within the Khedival state. Informed by a history of merchant councils and tribunals that were in existence since the late eighteenth century, and by a longer tradition of merchant guild practices, the merchant courts of 1845–1876 encapsulated a synthesis between merchant business networks and market knowledge, state plans to govern commercial activity, and consular strategies to defend the capitulations and promote European economic interests. This complex character was manifest in the merchant courts' composition and statutes, as well as the laws they applied and their capacity to enforce their decisions. The frequent reconfiguration of the merchant courts, especially in the 1850s and 1860s, witnessed the institutionalization of a system of appeals and of legal representation in court hearings. An interrogation of these structural features is the foundation for understanding the material realities that merchants faced and the logic behind the legal demarcation of "commerce" as an exclusive sphere of legal regulation.

In the next three chapters, we are going to explore the first point—i.e., material realities—following three merchants as they navigated the commercial-legal infrastructure, as well as a law practitioner who aided them in doing so. This exploration will not be limited to their time inside the merchant court. Rather, it will be an expansive examination of their life trajectories more broadly, with an emphasis on the moments in which they entered the commercial-legal infrastructure. Next, in the book's final chapter, we will return to a different kind of structural examination centered on concepts, not institutions. At that point, we will consider the overlap between nineteenth-century state-administered commercial law and *shari'a*, and the extent to which the merchant courts lived up to their promise, as it was articulated in the regulations discussed in this chapter. Hence, the demarcation of the law-defined realm of commerce—separated from other spheres of social activity, especially family and land—will become visible.

TWO

Butrus/Pierre

THE MERCHANT WHO AVOIDED THE LAW

THE COMMERCIAL HUB OF ALEXANDRIA was to the west of the city. Mina al-Basal developed in parallel to the growing prominence of Alexandria as a Mediterranean port city in the nineteenth century. Early in the 1800s, the area was unmarked on maps—an undesignated expanse with a few scattered hills and no sign of urban planning or agricultural development.[1] Still unlabeled on a midcentury map, the area's economic significance was evident. It was now the point where the al-Mahmudiyya Canal, arguably the most impressive infrastructural legacy of Mehmed Ali's era, opened into the recently improved western harbor of Alexandria. On both sides of the last stretch of al-Mahmudiyya stood large warehouses, multiple mills, and beyond that, the newly cultivated lands of al-Qabbari and the "Arab Quarter."[2] When Egypt's premier cartographer, Mahmud Bey al-Falaki, issued his authoritative map of Alexandria in 1865, Mina al-Basal was already an integral part of the metropolitan area, connected to it through two bridges over al-Mahmudiyya and containing the western harbor's longest piers—one in operation and equipped with its own railway, the other under construction (see Figure 2.1).[3] A decade later, the volume of cotton moving through the area would justify the establishment of Egypt's first cotton exchange in Mina al-Basal.

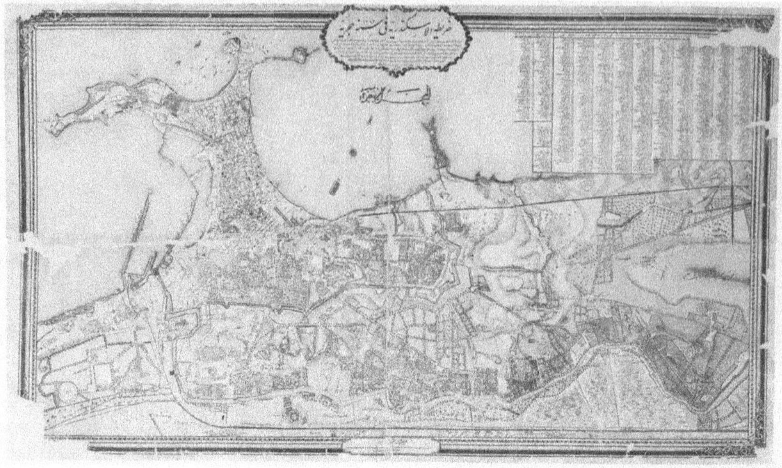

Figure 2.1. Mahmud Bey al-Falaki's map of Alexandria, 1865. Source: Gallica, Bibliothèque nationale de France.

Traveling frequently by horse carriage along Ibrahim Street, which connected the Place des Consuls to Mina al-Basal, Butrus Tawil knew this area well. A member of Alexandria's "Syrian" merchant community, he mostly traded in cotton, but in the autumn of 1862, he was preoccupied with a dispute over other commodities. He had discovered "outrageous and extraordinary deficits (*'ujuzat fahisha wa khariqa 'an al-'ada*)" upon the delivery of a shipment of grains and beans. He reported the incident to the police director of Mina al-Basal, who investigated the matter and, finding further evidence of "embezzlement," ordered the boatmen imprisoned. But for Butrus, imprisonment was beside the point. What he was after was compensation for the financial losses that resulted from this unsuccessful business deal. Therefore, he returned to the police station of Mina al-Basal to demand his money, especially since the whole incident was detailed in the police records (*al-jurnal allathi sar i'maluh fi al-dhabtiyya*). While Butrus was emphasizing the irrefutability of official documents, one of the boatmen "attacked the official who was holding the document, snatched it from him . . . tore it to pieces, put it in his mouth and chewed on it." The police guards who witnessed the incident could not stop the boat captain, but eventually the situation calmed down and the presiding official assured Butrus that he would be paid and that the boatman would be punished for his "terrible act (*l-irtikabih al-fazi'*)." Unconvinced by the police's ability to preserve the written evidence, Butrus took what remained of the torn and chewed-on document with him as he left the police station. Recounting the incident in a letter to the Italian consul, he wrote: "As for the document . . . yes, I took it with me out of fear that it might be damaged after [the boatman's] attempt to swallow it . . . I took it and am keeping it under my hands as a weapon [that protects] my rights (*silah ila huquqina*)."[4]

After this encounter, the dispute continued to play out on two levels. The first concerned the dispute over the shipment. That level witnessed the boatmen seeking expert opinions to establish that they were not responsible for the deficit and demanding that Butrus pay them the full freight bill (*nawlun*) and suggesting he take the matter up with the suppliers. The second level saw a battle over the documentary evidence. While a boatman tried to destroy it in the hope of nullifying Butrus's legal claim, Butrus and the police clashed over who was entitled to preserve it, and the Italian consul—Butrus was a subject of Italy—tried to track it down.

I will argue in this chapter that this concern about written documents became pervasive in the mid-nineteenth century both inside and outside of the commercial-legal infrastructure. On the one hand, widespread interest in documentation seems to be an inevitable result of the creation of a modern bureaucracy, one of the main tasks of which is the production and organization of a paper trail of its own activities. In the specific case of market governance, the creation of state-organized merchant courts to oversee the resolution of commercial disputes influenced the existing practices of writing contracts and related business documents. On the other hand, it is noteworthy that individual merchants like Butrus Tawil were at once committed to documenting their business activities, while at the same time adamant to avoid resorting to state-organized courts. In the next section, I explain the utility of Butrus Tawil's recordkeeping practices for the writing of his own history as well as for dissecting private business practices that coincided with the elaboration of a new commercial-legal infrastructure during the second half of the nineteenth century. The sections that follow are organized around different dimensions of Butrus's social and economic experiences, namely, his biography, the range of commercial activities he engaged in, his day-to-day business operations, and his interactions with the legal sphere.

Butrus's Archive

Among the holdings of the Rare Books and Special Collections Library at the American University in Cairo are business records belonging to a merchant named Butrus Yusuf Tawil and his family. The collection is divided into two parts. One consists of a number of accounting ledgers and receipt books covering sporadic time intervals between the late 1860s and the 1920s. The other part, which forms the foundation for this chapter, contains copies of Butrus's business correspondence during the 1860s. These letters are preserved in four bound registers, each including about 500 numbered pages. Taken together, the letters cover four stretches of time: March 1859–November 1859, June 1862–September 1863, January 1865–May 1866, and May 1869–September 1870.[5] They are written in three languages. The majority is in Arabic, but letters in French and Italian are common as well. Some of the letters are as short as three or four lines, while others run for several pages. Most letters are primarily concerned with quantities, prices, delivery dates, and loans related to the cotton trade. However, information about other crops, current events, disputes, and personal matters have also made their way into the letters.

In the context of Middle Eastern history, personal or private business archives are not easily found before the twentieth century.[6] To give one rather uncommon example, Terence Walz examined the private papers of the Asyut-based al-Jawhari family, which span from 1831 to 1866.[7] However, historians have more commonly relied on court records to reconstruct individual biographies or collective experiences. Nelly Hanna has done both in her studies of early modern Cairo, piecing together *The Life and Times of Isma'il Abu Taqiyya*, a prominent merchant, and delineating the city's book culture.[8] More recently, Zoe Griffith tested the limits of state documents by focusing on archival silences to understand commercial activities that fell outside the state's purview in what she calls "the Muslim Mediterranean" in the late eighteenth century.[9] Historians of later periods face a similar challenge. To write the social life of the nineteenth century, they could seldom escape the modern bureaucracy's paper trail. To locate aspects of social life outside the domain of modern state activity, these sources are read against the grain. But even the most critical reading of these sources depends on the individual or experience in question coming within the purview of the state. For example, a contract or a will has to have been deposited in a courthouse or a dispute must have been reported to the police.

Butrus Tawil, of course, appeared in Egyptian state records. But his private papers allow us a rare glimpse into the workings of a nineteenth-century merchant who, despite his extensive business activities, avoided the court system for most of his career. We know through conjecture that court documents, as extensive as they may be, are only a partial record of what goes on in society. It is always possible that agreements be carried out without registration and disagreements resolved without official intervention.[10] The survival of Butrus's records may be exceptional, but that quality itself presents a methodological opportunity. What is missing from this literature on the economic history of the Middle East is the individual experience of the merchants who inhabited the market. Butrus's business papers constitute a link between the "larger contextual dimension" that dominates the historiography and the "microscopic dimension" of one merchant. On this point, Carlo Ginzburg's description of the microhistorical approach is particularly apt.

> First . . . it hypothesizes the more improbable sort of documentation as being potentially richer . . . . Second, it demonstrates . . . that any social structure is the result of interaction and of numerous individual strategies, a fabric that can only be reconstituted from close observation.[11]

With this potential in mind, we now turn to Butrus Tawil—who was he? What commercial activities did he undertake? How did he run his business? And how, given the scantiness of his appearance in court records, did he engage with the law?

His Life

A biographical sketch of Butrus Tawil is bound to be incomplete. We do not know for sure when or where he was born, what kind of education he received, or how he entered the world of commerce. What we know with certainty are the personal details that are recorded in his business letters. More often, we get a sense of who he was as a person from the letters he received from his closest aide, Qustantin Qattan. For example, whenever Butrus spent time outside of Alexandria, Qustantin would write to him every day to update him on the performance of the market, share with him relevant political news that may affect it, and inform him of interactions with clients. He would also tell him about household-related matters. These details, together with knowledge of the broader history of Egypt's Syrian community and scattered references to Butrus in official documents, present us with a fairly clear arch of his life.

The earliest business letter in Butrus's collection dates to March 1859. At that point, he was already established as a merchant in Alexandria. The last record I found that mentioned his name was a lawsuit in the Mixed Court of Alexandria in 1906. Other documents in his collection suggest that at least some of his descendants stayed in Alexandria well into the twentieth century. These details are consistent with what we know of Egypt's *shawam* or Syrian community, especially the second wave of Syrian immigration to Egypt, which began gradually in the 1840s and intensified through the rest of the nineteenth century.[12] Scholars who have studied Ottoman-Syrian emigration argue that it followed from momentous economic transformations: the reorientation of the silk economy toward France, the dearth of agricultural land in Mount Lebanon that paralleled or resulted from this economic shift, and the rising numbers of those who were well-educated but with no suitable employment prospects locally. The majority of these migrants left for the Americas.[13] A smaller number emigrated to Alexandria, Cairo, and other Egyptian provincial cities.

It is likely that Butrus grew up amid the rising sectarian tensions that followed the defeat and withdrawal of Mehmed Ali's army from Syria in 1840, but that he did not witness firsthand the culmination of these tensions in 1860. Therefore, while the emigration of Syrian Christians accelerated during the "long peace" that followed 1860, primarily in search for economic advancement, one cannot rule out that the political instability and sporadic episodes of violence that preceded it may have factored into Butrus's decision to move to Alexandria in the 1850s.[14] That qualification aside, Butrus, like many Syrian immigrants to Egypt, was a well-educated Christian who established a commercial business. His relocation is consistent with Thomas Phillip's conclusion about the Greek Catholics' preference to move to Egypt where they stood a better chance of finding well-paying white-collar jobs, compared to the Americas, which was the more popular destination among the Greek Orthodox and Maronites.[15]

In Alexandria, Butrus lived with his wife and at least two children: a son, Salim, and a daughter, whose name is not mentioned in the letters. Educated himself, Butrus was careful to provide his son with a thorough formal school education. When Butrus was away from his family, he would check on Salim's studiousness and be reassured when his agent, Qustantin, confirmed that "Salim goes to school daily and returns home in the evening to study and write."[16] The pillar of this education was fluency in European languages in addition to Arabic. We see evidence of this tendency in a letter that Butrus wrote to his aunt, who most probably resided in Syria, in 1869. In it, he asked whether her son "is successful in his studies of the Arabic language" and if he "practices the [European] languages he has learned."[17] Butrus himself gallicized his name routinely when writing in French, signing his name as "Pierre Joseph Tawil" and shortening it to "P. J. Tawil."

Not surprisingly, Butrus's extended family was scattered throughout Egypt and Syria. While there is no evidence that Butrus left Egypt after starting his business, he was in touch with relatives by visiting the ones present in Egypt and corresponding with those in Syria. He had at least one brother, Nakhla, who probably lived in Alexandria as well. Nakhla rarely featured in Butrus's papers, but when he did, their correspondence was about family matters. During one of his trips out of town, Butrus's assistant, Qustantin, wrote to him that he met Nakhla and learned from him that "your neighbors . . . have complained to the governorate about a fence (*hajiz*) that you had built in the garden."[18] Butrus would have to take care of the matter when he returned home. On another occasion, Nakhla handed Qustantin a letter to deliver to Butrus. The letter was from their aunt Malaka.[19]

In addition to his brother, he had two uncles who lived in Egypt. His uncle Niqula Tawil lived in Cairo and was possibly engaged in business with Butrus. In June of 1859, one of Butrus's assistants, Salim Khawam, vanished, taking with him some papers. Among the missing documents was one that belonged to his uncle Niqula. When he lost hope of finding it, Butrus reported the loss to his uncle. Fortunately for him, Butrus stumbled upon the missing document the next day while sifting through his papers and wrote to his uncle right away to reassure him that the issue was resolved.[20] His other uncle, Jirjis Tawil, may have been a prominent figure in mid-nineteenth-century Alexandria and a leader of the city's Greek Catholic community. Like Butrus, he lived in Alexandria, and they both used the services of the same building contractor (*banna*), a certain 'Abd-Allah Haydar.[21] While the identity of the uncle is uncertain, the location and date of the interaction—Alexandria,

1863—makes it possible that Butrus's uncle was the Damascus-born Jirjis (the son of Butrus) Tawil (ca. 1794–1864), who commissioned the building of the Greek Catholic Cathedral of Alexandria on land that he endowed. If this connection is true, then Butrus was probably of Damascene origin and his emigration to Alexandria followed the presence of a wealthy and influential uncle in the city.[22]

Outside of Egypt, family relatives lived mostly in Beirut and Damascus. Some of them visited Butrus when they were in Egypt. For example, in the summer of 1864, his "aunt Warda Tawil and her son *khawaja* Jirjis Masamiri of Damascus" traveled by sea from Beirut to Alexandria, where they visited Butrus's wife and aunt, before continuing their journey to al-Mansura, another city with a significant Syrian community, in which they probably had relatives.[23] Short of actual visits, Butrus remained in touch—and in business—with relatives in Syria. He wrote to his cousin's husband, Ilyas Salhati, who lived in Beirut, to inform him that he could not collect the debt of a certain *khawaja* Jubran because the latter was short on cash and needed an extra month to pay back his debt. He ended his formal business letter on a friendly note, sending his greetings to his cousin (Ilyas' wife) and "your dear, well-protected children (*janab mahrusikum al-'uzaz*)."[24] On another occasion, Butrus asked an acquaintance traveling to Beirut to deliver money that he owed to a relative.[25] Needless to say, family relatives did not all share the name Tawil. In a letter to his aunt, Butrus asked her to convey his greetings "to the entire Ayyub and Tawil family (*li-kaffat al-'ayla al-Ayyubiyya wal-Tuliyya*)." The fact that he commonly specified his relationship to the recipients of his letters—"my beloved and glorious brother"[26] or "[my] uncle's honorable wife"[27]—rather than their full names makes it difficult to map his family relations comprehensively.

Butrus Tawil's letters contain no specific information on the location of his residence in the growing metropolis of Alexandria. However, they contain clues about what kind of residence it was. For example, Butrus did not own a house but rented it from the estate (*da'ira*) of Mustafa Pasha for 570 reals annually.[28] Incidental references point to a residence that was not a standalone unit. For example, for a week during the winter of 1865, Butrus's residence did not receive water through pipes. After visiting the landlord's office to inquire about the problem, Qustantin wrote to Butrus, "as for the elevation of the water (*tulu' al-ma'*) to [your] home, I think it will take a few more days . . . a new pipe needs to be installed because [the neighbor] Bernard's pipe is [now] connected to another home [as well] and has become insufficient."[29] Probably, the appearance of a new (third) neighbor strained the shared infrastructure. The fact that Butrus had a problem with water pipes does not mean that his rented residence was not well maintained. During this water shortage, painters (*mubayyidin*) were redoing the walls of his home. In addition, the building's owner had agreed to replace the tiles but only with a specific kind (*balat makhsus*) that they would order for that purpose.[30] On another occasion, the neighbors complained to the governorate when Butrus built a fence in the garden, which suggests that the residence may have been located on a land plot that included more than one house.[31]

In addition to his residence in Alexandria, Butrus owned an agricultural estate (*'izba*)[32] less than thirty miles to the southeast of Alexandria, near the town of Abu-Hummus in the province of al-Buhayra.[33] Official censuses from the late nineteenth century indicate that the estate had a population between 52 and 78 people.[34] If these numbers are a rough indication of land size and profitability, then Butrus's estate was on the smaller side. Adjacent estates had populations between 40 and 400.[35] The scale of Butrus's land investment is consistent with the trend among Syrian merchants in the nineteenth century who, generally speaking, did not count agricultural land among their principal investments.[36] This set them apart from a segment of the Egyptian merchant class that invested more heavily in land, such as the al-'Aqqads (discussed in the next chapter). Scale aside, Butrus's *'izba* contained a country house, where he would spend up to five consecutive weeks in a single visit.[37] While at the estate, Butrus would directly oversee some of the day-to-day operations, including the health of the cattle.[38] When the occasion arose, he would host relatives or his assistant Qustantin and his family, who would only go on Sunday, his day off from work.[39] More typically, Qustantin would be in Alexandria overseeing the business and updating Butrus in writing on a daily basis. Whenever Butrus needed something during his stay in the estate, he would ask Qustantin to send it by mail or with one of his servants. For several weeks in the summer of 1863, Qustantin struggled to find a building contractor who was willing to travel to Butrus's estate in order to do some construction work at his house.[40]

Qustantin Qattan was Butrus's right-hand man. Depending on the situation, he either carried out Butrus's decisions or supplied him with necessary information for decision-making, and, when Butrus was absent, he determined the best course of business action. Evidently, Qustantin played a role in Butrus's domestic life as well, updating him on family matters in the course of their ongoing correspondence and managing two servants in Butrus's employ. The first, Sulayman al-Barbari, traveled from Alexandria to deliver groceries such as meat and vegetables or accessories such as cigarettes or rosewater to Butrus at the *'izba*. He was also entrusted with moving larger items such as furniture, which Butrus needed to furnish his rural home. Qustantin and Butrus's exchange about this particular delivery shows both their camaraderie and the casual racism they directed at their black helper. On February 20, 1865, Qustantin ended his long business update with the following sarcastic note:

> I hope that he [Sulayman] has made it to you in time, since I have not seen his honor (*hadratahu*) yet. I do not know whether he stayed with you or returned [to Alexandria]. Most probably he is busy getting drunk, may God destroy him! (*wa lakin ghaliban mashghul bil-buza Allah yubiduh*).[41]

The other servant, Darwish, performed similar tasks, but his main duty was to be in charge of Butrus's horse-drawn carriage.[42] Apparently, Darwish earned the confidence of Butrus, who decided to raise his monthly salary and, at one point, to pay it to him in advance.[43]

Butrus then was well-established in Alexandria during the 1860s and 1870s. He was a member of the Syrian community of Alexandria while remaining connected to relatives in other Egyptian cities as well as in Syria. He was affluent enough to send his son to school, keep his home renovated, have at least two domestic servants, and own a horse carriage. He had a trusted deputy, Qustantin Qattan, who worked closely with him and took care of the business and the home when he was away. Butrus also made enough money to invest in an agricultural estate in al-Buhayra, Alexandria's rural hinterland. With this image in mind, we now turn to an examination of how Butrus pursued his interests as a merchant.

Buying to Sell

The nineteenth century witnessed the gradual transformation of Egypt into a major center for the cultivation and trade of cotton on the world stage. Mehmed Ali, Egypt's Ottoman governor, is credited with laying the foundations for this transformation when he introduced the cultivation of long-staple cotton on a wide scale in the early 1820s. Until at least 1838, Mehmed Ali and the state apparatus he presided over were the main beneficiaries of the sales of the new crops. The benefit derived from the fact that Mehmed Ali used the coercive power of the state to become the only legitimate buyer of locally grown cotton. Subsequently, he also became the price-setter. His profits came from the difference between the (low) price he paid to local cotton growers and the (high) price he charged to foreign merchants who sold the cotton in England, France, and Italy. This monopoly system started to break down in 1838, as a result of the sharp fall of cotton prices in Europe and low tax revenues in Egypt, and was formally abolished in 1841 in accordance with the terms of the Anglo-Ottoman Commercial Treaty. The end of the monopoly, however, did not mean the end of the cotton economy.[44] Cotton continued to be the most important cash crop in Egypt, constituting at least 70 percent of its annual export revenues from the early 1860s into the first decades of the twentieth century.[45]

Given the persistent position of cotton as Egypt's primary cash crop, the demise of Mehmed Ali's monopoly signaled "the return to a free market in agricultural produce."[46] From 1841 onward, an increasing number of merchants came to realize the profits to be made as intermediaries in the cotton trade. Both local and foreign merchants tried to create a space for themselves in the chain of transactions that connected cotton growers in the Egyptian Delta to cotton mills and factories in Europe, especially England. Money was to be made from buying cotton from farmers, storing it in warehouses, shipping it to various locations in Europe, and selling it on cotton exchanges, most famously in Liverpool. The profits made in the cotton trade were partly reinvested in other moneymaking activities as well. As Roger Owen wrote, "it would not be too much of an exaggeration to say that the economic history of Egypt during the nineteenth century was almost wholly shaped by cotton."[47]

These economic transformations correspond to the waning of Syrian immigration to Egypt during Mehmed Ali's era and its surge during the second half of the nineteenth century. The first immigrants in the late 1700s accumulated wealth through commerce, both privately and in key positions within the state's tariff administration. There was no place for them when a far-reaching monopoly was in place. With the re-marketization of the economic sphere, Butrus was one of a large number of Syrian merchants who moved to Egypt to seize the opportunity. What sets him apart from his peers is not that he was necessarily more successful but that his role as a merchant is fairly well documented. From the late 1850s until the early 1870s, Butrus performed and benefitted from the same commercial activities that Mehmed Ali had undertaken in the 1820s and 1830s, albeit on a much smaller scale. He was a transnational intermediary who connected cotton growers in the small towns of the Egyptian Delta, such as al-Zarqa and Mit al-Khuli, to the traders of the Liverpool Cotton Exchange. His commercial enterprise included different crops such as wheat (*hinta*), grain (*ghalla*), and beans (*ful*). Yet most of his activities revolved around cotton.[48] Even when presented with the opportunity to buy flax, a comparable textile fiber, he was willing to pass it out. "[A flax merchant] has to exclusively concentrate on it, personally (*bi-zatihi*) monitor it and waste all his time handling related work."[49]

To understand Butrus's role as a merchant, we need to unpack the two necessary steps of any commercial transaction: first buying a commodity, and then selling it. Butrus's business letters show him engaged in two kinds of buying. The first was straightforward. He acquired a specific amount of a certain commodity in exchange for a payment. In that case, Butrus's decisions regarding sales were his alone. The second kind of buying, more common in cotton-related transactions, was more complicated and therefore deserves closer examination. To put it simply, Butrus paid suppliers, be they cultivators or merchants, to sell their cotton through him. He made money in the form of interest on the amount he lent them originally and as a service fee once the cotton was sold.

Butrus's first step was to reach an agreement with a cotton supplier to sell cotton on his behalf. Preferably, the agreement would not be a one-time deal but would hold the promise of regular cooperation in the future. Several agreements that Butrus made in the summer of 1862 offer us a glimpse into the terms of such arrangements. In two separate but identical agreements between him, on the one hand, and each of two brothers, ʿAwad Rizq and ʿAbd-al-Masih Rizq, Butrus agreed to lend the Rizq brothers an amount of money they would specify for a monthly interest of 1.25 percent.[50] The exact amount of money ranged between two-thirds to three-quarters of the value of the goods to be bought.[51] To guarantee his money, Butrus did not send the actual payment until he received a bill of lading (*bulisat shahn*)—i.e., a document issued by the transporter specifying the amount of goods to be shipped to him. Most likely, the Rizq brothers were not cotton cultivators themselves but local merchants who needed the money to buy cotton. Once they bought it, they shipped it to Butrus in Alexandria, where he stored it in his warehouse—probably rented, as we will see later—before shipping it for sale in Europe.

Butrus usually insisted on the 1.25 percent monthly interest. However, it is important to note that the financial calculation was not the only factor he considered. Social capital, especially building trust and expanding his network, was as important. Therefore, Butrus made exceptions but was careful to be discreet about them. Shortly after his agreement with the Rizq brothers, he received a request from another two brothers, Muhammad and Mahmud al-Faraqawi. The al-Faraqawis wanted to borrow money in exchange for a one-time 2 percent fee and no recurring monthly interest. They would also rely on Butrus to handle the storage and sale of the cotton for a separate fee. Although the terms were less lucrative than those he was used to, Butrus agreed but clarified his condition:

> Your [proposed] terms do not suit us . . . but because you have shown an inclination to [work with] us . . . and due to your renown as honest and conscientious [merchants], we agree as long as you pay us through sending [cotton] shipments soon. But keep this [matter] a secret . . . because we cannot treat all our associates in the same way.[52]

Such an arrangement generated less money, but if the advance bills of lading were received, there was little chance that Butrus would lose his money.

Relying on reputation alone without taking the routine precautions could be risky. Indeed, on one occasion, Butrus agreed to lend money to the sons of one of his regular clients, *khawaja* Jubran Ishaq, who may have been new to this line of business. The Ishaq sons received more money than the value of the cotton they shipped to Butrus and were asking for more. Because Butrus agreed to extend loans without receiving advance bills of lading, he found himself in a weak position. Ultimately, he wrote to their father asking him to "let me know if you consider yourself responsible [for their debts] or not."[53] Butrus did not specify the possible actions he could take in response but seems to have been walking a tightrope between keeping *khawaja* Ishaq as a regular client and declining his sons' business.

For these agreements to take effect, payments took the form of promissory notes, were factored into future transactions, or included the exchange of actual cash. In the latter scenario, Butrus mailed the physical money to his associates, usually in a sack that was sealed with red wax. Consequently, any extended cash shortage amounted to a crisis. That was the case in January and February of 1863. In consecutive letters to his associates in al-Mansura, the Samnah brothers, Butrus repeatedly apologized for being unable to extend to them loans that they had agreed upon. "I plead with you (*natarrajakum*) to give me a few days until I could prepare the cash (*al-naqdiyya*). Currently, cash is very dear because the most recent ships did not bring any from Europe. Therefore, all banks and merchants have very little cash."[54] Ten days later, Butrus was still apologizing. "I plead with you not to hold us responsible for this delay . . . I swear it is not the result of any shortcoming [on my side] but is part of a general crunch (*zanqa*) that is affecting all merchants." Butrus himself had financed several cotton purchases but was having difficulty in locating buyers due to the cash shortage.[55]

Most of the cotton that Butrus acquired from various locations in the Delta was shipped to Europe. Price quotes were always made in reference to the Liverpool Cotton Exchange. Butrus also shipped directly to cotton buyers in other English cities and elsewhere in Europe.[56] Along with the cotton, Butrus provided each buyer with a description of the shipped goods and a list of the expenses. In a representative example from 1863, he wrote to business associates in London: "Now, I send to you . . . a bill of lading for 220 bales of *zawati* cotton . . . shipped on the English ship *Cossack* [led by] Captain Ford . . . . The freight fee was 3/8 pence [*sic*] although we actually paid half a penny because there was no room."[57] Butrus's note reflects his particular position as a merchant—he bought in order to sell, and just as he expected a bill of lading from his suppliers in the Egyptian countryside before paying them, he offered the same kind of evidence to his buyers in Europe when it was his turn to supply the cotton.

How Did He Do It?

At any given time, Butrus Tawil was engaged in diverse and rather complicated business dealings. A closer examination of the tools he used to manage these multiple simultaneous transactions brings us closer to understanding how the commercial sphere in mid-nineteenth-century Egypt operated. Specifically, it brings to light the interconnection between contemporary means of communication, the knowledge of markets and politics, and the role played by merchants within the commercial sphere. In this section, we examine each of these aspects. First, to use the available means of communication effectively, a merchant had to possess a certain level of organizational skill and capacity. Second, political knowledge was inseparable from market knowledge, and both shaped business decisions. Third, a merchant's success in navigating the commercial sphere largely depended on the ways in which he acquired, recorded, and disseminated knowledge, as well as on his ability to maintain a network of agents and clients.

Tools of Communication and Transportation

In 1859, the date of Butrus Tawil's earliest extant letters, no centralized postal agency existed in Egypt. Yet several privately owned postal companies had been operating since the 1820s. A regular postal service between Alexandria, where Butrus lived, and Cairo was in place by the mid-1840s.[58] Because the international postal service traveled by ships, Alexandria became Egypt's most important postal center. Inside Egypt, the speed and reach of postal traffic benefitted from the establishment of two railroad lines that connected Alexandria to Suez via Cairo in 1854 and 1858.[59] Additionally, in 1866, the telegraph lines installed alongside the railway tracks connecting Alexandria, Cairo, and Suez were linked to the Atlantic submarine telegraph cable.[60] In short, from the 1860s onward, being in Alexandria entailed the possibility of receiving and disseminating news with speed that was unthinkable only several years earlier. Such was the environment in which Butrus lived and worked.

An essential feature of Butrus's communications with his agents and clients was the ability to keep a comprehensive record of these exchanges. To this end, he made copies of every letter that he, or his primary assistant Qustantin Qattan, sent out. Using a duplication process—probably carbon copying—saved Butrus and Qustantin time and minimized the possibility of copying errors. The accuracy of the copies served as assurance against future contestations over the content of letters. This record-keeping practice mirrored the prevailing norms within the government bureaucracy, which archived "incoming" (*warid*) communications and, more importantly for this comparison, preserved "outgoing" (*sadir*) responses and orders into official registers. The ongoing production of this paper trail was not a mere formality in private or government operation. In Butrus's letter collection, there are dozens of cases in which Butrus or Qustantin went over the copy to clarify key words, numbers, or phrases that came out faint or blurred. In some cases, they even wrote over an entire carbon copy to make sure that the original text of a correspondence was clear. Occasionally, they added notes to provide context, correct a wrong piece of information that was mentioned in the original text, or indicate that the copied letter was never sent out.

For example, an unsigned letter, most likely from Butrus Tawil, is addressed to one of his associates probably based in al-Mahalla. It informs the associate that the money he had asked for was transferred to him and lists that day's prices for different kinds of cotton. Because prices could change from one day to the next, a handwritten note was added to the copy to highlight the crucial detail that the letter "was sent on July 14 because it did not make it to yesterday's mail[.] The prices of cotton are the same and have not differed from those of yesterday."[61] On another occasion, Butrus wanted to follow up on bad advice he had provided to his clients in al-Mansura. The Samnah brothers had sent Butrus thirty-three bales of cotton and asked him not to sell them at less than a certain price. Butrus wrote back three days later to inform them that he had decided to keep the cotton in store for the time being because market prices were considerably lower than the minimum price that they deemed acceptable. After mailing them his response, Butrus decided that he should offer them another option to consider. He added in pencil, "correction (*sahh*). For now, it is not expected that the prices will change. Most [cotton merchants] are shipping their cotton to England . . . if you wish to ship [your cotton to England] let us know."[62] Butrus could have included that addition in the original letter after the duplicate was made or through a separate telegraph. In any case, the attention he gave to the preservation of the original text through clarifying, correcting, or adding to the copy demonstrates a genuine effort to keep complete and accurate records.

The possibility of exchanging information accurately and quickly was paralleled by the ability to move goods and people. Butrus Tawil's engagement in commerce as early as 1859 made him a member of the first generation of merchants to use trains. The new railroads allowed Butrus and his peers to travel and send their goods and letters over vast distances of land in short periods of time. This new infrastructure enabled Butrus to spend extended periods in his rural estate while being in touch with his business (through ongoing correspondence) and home in Alexandria (his domestic servants traveling by train to deliver groceries and other items). More importantly, the completion of the Alexandria-Cairo-Suez railroad in 1858 enhanced the centrality of Alexandria to the exportation of locally produced cotton and the travel of individuals. Yet it is worth noting that the railways were introduced into a geography that was integrated along riverine routes.[63] Between the 1850s and the 1870s, Butrus cultivated a network of, mostly, cotton suppliers along the rail and riverine networks. His warehouses in Mina al-Basal were near the point of convergence of the railroad, the al-Mahmudiyya Canal, and the Port of Alexandria. Given his commercial interests, the location was ideal. He would receive cotton shipments from many towns around the Delta, store them near the port in Alexandria, and load them on ships leaving for Europe.

Butrus could be thorough with the processes under his own control. To run a commercial business like his, however, he had to rely on the existing communication and transportation infrastructure. Butrus's experiences in both domains provide evidence of their far reach but also of their susceptibility to personal influence. For example, both Butrus and Qustantin were concerned about the regularity and punctuality of postal deliveries. Delays were likely, especially when Butrus traveled to his estate in al-Buhayra and left Qustantin in charge of the business in Alexandria. At one point, Qustantin suspected that when the postal worker saw that letters were addressed to him—i.e., to Qustantin—he did not care to deliver them promptly. Therefore, he suggested to Butrus that when he sends a letter to his business office in Alexandria, he should still write his own name, "Butrus Tawil," as the recipient.[64] Qustantin assumed that the status of the customer influenced the quality of the service.

Similarly, Butrus sometimes interjected with river transportation employees to make sure that his shipments were delivered on time.

In one striking instance, he threatened the deputy director of a local station because he caused the delay of a cotton shipment. Butrus had learned that the cotton that was shipped by boat from al-Mansura by his associate, Rufa'il Musili, did not make it past Samannud some twelve miles west of al-Mansura. Protesting the delay of the shipment, Butrus wrote directly to Surur Afandi, the deputy of the Samannud station, to urge him to move the shipment along but also to threaten him. A long quote from the letter, which was written on December 10, 1862, conveys Butrus's threatening tone and lends further evidence to the impression that a customer's status could influence the quality of a presumably impersonal service.

> I have learned that you are causing the delay of goods that are being shipped in my name through Rufa'il Musili and that other merchants are receiving a preferential treatment (*hasil imtiyazat lil-ghayr*) . . . . Truly, I did not expect that from you. At the time that others would complain directly to the general director (*nazir al-'umum*), I have decided not to do so and to get in touch with you directly in a friendly way (*aradna nukhatibukum ra'san 'ala sabil al-mahabba*) . . . . Now, I hope that no further delays will occur and that you will hurry in shipping my goods. The delay thus far has been enough. I hope that you will not lead me to resort to non-friendly ways (*wasayit kharija 'an tarayiq al-mahabba*). Because in that case I will prove that the others' goods, which arrived at the station after mine, were shipped as soon as they arrived, while mine remained. But I do not believe that I will need to do so because of the friendship between us.[65]

Like the railway, telegraphs were part of a larger British scheme to secure communication lines between the imperial British center and British-ruled India. By the time they were installed and functioning in 1866, Butrus Tawil was already an established merchant with a significant network of business associates in Egypt and Europe. The speed of this new technology made it indispensable for making successful market decisions. Merchants who focused on exporting cotton to Europe would use the telegraph to follow the commodity's changing prices in European markets and remain up to date on competing supplies originating in North America and South Asia. It is important to note, however, that the reach of this network of telegraphs was uneven and that it increased over time. Therefore, Butrus's letters from the early 1860s include the texts of telegrams that were sent by post. This fusion of communication modes demonstrates the advantage that Butrus, and other merchants based in Alexandria, enjoyed over their associates in the Egyptian interior over access to information.

To be more specific, until the second half of the 1860s, merchants who were based in Alexandria enjoyed a privileged position with regard to information in two ways. First, the closest location to which messages could be transmitted via telegraph was Malta. Telegrams sent from Europe to Egypt were transcribed on paper in Malta and sent by ship to the port of Alexandria. Butrus was a member of that Alexandrian community of merchants who acquired those transcribed telegrams as soon as they arrived and could then convey their content to their associates in the countryside via postal service. Second, even though all telegrams coming from Europe traveled through the same cables, they fell into one of two categories: public (*'umumi*) and private (*khususi*). The first category of telegrams included the latest news on the cotton market of Liverpool and were displayed "in the bourse or other public spheres."[66] A merchant based in Alexandria would be the first to learn about this valuable information and the first to act upon it. The private telegrams were transmitted to a specific recipient, most likely a merchant, who may choose to share its content with some of his peers. In this way, Butrus Tawil was in a position to learn about market or political developments that would be publicly disseminated later.

When conveying the contents of a telegram, he would typically sign his message and date it but not specify an addressee, since the exact message would be disseminated to several recipients. Consider the following example:

> Alexandria on 26 July 1863. Sunday noon.
>
> An English ship arriving from Malta brought with it a telegram from Liverpool dated 21 July. [It states that] the market is steady (*mutamasik*) and that the sales on that day reached 6000 bales [of cotton]. These include 800 from Egypt selling at an extra half penny. It was necessary to notify you. We will inform you of later developments.
>
> Butrus Yusuf Tawil[67]

It is noteworthy that Butrus did not only convey to his collaborators the central piece of the information in the telegram, namely, the quantity and price of Egyptian cotton sales. He also specified the date and means of communication. It was also common for Butrus to integrate a telegram he received within a longer letter. For instance, a letter mostly dedicated to financial transactions and interest calculations included the following passage:

> The cotton market . . . is calm today. Prices are largely unchanged compared to yesterday. [But] after the market emptied out, a telegraph arrived from Liverpool that an American ship has arrived in England and that it is carrying dreadful news (*akhbar radiyya*) about cotton . . .[68]

Butrus did not specify the details of the "dreadful news," which must have concerned the developments of the American Civil War and its effects on the cotton market. He did, however, show his ability to relate the knowledge of politics and markets.

Explaining International Politics

Cotton was a global commodity. It was cultivated to be exported and was processed far from the lands where it was grown. By 1880, more than half of all the cotton produced locally was sold transnationally. European stock exchanges were the main markets for cotton grown in the Indian subcontinent, the American South, and Egypt. Cotton merchants like Butrus Tawil were keenly aware that political events or crises unfolding anywhere near the nodes of this global trade network could affect their commercial businesses.[69]

On the eve of the American Civil War (1861–1865), cotton was the largest cash crop in the American South. Collectively, the southern states constituted the largest exporter of cotton in the world, with most of their cotton shipped to textile factories in England. In the buildup to the Civil War, large cotton growers were convinced that Great Britain and France would rush to support the confederate states of the South in order to ensure the continuous flow of cotton to European factories. While the predictions of this so-called cotton diplomacy proved wrong, its main assumption held true. Shortly after the war broke out, the federalist states of the north imposed a blockade on southern ports, thus imposing an embargo on southern cotton exports, which lasted for the entire duration of the war. During these years, British cotton importers replaced the American cotton that was no longer available with Indian and Egyptian cotton. Accordingly, the cotton producers in these two countries dramatically increased their share of the global market during the first half of the 1860s. The reconfiguration of this global market of cotton was also accompanied by a surge in prices, further benefiting export-oriented merchants in India and Egypt.[70] It was in this context that Butrus Tawil was buying cotton from various suppliers in the Egyptian Delta and selling it on the Liverpool Cotton Exchange.

Profiting from the blockade, Egypt's cotton merchants wished that the American Civil War would continue for as long as possible. They expected that when it ended, the global market of cotton would be reconfigured once again to factor in the reintegration of American cotton. The future crisis would not only entail the plummeting of cotton prices but also the reduction of their share in the global market. Therefore, Butrus Tawil's interest in the war was not that of a curious outside observer who consumed international news in general but rather of a merchant whose business fortunes depended on it. His business letters from this period reveal how he learned about the war's developments promptly, tried to distinguish actual events from rumors, disseminated relevant details to his associates, and made business decisions in light of his understanding of war's implications.

Reuters and Havas, the major global news agencies of the nineteenth century, only opened an office in Alexandria in 1866, after the end of the American Civil War. Following international news in the city was possible through several privately owned newspapers published in French and Italian since the late 1840s.[71] Butrus Tawil, however, did not rely on those because they probably focused on the European diplomatic scene. Instead, Butrus and his right-hand man, Qustantin Qattan, relied on their membership in Alexandria's merchant community and related access to private and public telegrams. When one of them learned a piece of news, they discussed it together, comparing notes and verifying details. At one point in the spring of 1863, unverified news that the American Civil War was coming to an end was circulating in Alexandria. Butrus understood that if true, this development would upend the market. Still, a rumor that is widely believed would have a similar effect. Unsure of its truth, he was inclined to dismiss this piece of news based on an approximation that he explained in a telegram to his clients:

> Alexandria, 22 May 1863. On the said date, a telegram arrived from Liverpool informing [us] that a decision had been reached in America that the war between the Northerners and the Southerners would

> be stopped. But this news is not being believed in England among the public. The cotton market is completely calm. The price of cotton has dropped one penny.[72]

A week later, he was at his estate in al-Buhayra, when Qustantin wrote to him that a certain Shumayyil had received a private telegram informing him that the American warring parties had agreed to an "armistice." Qustantin doubted the validity of this news, explaining that:

> Since this piece of news was only transmitted to Shumayyil, we did not endorse it (*lam i'tamadnah*) . . . if news like this was true it would have reached the general community of merchants (*'umum al-tujjar*). It would have also been reported in the public telegram, which does not mention anything about this piece of news. From these [indications] it became certain that Shumayyil's telegram is incorrect.[73]

Thus, Butrus and Qustantin followed different, but not contradictory, logics to deal with the avalanche of information about the war, upon which their commercial business depended.

Major events such as a peace treaty or even an armistice were not imminent in 1863. More worrisome for Butrus was the phenomenon of blockade runners that were frequently bringing limited amounts of American cotton to Britain and therefore threatening short-term price drops. In a letter to the Samnah brothers, he wrote:

> Thank God[!] The news that cotton was smuggled from America did not influence [cotton prices] to the extent that merchants had surmised (*tawahhamu*). The prices are still stable . . . . Until now the news has not been confirmed. There are no reports about it from England . . .[74]

In other cases, he wrote what appears to be a template that he prepared to send to several business partners dismissing a certain rumor about a blockade runner based on the "illogical (*al-ba'id 'an qiyas al-'aql*)" route that it contained.[75] It would be another two years before the war ended and the blockade was lifted. Even then, concern about competition with American cotton exports would continue. In 1870, Butrus sent Qustantin to visit several Delta towns in search for new cotton deals. Even though Qustantin had secured at least one, Butrus still felt that the job was not being carried out quickly enough. He wrote to Qustantin to urge him to ship more cotton as soon as he could because even though the market was calm at the moment, prices were likely to drop. "Our view (*malhuzina*) is that the prices will go down soon because of the quality [of the cotton harvest] this season in America and here [in Egypt]."[76]

It is important to note that even though the competition with American cotton was Butrus's biggest concern on the international scene, it was not the only one. In the few days preceding the outbreak of the Franco-Prussian War (1870–1871), Qustantin and Butrus were already debating what the impending war could mean for the stock market.[77] On the eve of the war, Qustantin wrote to Butrus that:

> Yesterday Sunday [July 17] at 5 in the afternoon, Napoleon ordered fifty thousand soldiers to march toward Prussia. Today, one hundred and fifty thousand [soldiers] will follow and tomorrow [another] eighty thousand [soldiers] will [join them]. After [the announcement] of the news, stock prices stayed the same.[78]

However, Qustantin was not confident in his assessment of market conditions. Later that same evening, he worried that Russia might join the war on Prussia's side, a development that "if proven correct would cause the [value of] stocks to drop."[79] The Russian Empire did not join the war on either side, but Butrus's close following of the war continued until at least September 24, 1870, a few days after the Prussian army started its four-month siege of Paris.[80] The last letter in the Butrus Tawil business letter collection is dated September 27, 1870.

Agents and Organizational Capacity

From his base in Alexandria, Butrus Tawil undertook commercial transactions in several places and with various individuals at the same time. To attain a more complete understanding of his mode of operation, we need to learn about his organizational strategies and, especially, the network of individuals he relied on in running his commercial enterprise. Parallel to exploring these topics, we need to situate Butrus geographically within Alexandria. While he never mentioned the exact locations where he kept his records or met with clients, we can glean some information about his work routine from his surviving correspondence. First, a minor crisis that took place in 1865 indicates that he rented a warehouse (*shuna*) in the port of Alexandria's vicinity. The crisis ensued when the warehouse's owner, *khawaja* Mashaqah, decided that he would not renew the lease. Butrus used the warehouse to store cotton, some of which he did not own but was selling on behalf of other cotton merchants. His concern was to keep the cotton stored somewhere until it was transported to prospective buyers.[81] It took more than ten days to arrive at an agreement. Mashaqah would allow Butrus to use a compartment which occupied one-fifth of the warehouse's area for an extra month until Butrus found other storage.[82] Since the warehouse was used exclusively for storage, the responsibilities of its supervisor, Sulayman al-Makhzanji, were limited to ensuring the security of the stored cotton.

Alongside his closest aide, Qustantin Qattan, Butrus made and recorded his commercial activities in an office that was far from the warehouse. It was also in this office that he met with clients. When he was not available, Qustantin filled in, identifying himself as the office manager (*mudir mahal*).[83] Butrus even considered opening another office somewhere in the Delta. He stated this idea to Yusuf Hanna Kahil, a potential partner or a prospective employee. "You have explained to us that you intend to move to the countryside [i.e., the Delta] to search for work (*li-muʿatat al-asbab*) and that you are relying on the support of friends to achieve this goal. We too are looking into opening a commercial office (*mahal matjari*) in a location that we deem suitable and are inclined to the place where you are headed . . . visit us soon and here we will talk [more] and hopefully reach an agreement."[84] There is no evidence that such an agreement was reached or that Butrus opened any offices besides his main one in Alexandria. However, it is likely that within the city, Butrus moved among three different locations: home, office, and warehouse.

Thus, as his contemporaries were increasingly doing, he kept the locations of home and business separate.[85] Besides himself, one other person was allowed to cross this boundary, namely, his closest aide, Qustantin Qattan. As we have seen earlier, Qustantin was not only Butrus's business associate. He would be invited alongside his family to visit Butrus at his rural home. He would also look after Butrus's son, Salim, during his absences. Moreover, Qustantin was put in charge of supervising Butrus's domestic servants and was authorized to assign them household-related tasks. In the office and the warehouse, Qustantin played an even larger role. He was Butrus's primary deputy in all commercial matters and was the only person authorized to sign letters on his behalf. Qustantin penned and signed a substantial percentage of Butrus's correspondence with other merchants and associates, using the formula "Qustantin Qattan on behalf of (*'an*) Butrus Yusuf Tawil." These signatures convey more than secretarial responsibilities. Certainly, Qustantin wrote many of these letters according to Butrus's general orders or verbatim dictation. However, he consistently carried out correspondence with merchants himself and informed Butrus of the details later.

Qustantin's prominent position in Butrus Tawil's business was occasionally challenged. One kind of challenge came from formal exchanges with government agencies as well as private merchant banks. Organized as joint-stock institutions, these banks had started to appear in the 1840s and came to occupy a central place within the economy during the second half of the 1850s, with the establishment of the Bank of Egypt (1855) and the Ottoman Bank (1856).[86] Landau Bank[87] was one such bank that Butrus Tawil owned stocks of. During one of Butrus's absences, Qustantin had difficulty completing a transaction because the bank did not approve his signature. As a client/stockholder of the bank, Butrus needed to notify the bank that he had authorized Qustantin to perform financial transactions on his behalf. The delay and the need to do more paperwork with the bank worried Butrus, who mistakenly assumed that he needed to issue Qustantin a power of attorney. To assure Butrus that the matter could be resolved in a simpler manner, Qustantin explained to him: "Sir, I do not need a general power of attorney (*tawkil 'umumi*) . . . . My hope is that you write to [the bank] two lines indicating that you authorize me to sign the transfer. Other than that I want nothing other than your safety."[88]

Another kind of challenge came from business associates who were dissatisfied with Qustantin's decisions. This was the case when *khawaja* Majar Ya'qub wanted to renegotiate the terms of a promissory note (*kambiyala*). Since Butrus was in his rural estate, Majar was forced to negotiate with Qustantin. He persistently asked that the repayment date be extended for an additional three months. Qustantin agreed on the condition that Majar paid a 17 percent advance fee each month, which Majar refused. Realizing that Qustantin was not showing sufficient flexibility, he decided to go over his head and directly negotiate with Butrus. To preempt Majar's move, Qustantin wrote to Butrus immediately. "Finally, he told me that he will head to [your estate] tomorrow in order to bring a [direct] order from you that dictates the fulfillment of his request. I had to inform you (*lazim ifadatikum*)."[89] Accordingly, Butrus and Qustantin were able to coordinate their actions.

For the most part, Butrus and Qustantin were able to operate the business from Butrus's office in Alexandria. They communicated with a network of merchants and cotton suppliers, received and stored shipments of cotton among other goods, negotiated prices, and exchanged opinions on the best course of business action (see Figure 2.2). However, in order to maintain their position in the market, if not improve it, they adopted three additional strategies, namely, relying on agents who traveled between different towns in the Delta, soliciting the help of existing clients, and acquiring insurance against the damage of cotton they stored in warehouses pending sale to buyers in England.

One of Butrus's most active agents was Qustantin's brother, Bishara, who was sometimes in Cairo but was based mostly in al-Mahalla, some ninety miles to the southeast of Alexandria. Just as Butrus's business

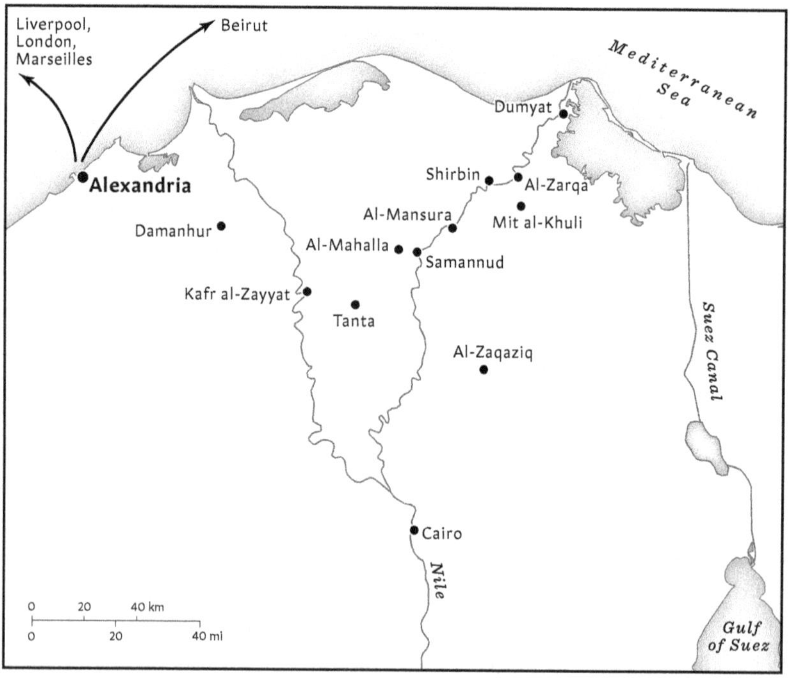

Figure 2.2. The geographical extent of Butrus Tawil's commercial activities as constructed from his business letters.

letters touched on familial matters, so did Qustantin's. It was not strange, for example, for him to end a letter to his brother with the postscript: "If you need any clothes or food let me know and I will send it [to you]."[90] These written exchanges were marginal to the role that Bishara played in Butrus's business. Bishara's main task was to locate suppliers who were selling various kinds of goods, especially cotton, around the Delta and to buy them for Butrus. Typically, he would visit marketplaces and survey prices, then write to Butrus in Alexandria to tell him of the findings and possibly recommend certain deals. If Butrus agreed, he would encourage Bishara to negotiate a specific deal but would also set the highest price he could pay. Upon receiving this response, Bishara would proceed with the negotiations and, if successful, conclude the deal. Subsequently, he would write again to Butrus to inform him of the results and ask him to send the exact amount of money needed to conclude the deal. The money arrived in the mail along with instructions regarding the shipping of the goods to Butrus's warehouse in Alexandria. It took up to a week between the day Bishara first identified possible commercial deals and the day he received the money needed to execute the final transaction. To save time, Butrus often authorized Bishara to seize good opportunities without getting back to him first. When Bishara wrote from Cairo with the current prices of grain and beans, he received the following response:

> The prices you sent to us will generate very limited profits . . . . In light of your intelligence and alertness, we hope that you will find the least possible prices, pay attention to weights and reduce the costs of handling so that [the deal] becomes profitable. Given the situation, we authorize you to immediately shop for grain and beans with the utmost effort. Let us know each time you can conclude a deal and we will send you the needed money in the mail. Tomorrow, I will let you know whether you should ship any goods you buy to me, or if you should store them [for the time being].[91]

Three days later, Bishara confirmed that he found a suitable deal.[92] Butrus also relied on Bishara to actively search for individuals who were willing to borrow "at any interest rate" as long as they were "trustworthy."[93] In this way, Bishara enabled Butrus to expand his business network and moneylending activities that were not tied directly to commercial deals.

The organizational capacity of Butrus Tawil extended beyond the significant efforts of the Qattan brothers to include an essential market tool, namely, insurance. An incident that occurred in February of 1865 sheds light on how insurance arrangements worked. A limited fire broke out in the warehouse leading to the destruction of eight bales of cotton that belonged to *al-sayyid* 'Ali al-Haki', a cotton merchant in al-Mansura. Butrus stored the cotton in his warehouse in the port of Alexandria until he sold it on behalf of *al-sayyid* 'Ali. As soon as the fire was extinguished, Butrus's assistant, Qustantin, wrote to *al-sayyid* 'Ali to inform him of what happened and assure him that the insurance covered the damages.[94] Afterward, Qustantin contacted the insurer about the correct course of action in this situation. He was instructed to sort the cotton and report to them the amount of "damaged and lost" cotton in order to calculate the compensation.[95] Indeed, several days later, Qustantin reported to *al-sayyid* 'Ali that he had received the full price of the damaged cotton according to the terms of the insurance.[96] Butrus's success in handling the crisis must have augmented his image as a trustworthy merchant. *Al-sayyid* 'Ali al-Haki' continued to rely on him to sell his cotton until at least the summer of 1869.

Engaging with the Law

Based on the previous discussion, it should be clear that Butrus Tawil was a competent merchant. He owned and oversaw a sophisticated commercial enterprise, pursued varied economic interests—exporting cotton, money lending—and maintained a network of business associates in Egypt and abroad. To do so, he relied on at least two agents, Qustantin and Bishara Qattan, systematic recordkeeping, and an awareness of world affairs. He belonged to the large and established Syrian community of Egypt, through which he had business, as well as social, connections. He was also a subject of Italy, which meant access to business opportunities and legal privileges through the extant capitulations. Butrus Tawil's far-reaching business presence was spent under Egypt's centralized modern state and its expansive bureaucracy. Throughout his career, which encompassed the second half of the nineteenth century, he was obligated to answer to the existing laws when others mobilized them against him. However, when he was in a position to take the initiative, he seems to have avoided resorting to the courts whenever possible. When dealing with business disputes, there is no evidence that he had used the specialized merchant courts.[97]

Explaining this limited engagement with the legal regime is essential for understanding the history of market governance of nineteenth-century Egypt in general. The most pressing question to answer in this regard is: Was Butrus Tawil's refrain from utilizing the existing commercial-legal infrastructure a sign of its ineffectiveness or unreliability in the eyes of the merchant community? If so, how do we explain the creation and persistence for three decades of this commercial-legal infrastructure, with the merchant courts at its center?

Historians of the early modern Ottoman Empire face this kind of question frequently. Because they are often reliant on *shari'a* court records as the primary source for writing social history, they are sensitive to the ways in which these sources are skewed and are keen to read what unfolds inside the courthouse as one scene in a longer drama that unfolded outside of it. Leslie Peirce's *Morality Tales: Law and Gender in the Ottoman Court of Aintab* is exemplary in its interrogation of relatively short court summaries to construct plausible scenarios of what occurred before and after the litigants walked into the courtroom.[98] The volume and level of detail that characterize court documents under the modern state should not make us overlook the fact that legal disputes are part of a larger social context. Butrus Tawil, like his peers within the community of merchants, was constantly engaged with the existing legal regime even as he tried to avoid entering the commercial-legal infrastructure. In other words, there was a legally informed logic to his near-total absence from court records.

Butrus was cautious not to get involved in actual legal proceedings against his associates. Even when legal action seemed inevitable, he preferred to let someone else handle it. In a case which involved him as a middleman between two of his long-term clients, *khawaja* As'ad Qalush and *khawaja* Zughayb, he had to do exactly that. The business deal consisted of Butrus selling 246 bales of cotton to As'ad on behalf of Zughayb. A few days after delivering the cotton, the buyer, As'ad, discovered that the shipment was missing two bags. Butrus promised to take care of the problem, contacting the seller, Zughayb, who ordered a search of his warehouse. Ultimately, he found only one missing bag that was marked with a different label (*nishan*). Yet As'ad was not satisfied and insisted that Butrus pursue Zughayb until the entire amount was retrieved. If this attempt failed, he planned to sue Zughayb in court. Realizing that the situation would soon become the subject of a legal case, he wrote to As'ad:

> If you want to pursue this problem further, you will have to do so in an official manner. If you so choose, I implore you to assign someone else with this task . . . . As for me, I cannot pursue this case officially with *khawaja* Zughayb, not because serving you is burdensome but because of personal reasons (*li-asbab dhatiyya*). If this case involved someone else [other than Zughayb], I would not have turned you down. I would not turn down a chance to serve you. But on this one, I hope you will excuse me and accept my justification (*inama hadhihi narjukum tu'funa minha wa taqbalu al-'udhr*).[99]

Thus, he tried to maintain an amicable relationship with two business associates headed toward a legal confrontation.

Even in cases where Butrus was more directly involved, he was reluctant to resort to the courts. As someone who extended loans to local cotton merchants, Butrus was aware that delays in payment were not unusual. However, Muhammad 'Abd-al-Raziq was extremely slow to pay what he owed. The amount of cotton he supplied in seven months was so small that Butrus described it as "less than the pay of a black slave." To make Muhammad's delay costly, Butrus continued to charge him an interest of 1.25 percent for each month of delay. Muhammad protested what he deemed to be an unfair expense. Although intensifying, this business dispute was not about to turn into a legal confrontation. Instead, Butrus turned to a longtime business associate, *al-sayyid* 'Ali al-Haki', who also happened to be a relative of his debtor. He was disappointed when *al-sayyid* 'Ali sided with his relative. Butrus's letter to him is remarkable for its avoidance of any mention of the law.

> I found your response very surprising . . . . I never expected such a response because I am used to you being fair . . . . If you recount the events properly (*kama yajib*) you would find me in the clear . . . . My job is commerce (*shughluna huwa al-tijara*) and I only give out loans against ready cotton . . . . If all my clients act in this way it would not be worthwhile to engage in commerce (*tabqa al-tijara zayy ba'daha*) . . . . My right is as clear

> as the sun and it is impossible that I would disregard it. I only want to end everything between him and me in a friendly and peaceful manner without disputes and needless talk (*bidun munaza'at wa kalam wa hadith*).[100]

Butrus stopped short of threatening to sue, which was only a strategy of last resort.

Butrus's lack of formal engagement with legal institutions does not mean that he was ignorant of the law.[101] One way in which we can be certain of his familiarity with the realm of law, with its overlapping jurisdictions, is that his associates often turned to him to recommend lawyers (*avukatiyya*) they could hire, especially to help with ongoing consular court cases. For example, in April 1870, he helped a Cairo-based merchant, *khawaja* Jubran Ishaq, with an ongoing case that was being decided by an unspecified consular court in Alexandria. Butrus met with the lawyer, *khawaja* Girondin, and "urged him to bring [Jubran's] case to a favorable conclusion." He also delivered a message from the lawyer to Jubran: "You would do good if you come to Alexandria to resolve this case. The vice consul who opposed you has travelled and the old consul was . . . replaced by a new one who is willing to accommodate you[r request]."[102] In another instance, a merchant in al-Mansura, Faransis Tadrus, rented out a boat, but the lessees stopped paying, claiming to have gone bankrupt. Faransis sought Butrus's help, who in turn reached out to Girondin. The latter studied the case and advised Faransis that it was winnable in the consular court.[103] These two cases offer us a glimpse into the ways in which merchants sought to learn the likely outcome of a legal suit before deciding on taking someone to court through asking lawyers—a subject that will be discussed in more detail in Chapter Five.

In addition to his familiarity with the overlapping jurisdictions of Egypt's courts, in at least one instance Butrus found himself part of a prolonged trans-Ottoman commercial case. The case started in 1854, five years before the earliest extant business letter that survived in his archive. The correspondence contains no details about Butrus's whereabouts in that year. Significantly, however, one of the promissory notes at the center of the dispute was certified in the merchant court of Damascus (*majlis tujjar al-sham*), which may point to Butrus's whereabouts before he moved to Egypt. In 1854, Butrus had extended a loan to a certain *khawaja* Yusuf Maysir, a subject of France, but was never paid back. Nine years later, from Alexandria, he contacted two of his business associates in Beirut to help him collect the debt. With the approval of the French consulate, it was legally possible for Ottoman government officials to sequester Yusuf's possessions in order to pay his outstanding debts. Butrus reluctantly issued his two business associates in Beirut a power of attorney to authorize them to launch this debt repayment process on his behalf.[104] Legal action of this kind across the different provinces of the Ottoman empire was facilitated by the universal authority of the Ottoman Code of Commerce, including in Egypt.

Unlike his approach to business disputes, Butrus Tawil was more ready to settle non-commercial matters through the Italian consulate or in the courts. Sometimes he had no choice, as when he wanted to pay the land tax that he owed to the government in kind rather than in cash. As an Italian subject, this dispute was mediated through the Italian consulate in Alexandria. Given that this dispute emerged in 1863 and again in 1870, it does not seem that it was resolved definitively or that it escalated into a formal legal suit.[105] In the following decades, Butrus Tawil was a litigant before the Mixed Court of Alexandria four times. None of them were about commercial matters. He lost all four. In 1882, he was ordered to pay damages to his neighbor Muhammad al-Sawah because of a steam engine that exploded and destroyed the neighbor's house.[106] In 1889, his effort to reduce the payments he was owed for a *waqf* land that he had been renting since the 1860s failed.[107] The following year, he lost a legal suit against the government over the fair valuation of a part of his land that was expropriated to build a road.[108] Finally, in 1906, he sued the government because its agents did not fully clean a draining canal that passed through his land in al-Buhayra. The Mixed Court dismissed his case.[109]

Concluding Remarks

Like his peers, Butrus kept records of his commercial dealings. He did so systematically and neatly. His meticulousness made writing his history possible. But more importantly, Butrus's attentiveness to keep his records in order was not only about his competence in business but also about his awareness of commercial law. As long as commercial operations were proceeding smoothly, there was no legal use for these business records. But if a debtor refused to pay what he owed or an associate disputed the details of a shipment, Butrus would be prepared to go to court or to credibly threaten that he would do so. Except for one case presumably in the beginning of his career in Damascus, there is no evidence that he actively utilized the commercial-legal infrastructure. However, this absence from court records is not inconsistent with the claim that Butrus was familiar with the law and was ready to engage with it if he had to.

As will become apparent in the next chapters, potential litigants were sometimes denied permission to sue their adversaries in specialized state-organized merchant courts. A common reason why the court rejected their cases was because it did not recognize them as merchants in a strict legal sense despite their engagement in buying and selling in the marketplace. In the view of these courts, a merchant did not only engage in these market exchange activities but also, necessarily, kept business records regularly and legibly. These records could be demanded by the court and treated as legal evidence in the case of litigation. Therefore, by keeping his records in a certain way, Butrus had under his hands the essential tools that would allow him to engage the commercial-legal infrastructure and, more broadly, to inhabit the law-defined realm of commerce. This is also why his failed legal engagements in relation to land-related disputes before the Mixed Courts in the last two decades of the nineteenth century are to be understood as qualitatively different pursuits.

Butrus Tawil lived in Alexandria but was never confined by its physical borders. His familial relations linked him to Ottoman Syria and his business associates to the towns of the Egyptian countryside and to the cotton markets of England. He belonged to the first generation of merchants in the Ottoman Middle East that relied on the railroad and telegraph in transport and communication. To cope with the volume and diversity of his commercial activities, he was dependent on aides who oversaw day-to-day transactions and traveled the countryside in search for good deals. Thus, whether he was at home in the city or spending a few weeks in his rural estate, Butrus continued to operate as one node in an expansive transnational network of commerce. He also acquired extraterritorial privileges as a subject of Italy. His privileged legal status posed a particular problem to market governance, namely, the co-existence of multiple jurisdictions in relation to what was supposed to be universal governing mechanisms of the market.

To put Butrus's profile and circumstances in perspective, we turn next to two very different figures. In contrast to this Syrian Christian merchant with trans-Mediterranean commercial links, Musa and Hasan al-ʿAqqad were Muslim merchants, most likely from Upper Egypt, with business connections in Sudan. Their business strategies entailed a direct and sustained engagement with the commercial-legal infrastructure.

THREE

Musa and Hasan

THE MERCHANTS WHO USED THE LAW

ON PAPER, MEMBERSHIP OF THE merchant court was not open to all. The European consulates elected a portion of the members from among their subjects, while Cairene and Alexandrian merchant guilds chose the rest from among their ranks. These elections presumably took place regularly every six months for half of the members to ensure continuity, and the archival record preserved instances of these transitions.[1] This mechanism, as I have argued in Chapter One, likely kept influence over the court among an exclusive group of merchants—both local and foreign. The 1860s present us with concrete evidence of a related occurrence: the passing on of court membership from father to son.

Musa al-ʿAqqad, a well-known merchant, was among the court's members until his death in 1867. Within two years, his son, Hasan Musa al-ʿAqqad, who was careful to always sign using his full name lest his connection to his father be unnoticed, occupied the same position. The al-ʿAqqads were not only wealthy merchants but they had landed interests as well. By joining a select group of merchants who presided over the Cairo Merchant Court, they added a different kind of power to their repository of social influence. Over the period of a decade, one of them always held the privilege of interpreting the law and deploying it to his own advantage when the opportunity presented itself. Legal interpretation in this context was not simply an intellectual undertaking but also a consequential social activity that involved hiring experts to evaluate the current prices of commodities and auditors to review commercial ledgers. Membership of the Cairo Merchant Court allowed father and son to serve as arbitrators or bankruptcy trustees. Their position must have also influenced their business relationships because they enjoyed permanent access to the commercial-legal infrastructure, whereas their rivals only appealed to it. Reconstructing their history adds an important dimension of the study of market governance in the middle decades of the nineteenth century.

In the previous chapter, the survival of a part of Butrus Tawil's archive enabled the reconstruction of his business history. Combining the broader historical context and his norms of recordkeeping allowed us to understand aspects of his practices as a merchant. Musa and Hasan present a different methodological challenge. They were known figures who were written about by their contemporaries as well as by modern-day historians. Although these writings identified them first and foremost as wealthy Egyptian merchants, they mentioned them almost exclusively because of their incursions into the sphere of politics. In this context, Musa's Khartoum-based business was broadly understood as a proxy for growing Egyptian political influence in Sudan under the Khedives, while Hasan's wealth was presented as the reason for his involvement in the 'Urabi movement. This chapter paints a more complex picture of the father and son merchants, placing their diverse commercial and (related) legal activities at the center of their biographies. This approach will bring us closer to understanding market governance as a sphere of commercial and legal activity that is embedded within a broader social and political context. Following the traces of Musa and Hasan will allow us to grasp who populated the commercial-legal infrastructure, and how they negotiated their positions within it while living through a politically turbulent time outside of it. It also sheds light on what managing a corner of this infrastructure actually entailed.

In the next section, I provide a biographical sketch of Musa and Hasan, highlighting their relationships to political authority. Musa's most notable business was a family partnership in Khartoum. It existed at the geographical boundaries of Khedival authority, brought him into contact with local power brokers and European explorers, and included trading in ivory and enslaved persons. Yet Musa also maintained a strong presence in the economic life of Cairo until the mid-1860s, including a permanent position within its burgeoning commercial-legal infrastructure. Hasan inherited financial wealth, land, and a position on the merchant court from his father but followed his own path, basing himself more firmly in Cairo, throwing himself into the contentious politics of Khedival Egypt, and returning to Sudan, and later Massawa, as a political exile only to join the ranks of local elites in their fight against European colonialism. This dual biography will provide the basis for the following two sections, which trace Musa and Hasan's commercial-legal activities—that is, their practical contributions to market governance—first in the Cairo Merchant Court and second under the new realities of sovereign debt and bankruptcy that preceded the British occupation of Egypt.

Their Lives

Musa al-Aqqad died in 1867. For at least the last thirteen years of his life, he had significant business interests in Sudan. Richard Hill's *A Biographical Dictionary of the Sudan* states that Musa was "originally from Aswan."[2] It may be the case that south-oriented trade networks were his entry point into the realm of commerce. Be that as it may, the particular character of Musa's commercial activities in Sudan suggests a significant overlap between his moneymaking enterprise and the ongoing efforts to expand the Khedival colonial project deeper into Sudan. Mehmed Ali's army had invaded Sudan in 1821 and managed to absorb the lands of the Sultanate of Sennar into his domain. The first few years of what the Sudanese came to refer to as the "Turkiyya"—i.e., the regime of Turkish-speaking Ottoman officials who took their orders from Cairo—were marked by attempts to conscript men, mine for gold, impose a tax-based administration, and monopolize Sudanese exports. For several decades, it seemed that Cairo's hegemony reached its geographical limits with the Ethiopian marshes in the southeast and Darfur in the west. Egypt's rulers' wish to take control of the Ottoman Red Sea ports of Suakin and Massawa materialized briefly in the mid-1840s, and more permanently in 1865.[3]

Starting in the 1850s, however, a wave of predatory commerce was opening up the possibility of colonizing areas in the south and southwest of Sudan, along the White Nile and Bahr al-Ghazal. Dominated at first by European merchants and missionaries, Khartoum-based Ottoman-Arab merchants from Egypt, Syria, and Sudan itself eventually took control of the most extensive commercial activities in the region: the trade in ivory and slaves. Their *modus operandi* centered on fortified stations referred to as *zara'ib* (sing. *zariba*), which "served as headquarters, entrepôts, and garrison-posts"—the points of departure for armed bands to raid southern territories in search of ivory to obtain and people to enslave, and the sites for storing these "commodities," which were ultimately transported to northern markets.[4] Some of those predatory merchants operated on a small scale, while others, like Musa al-ʿAqqad and his brother Muhammad Ahmad, used their profits to establish lucrative businesses—in their case, Agad & Co.—with headquarters in the new capital of Khartoum in the north and a network of *zaribas*, commercial agents and armed bands in the south.

The al-ʿAqqads were not simply resourceful entrepreneurs but were connected to the state apparatus in Cairo in multiple ways (see Figure 3.1). A series of orders that Saʿid Pasha issued in February 1859 highlight aspects of Musa's role in supporting the Khedival rule of Sudan. First, Saʿid notified the governorate of Asyut that Musa al-ʿAqqad would send items that were needed for government operations (*lawazim matluba lil-miri*) from Sudan. He ordered the governorate officials to facilitate the work of Musa's associates and to accept promissory notes for the customs charges that were due on the imported goods.[5] Two days later, Saʿid issued an order to his minister of interior, in which he referred to Musa's mission and ordered him to allow Musa to acquire a portion of "*kharaz ajnas* [*sic*]" that was seized and offered for sale by auction. Saʿid explained his decision in terms of an exchange. Since Musa was supplying necessary items from Sudan:

> He [i.e., Musa] requested to take what is needed from the aforementioned kind [i.e., *kharaz ajnas*] at the price of the highest bid. His request was met by our [i.e., Saʿid Pasha's] support, and we issued this order of ours to you so that he is given what he asks for . . . a promissory note to be accepted in exchange, and the price to be deducted from that of what he will supply [to the government] . . .[6]

In these orders, we see evidence of a continuous exchange between Musa and Saʿid. Musa supported Khedival authority from his base in Sudan. Saʿid offered him access to government-confiscated possessions, oversaw and facilitated his interactions with the Khedival bureaucracy, and employed credit-based exchanges in a way that suggested trust and

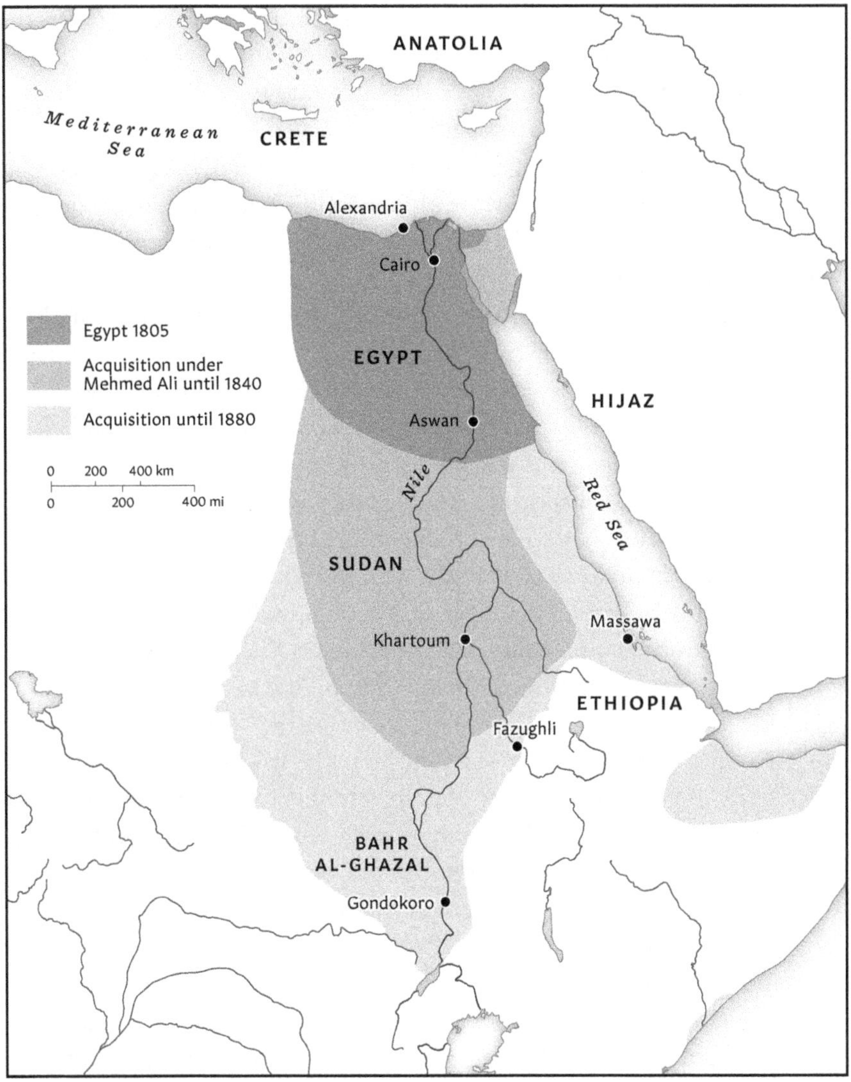

Figure 3.1. Cairo's political domain under Khedive Isma'il (r. 1863–1879) included locations that shaped the lives of Musa and Hasan al-'Aqqad: Cairo, Khartoum, and Bahr al-Ghazal where Musa built his wealth; Fazughli and Massawa where Hasan was exiled.

an expectation of continued cooperation. That same day, February 14, 1859, Sa'id sent another order to the minister of interior, which included the details of a new infrastructural project: a 600-mile road that would connect Wadi Halfa, at the border between Egypt and Sudan, to Khartoum, via Dongola. A certain Husayn Khalifa would manage the project with the endorsement of Musa al-'Aqqad.[7] The Khedival order does not contain the specifics of Musa's role, which may have been that of liaison or financier.

Some significant connections existed between the state and Musa's Khartoum-based business, Agad & Co., that did not involve him directly. For example, in 1860, the governor of Sudan farmed out taxation on the *zara'ib* to Musa's brother and business partner, Muhammad Ahmad al-'Aqqad. The privilege was extended on the condition, never fulfilled, that Agad & Co. would cease its raiding and slave trade activities in the south.[8] After Musa passed away, his brother and his nephew, Abu al-Su'ud, would maintain close contact with the Khedival administration of Sudan. In the 1870s, the latter would occupy the positions of lieutenant governor of Gondokoro along the White Nile and as director of accounts in the central treasury in Khartoum. Abu al-Su'ud would even join the failed government campaign to capture the Mahdist stronghold of Aba and arrest the Mahdi himself in 1881.[9] It is worth noting that while the al-'Aqqads continued their involvement in Sudanese politics on the side of the Khedival state, some of those working for Agad & Co. eventually joined the Mahdist revolt.[10] Evidently, the company, which included an armed wing, was not only a privately-owned extension of Khedival power in the south of Sudan but also, unwittingly, a training ground for loyalists of the Mahdist state.

To get a sense of the scale of Musa's business operations in Sudan, it is instructive to examine his relationship with Andrea Debono, another wealthy merchant active in Sudan from the 1840s to the 1860s. Debono was a Maltese subject of the British Empire who had established himself initially in Khartoum as the owner of "a corn mill" and a manufacturer of "lime and kiln-dried bricks." A few years later, he directed his investment toward the south of Sudan, "exploring" the Upper White Nile and engaging in trade in the same region that Agad & Co. was active in.[11] A British consular document from 1862 recorded the existence of a business partnership that included the al-'Aqqads, Debono, and others with a capital of 2.8 million *piasters*, which "were placed in the hands of the al-'Aqqads."[12] Shortly after Musa passed away, Debono wrote to the government-appointed commissioners responsible for auditing Musa's businesses (*majlis kumisyun ashghal Musa Bey al-'Aqqad bi-Misr*) about the partnership of which he owned one-third. According to the letter, Musa had not sent the annual business statements (*kushufat*) to the partners the year before, and Debono was unable to determine his "share of the profits" (*miqdar arbihana*). He hoped that the commissioners would help him claim his money "since commercial capital cannot be left unused (*bima ann mal al-tijara la yumkin tarkuhu bidun tashghil*)."[13]

The fact that Musa was not only a partner but also the manager of this large-scale business operation is understandable because he had a strong presence in the commercial circles of Cairo and Khartoum simultaneously. Debono explained in his letter that he relied on Musa to send him the statements because he was based only in Cairo while his late partner moved between Egypt and Sudan. Indeed, Musa's commercial activities in Sudan did not prevent him from appearing as a litigant in the Cairo Merchant Court from the mid-1850s onward or his appointment as one of the merchants presiding over the court from at least 1863. Outside of Cairo too, Musa's influence as a merchant with strong connections to the Khedival state manifested in his enjoying a government-sanctioned monopoly over commerce within a certain vicinity in the province of al-Fayyum and Bani Swayf in the early 1860s. An official correspondence from 1864 documents his decision to forgo his "right of usage" from [all] five streets, which allowed him to collect a fee from merchants bringing goods into the part of the market that was under his control.[14]

Musa also aimed to channel some of his commercially generated wealth toward acquiring a higher social status in Cairo and agricultural land within its rural hinterland. Therefore, in 1862, Musa oversaw the manufacturing of the *kiswah*, which was transported annually from Cairo to Mecca in a public procession that marked the beginning of the *Hajj* season.[15] He also left material traces in Cairo, most notably *wikalat Musa al-'Aqqad*, which he established on part of the *waqf* of Sidi 'Uqba in the old part of the city. The *wikala* was still standing but under the control of *Diwan al-Awqaf* when 'Ali Mubarak published his *al-Khitat* in the late 1880s.[16] Musa also paid for the renovation of a small thirteenth-century mosque, making it suitable for holding Friday prayers.[17] By the mid-1860s, Musa had acquired a total of 1,249 *feddans* in "Bani Swayf, al-Fayyum, al-Gharbiyya and al-Jiza." In other words, at the time of his death, he was part of a new trend which saw wealthy urban-based merchants turn their profits from commercial activities into land acquisition.[18]

Hasan left more traces in the historical record than his father (see Figure 3.2). An account of his life can be constructed with a greater level of detail. Yet, curiously, Hasan's exact dates of birth and death are unknown. He appears in the historical record only a few years after his father's death, and he was evidently alive until at least the first decade of the twentieth century. Despite the lack of an overlap in the historical record, certain aspects of Hasan's relationship with his father are certain. Like Musa, Hasan was a merchant, landowner (at least partly through inheritance), and a member of the merchant court. During an official interrogation in the aftermath of the 'Urabi revolt, he was eager to explain that his wealth was inherited and not a result of his connections with 'Urabi sympathizers within the Khedival family. Later, in the 1890s, he would resort to multiple courts to reclaim portions of that inheritance from his sisters, Fatima and Nafisa. His name would also continue to be associated with wealth for a long time afterward. In 1908, when 'Abbas Mahmud al-'Aqqad was a newcomer to Cairene literary circles, he was asked if he was related to Hasan Musa al-'Aqqad because they shared the last name, an anecdote that he recounted to highlight how the writer may have been mistakenly associated with pedigree and wealth when he lacked both.[19]

The fact of Hasan's wealth opened certain paths for engagement in the rapidly expanding public sphere of the 1870s. Those were the early years of the Nahda, a period of intense cultural dynamism manifested in new forms of literary and journalistic writing, scientific associations, and politicization.[20] Hasan's name appears in literary and historical studies of the Nahda.[21] These references are too brief to tell us the extent or quality of Hasan's participation. He may have contributed money or coincidentally existed in the same social circles as individuals who were active in cultural and scientific activities. Either way, his presence within these Nahda circles, even if on their margins, must have influenced his political imagination and understanding of what he as a wealthy Egyptian merchant and landowner could and ought to do in relation to society. Specifically, Hasan was simultaneously aware of his position as a member of the *a'yan*, "indigenous Egyptians, distinguished from the general public by their wealth and their closer access to the

Mussa-el-Accad.

Figure 3.2. Hasan Musa al-'Aqqad, ca. 1890. Source: HathiTrust. Reproduced from Achille Bizzoni, L'Eritrea nel passato e nel presente: ricerche, impressioni, delusioni di un giornalista (Società editrice sonzogno, 1897), 237.

central authority,"[22] and the *khassa*, whose power partly relied on "constructed legal systems intended to homogenize and control every aspect of human life from the personal to property to business."[23]

By 1871, Hasan had become one of the local members of the Cairo Merchant Court and would continue to occupy this position until the court itself was closed down in 1876. We will take a close look at his activities in the court in the next section. For the purpose of understanding his life's trajectory, it is worth noting that what might appear as Hasan following in the footsteps of his father actually entailed different choices in a rapidly changing historical context. First, while Musa's wealth base was, at least initially, a family partnership in Sudan, Hasan appears to have been more firmly established in Cairo. The first half of the 1870s was a busy time for the branch of the family residing in Sudan that continued to run Agad & Co. after the death of Musa in 1867 and his brother and partner, Muhammad Ahmad al-'Aqqad, in 1870. Muhammad Ahmad's son-in-law, Abu al-Su'ud (al-'Aqqad), took over the business and entered a period of intense—sometimes cooperative, other times adversarial—relations with the British representatives of the Khedival state in Sudan and Equatoria. For example, Abu al-Su'ud was tried for engaging in the slave trade at the behest of Samuel Baker Pasha, the Khedival governor-general of Equatoria in 1873, before being appointed as lieutenant-governor of Gondokoro by Baker's successor, Charles Gordon Pasha, in 1874.[24] The scholarship on the Khedival colonial project in Sudan and Equatoria documents the political and economic roles played by Agad & Co. under Abu al-Su'ud but does not mention Hasan al-'Aqqad, who appears not to have been directly involved in the business by that point.

Second, Musa al-'Aqqad resorted to the Cairo Merchant Court as a litigant in the 1850s and later served as a judge on the same court. Hasan was more heavily present in the merchant court, serving as judge and on several occasions as bankruptcy trustee during his tenure in the 1870s. Remarkably, while maintaining his position as a judge on the court, he also appeared before the merchant court as a litigant in several attempts to use the institution to recoup money from former business partners. Among the questions that his actions raise about the function and efficacy of the merchant courts as key institutions of market governance in the mid-nineteenth century is one about the notions of conflict of interest that were thinkable at the time.

Politicized and economically powerful, Hasan's engagement with politics took several forms. Following in the footsteps of his father, he was elected to the Consultative Assembly in 1870.[25] The actual influence of the assembly notwithstanding, his membership gave him an opportunity to understand the dynamics of elite alliances and formulate his interests in light of them. At roughly the same moment, an anti-imperialist discourse was growing among informal circles of politicized youths in Cairo. Hasan was not far from these. In 1874, he probably met with the central figure within these circles, Jamal al-Din al-Afghani (d. 1897), who had arrived in Cairo from Istanbul three years earlier.[26] Afghani's teaching and oratory had earned him a reputation as an intellectual of broad interests ranging from medieval philosophy to contemporary politics. He was also an anti-imperialist agitator who recognized Khedive Isma'il as an enabler of European domination in Egypt. At that moment, Afghani's disciples were claiming more of the nascent public sphere to themselves primarily through publishing.[27] Taken together, Hasan's awareness of his class interests and the growing anti-imperialist discourse provide the context for his deeper engagement in politics in the wake of Egypt's declaration of bankruptcy and the subsequent handing over of the state's finances to European powers in the form of the Public Debt Commission, which was established in 1876.

As a landowner, Hasan al-'Aqqad was among the local elites who benefited from the policies that the Khedival government adopted to stave off its deepening debt crisis in the 1870s. The most famous of these was the Muqabala Law of 1871. The law offered landholders the chance to permanently claim a 50 percent annual tax reduction in exchange for an advance payment of six years of land taxes. The influx of tax revenue was meant to pay off the government's outstanding debts to European creditors.[28] Yet the debt crisis continued, and faced with the conundrum of continued indebtedness and lower annual tax revenue, a struggle ensued between government leaders who wanted to abolish the Muqabala Law and return to a more regular land tax system and the landholding elite, including Hasan al-'Aqqad, who wanted to preserve the status quo. This struggle intensified between May 1876, when the government repealed the Muqabala Law for a few months before reinstating it under pressure from the landholding elite, and January 1880, when the government succeeded in abolishing the law permanently. These three and a half years were transformative for Hasan. In 1876, he was both a landowner and a wealthy Cairene merchant, who interpreted and enforced commercial law. He was also connected to political and intellectual circles but was by no means a dominant figure within them. By 1880, he became a prominent political figure in Cairo.

Hasan was one of four Cairo representatives during the second session of the Consultative Assembly (1870–1873). The Muqabala Law, issued on August 30, 1871, is conspicuously absent from the minutes of the Assembly. One historian suggested that the representatives did not discuss it because its terms were favorable to them.[29] This absence may tell us something about the scope of the Assembly, but it does not preclude the likelihood that the representatives discussed the matter off the record. Although the Assembly is described largely as a club of large landowners, all four representatives of Cairo—Hasan al-ʻAqqad, Yusuf al-ʻAqabi, Amin al-Danaf, and Muhammad al-Shurbaji—were major merchants who sat on the Cairo Merchant Court. One of them, Yusuf al-ʻAqabi, left the Assembly to serve on the Muqabala Committee in 1872.[30] In other words, Hasan must have been closely following the politics surrounding the Muqabala but, like his peers, if he was influencing them it was not through an official government channel. He was no longer a member of the Assembly when the struggle over the future of the taxation of land intensified in 1876 after the government's first (temporary) repeal of the Muqabala took place. With this background of the deepening Egyptian debt crisis and his own insecurity about his financial future, Hasan tried unsuccessfully to become a French subject with the help of a French business associate.[31]

Edouard Dervieu (1824–1905), whom Hasan asked for support with this matter, was not an ordinary businessman. He became Khedive Ismaʻil's private banker and later a central figure in the trading of the Khedival government's debt certificates.[32] In fact, Hasan invested in Egypt's public debt through Edouard Dervieu et Cie.[33] In retrospect, this dimension of Hasan al-ʻAqqad's investment strategy, together with his failed attempt to become a French subject, stands somewhat in contrast to how he became remembered later on, namely as an Egyptian nationalist, who spent his wealth to further the cause of national independence. When the Public Debt Commission was preparing to issue an authoritative report on the state of Egyptian finances and to establish a plan for debt repayment in 1879, Hasan had no formal affiliation with the government. He was no longer a member of the Cairo Merchant Court, which was abolished in 1876, or the Consultative Assembly. Yet he was a member of the coalition of national forces, which presented the National Program (*al-Laʼiha al-Wataniyya*) to Khedive Ismaʻil that included a roadmap for financial and political reform that would render the Public Debt Commission's mandate redundant. This political action led to "the return of the traditional elites to power and their initiation of a brief attempt to fulfill their political and fiscal agenda . . . ."[34] In concrete terms, the appointment of Sharif Pasha (1826–1887) as prime Minister in April 1879 was the political manifestation of that movement.[35]

Sharif's cabinet would only survive until the summer. His dismissal marked the reassertion of European control of the Khedival government and particularly its finances.[36] In 1880, with Khedive Tawfiq (r. 1879–1892) in power, the government finally abolished the Muqabala Law. This was the moment that brought Hasan al-'Aqqad into the limelight. He wrote to the Liquidation Committee, which was responsible for scheduling the reimbursement of Muqabala beneficiaries, to object to the measure and eventually published his objection in a French-language newspaper issued from Alexandria. He also encouraged other landowners to resist the work of the Liquidation Committee and to demand the reinstatement of the Muqabala Law. Such agitation led to Hasan's arrest, conviction, and imprisonment before *Majlis al-Ahkam* revised the decision to exile him to Fazughli in Sudan.[37] Thus, from a prominent merchant who inherited capital that was originally accumulated by Musa al-'Aqqad in Sudan in the 1850s and whose political outlook may have been ambiguous, Hasan was sent to Sudan almost three decades later as a political exile associated with a national coalition that resisted European control.

It is difficult to assess what power Hasan may have had during this initial period of exile. He was now physically distant from Cairo, the city from which he managed his commercial business. The documents of the Liquidation Committee show that he was being reimbursed for the land taxes he had paid in advance under the Muqabala Law.[38] Being in Fazughli, he was also far away from a new round of anti-imperial mobilization that commenced after the termination of Sharif Pasha's cabinet in the summer of 1879. While he became geographically closer to Abu al-Su'ud al-'Aqqad, who had taken over the leadership of his late father's Sudan-based company Agad & Co., there is no evidence that they were in contact. This lack of communication should not be surprising, for while Hasan arrived in Fazughli (on the border with Ethiopia), Abu-al-Su'ud had become an official within the Khedival administration in Khartoum and, in 1880, took part in the failed campaign to arrest al-Mahdi from his home of Aba Island.[39] Yet Hasan was not totally forgotten. For example, Ya'qub Sannu' praised him in *Abu Naddara* during his exile for his patriotism.[40] Significantly, soon after Ahmad 'Urabi was appointed Minister of War in February 1882, he intervened to end Hasan's exile and facilitate his return to Cairo. From that point onward, Hasan's name would be tied to the 'Urabi revolt, albeit in ambiguous ways.

The role that Hasan played in the 'Urabi revolt and the nature of his relationship to its leader are subjects of scholarly debate. 'Urabi, as Minister of War at the center of an acute political crisis and fearful of a British invasion, interfered to end Hasan's exile and bring him back to Cairo. His move was at least partly motivated by a desire to reunify the broad social coalition that included local notables like Hasan al-'Aqqad and army officers like himself, who resisted European financial control in 1879 and who constituted the political depth of the anti-imperial movement he was leading in 1882. Hasan's return also promised financial backing for the 'Urabists either through his own wealth or, as some sources suggest, as a liaison between 'Urabi and Halim Pasha (1831–1894), the former heir presumptive of Egypt, who opposed Khedive Tawfiq. Allegedly, Hasan also "had some hand in" facilitating an offer from the deposed Khedive Isma'il to purchase "light artillery from Germany" for the 'Urabists.[41] Consistent with this supportive role, Hasan's residence became a meeting place for the leaders of the 'Urabist movement, where they discussed their politics. During one of their dinners, the idea of republicanism was discussed, and so was a plan that never materialized for Hasan to join Muhammad 'Abduh (1849–1905), then editor of *al-Waqa'i' al-Misriyya*, to England to meet with the British Prime Minister William Ewart Gladstone on behalf of the 'Urabists.[42]

Despite his clear presence among the 'Urabists on the eve of the revolution, some of his contemporaries and later historians doubted his intentions. Most notably, Hasan al-'Aqqad's presence in Alexandria on the eve of the riots that became the pretext for the British invasion of Egypt in July 1882 remains an unsettled question. British sources accused Hasan of being behind the riots, while 'Urabi and his sympathizers dismissed his visit to the city as a coincidence. As the military confrontation between the invading British army and the Egyptian army under 'Urabi approached its end, Hasan disappeared only to be arrested by the Ottomans in Crete and returned to Egypt where he was tried with the leaders of the revolution. His activities during these fateful days in the late summer of 1882 must have colored how the 'Urabists' lawyer, A. M. Broadley, described him:

> Hasan Moosa was nothing more or less than a very clever political adventurer, with a keen eye to the main chance, and a strong determination to turn the existing complications to the best possible account. Although a man of considerable means, he looked on politics only as a means of increasing his riches, and he imagined he saw in the friendship of Arabi a veritable El Dorado of intrigue . . . . He frequented Arabi's society merely in order to pretend to the possession of a certain influence over him which he in reality did not possess . . . . Arabi did not fathom the wily scheme of Hasan Moosa . . . [who] was, I fear, a weak spot in Arabi's armour . . .[43]

Despite Broadley's defense of Hasan in his trial, he was exiled this time to Egyptian-ruled Massawa (in modern-day Eritrea) on the Red Sea.

In exile, Hasan seemed to have quickly found his place among the Massawan elites (see Figure 3.3). The port city had been ruled from Cairo since 1865. As a site of Khedival state-building efforts, Massawa witnessed infrastructural developments and administrative reforms for almost two decades. It had also become an attractive destination, particularly for Yemeni (Hadhrami) and Egyptian entrepreneurs.[44] By the time Hasan landed in Massawa for the first time, it must have appeared familiar. With a long experience in commerce, state administration, and political organization, he recognized how the newly-established Arab elites gained wealth and political power. Their path to acquire this influential status went through the institution of the *waqf*. Alongside buying property, those wealthy merchants also endowed property in Massawa. As *waqf* holders, they then utilized the expansive bureaucratic arm of the Khedival state to establish and dominate a centralized *Waqf* Committee (Ar. *Lajnat al-Awqaf*) in 1882–83 that not only oversaw the newly constituted *waqfs* but would also oversee those that predated Khedival control.[45] As a newcomer to Massawa, Hasan became the first chair of this committee together with a Hadhrami merchant, 'Abd-Allah Ba-Junayd.[46] With this official status, Hasan would soon resume his economic activities and augment his elite status through public acts of beneficence, such as the manumission of slaves.[47] To put it differently,

Figure 3.3. Hasan Musa al-ʿAqqad's house in Massawa during his decade-long exile in the aftermath of the defeat of the ʿUrabists. Source: HathiTrust. Reproduced from Achille Bizzoni, L'Eritrea nel passato e nel presente: ricerche, impressioni, delusioni di un giornalista (Società editrice sonzogno, 1897), 233.

as soon as Hasan arrived in his new exile, he envisioned his place in Massawan society as a continuation of his prominent status in Cairo.[48]

Three years later, Hasan had to negotiate a different political landscape in order to maintain his status. In 1885, Khartoum finally fell to the Mahdists, which put an end to the era of Khedival control in Sudan. Within the same year, Italian troops occupied Massawa, launching its colonization campaign in East Africa. Hasan, in exile on account of his resistance to British colonialism, chose at that moment to prove publicly his acceptance of its Italian equivalent. When Ethiopian forces decisively defeated an Italian battalion, killing about 500 troops, in the Battle of Dogali in January 1887, Hasan donated one thousand Italian *liras* to the families of the fallen Italian soldiers.[49] Yet this public act of generosity did not signal loyalty as Hasan must have hoped. Instead, it led to a series of events that, reminiscent of his 'Urabist experience, placed him closer to political power and eventually behind bars. Dogali soon metamorphosed from a military defeat into a rallying cry for Italian colonialism.[50] As the public discussion intensified in Italy over what happened and who was responsible for the defeat, the idea that the fallen Italian troops were betrayed gained currency.

Hasan's name circulated as a suspect on the pages of Italian newspapers. After all, Hasan's political allegiances had been questionable to both enemies and allies in the years leading up to his exile from Egypt. The British had accused him of planning a massacre of Europeans in Alexandria on the eve of their invasion. Some of the 'Urabists, including his own lawyer, were never sure of his loyalty to the movement. In comparison, Hasan's efforts to vindicate himself in the eyes of the Italian colonial administration were impressive. "In August 1889, [he] visited Rome, ingratiated himself with government officials, met with [the Italian] prime minister . . . procured a cautiously favorable interview from a [liberal newspaper] reporter, and missed being named a *Cavaliere* of Italy by a narrow margin of votes in the Chamber."[51] Soon after he returned to Massawa with a sense that his position was now secure, Hasan was arrested by colonial officials on the suspicion that he participated in a plot against the Italian colonial presence. Two days later, he and his alleged co-conspirators were sentenced to death by an Italian military tribunal, but the Italian prime minister, who had just met Hasan recently, ordered a stay of the sentences and a reexamination of the trial. In October 1890, after seven months in prison in which he continued to plead his innocence in interviews to the Italian press, he was released. The examination of the military trials revealed that the colonial administrators had manufactured evidence and used false testimonies. Hasan's case was now closed, but the question of the possibility of administering justice in the colonies continued to dominate Italian newspapers for years to come.[52]

A decade into his Massawan exile, Hasan returned to a changed Cairo. The British were firmly established and Khedive ʿAbbas II (r. 1892–1914) succeeded his father, who was the ʿUrabists' archenemy. On April 5, 1893, Hasan returned to Cairo having been pardoned by the new Khedive.[53] The documentary traces from his post-exile years show him concerned with consolidating his personal wealth, especially agricultural land, while rebuilding his connections to powerful individuals within the Khedival state structure and occasionally dabbling into politics, mainly through contributions to the growing journalistic scene. Like many ʿUrabists, he appeared to have made his peace with the reality of the British occupation.[54] He would be involved in at least two lawsuits: a ten-year-long dispute with his sister Fatima over the division of family inheritance[55] and a private land dispute.[56] There were moments when he influenced local politics, such as in 1897 when he intervened to protect the mayor of al-Matariyya, north of Cairo, where he held significant land.[57] He dedicated some of his energy toward agricultural matters, writing in newspapers about the price of cotton and reaching out to the government to offer his services in the campaign to eradicate the cotton worm.[58] His main journalistic forum was the British-backed *al-Muqattam* newspaper,[59] which he only broke off with on account of its inciting coverage of the Dinshwai incident of 1906. This political shift should not be surprising not only because of Hasan's long history of political ambiguity but also because the aftermath of Dinshwai, as historians have argued, was the moment in which Egyptian nationalism would be articulated most clearly. In the following years, he supported the establishment of the al-Umma Party in 1907 and would, apparently, try to toe the newly formulated nationalist line.[60]

Hasan Musa al-ʿAqqad appears an enigmatic figure in the scholarship because of his ambiguous political stances. Referring to him simply as a wealthy nationalist who used his influence to resist imperialism, as some nationalist historians suggest, is unconvincing. As AbdelAziz EzzelArab observed, Hasan and other members of his class did not represent a unified mercantile interest in pre-ʿUrabist politics. That observation holds, for Hasan at least, in the first quarter century of the British occupation. Figures like Hasan may become more legible if we approach them initially not through the lens of politics (i.e., how they used money to intervene in politics) but through that of law (i.e., how their ability to navigate the legal system allowed them to generate wealth). With that in mind, let us now turn to the traces left by both Musa and his son Hasan within the commercial-legal infrastructure. The Cairo Merchant Court was one site where the al-'Aqqads' private wealth allowed them to work with and through the Khedival state structure, years before nationalism became thinkable or the engagement with direct European imperialism became a necessity.

Musa and Hasan in the Merchant Court

The period from the mid-1840s to the mid-1870s witnessed the rise of Musa al-'Aqqad among Egyptian and Sudanese merchant networks as well as the prominence of his heir, Hasan, as a merchant and landowner. During these years, they also played a political role through their membership of the Consultative Assembly in the 1860s and 1870s, respectively. The full extent of their power can only be appreciated fully with the consideration of their participation in the merchant courts, which served as a key component of market governance during these decades. In Chapter Two, we learned about Butrus Tawil, a merchant who avoided going to the merchant court yet kept his records in such a way that prepared him for any lawsuit that would force him to the judicial arena. In this section, we pay attention to Musa and Hassan al-'Aqqad, who chose a different approach, namely, to join the ranks of the presiding members of the Cairo Merchant Court. Their strategy is noteworthy because it sheds light on how wealthy local merchants sought to take charge of the interpretation and implementation of commercial law at the moment in which the state had co-opted the guilds and extraterritorial privileges enjoyed by European subjects and protégés were widely applied. The al-'Aqqads did not only serve in these judicial leadership roles; they also resorted to the merchant court as litigants. In the case of Hasan, this dual approach demonstrates how potential conflicts of interest arose in the merchant courts.

Musa's business presence in Sudan began around 1854. It was a family partnership characterized by a close relationship to the Cairo-based Khedival state, and it focused on the ivory and slave trades. The business brought Musa into communication with European "explorers"—individuals who were after fame or money and who practically spearheaded the colonization of the Upper Nile regions beyond the Khedival-ruled domain. That same year, 1854, as can be gleaned from a merchant court case, Musa was simultaneously engaged in a different business deal in Cairo. Together with his business partner, Mahmud ʿAbd-al-Muʿti, Musa signed two contracts with a Sardinian merchant who imported silk and quilts (*battaniyat*) from England (*bilad lundra*).[61] The silk deal almost fell through. The Sardinian merchant could not deliver the agreed-on amount. He could only acquire a portion of what he had planned to purchase in England and, to make things even more complicated, he had agreed to supply an additional quantity of silk to yet another merchant. When the goods arrived, Musa and his partner refused to receive it, citing the shipment's delay, its incorrect quantity, and its inconsistency with the sample that was used to sign the contract in the first place. As a result, the Sardinian merchant sued them before the Cairo Merchant Court. After deliberating in court, the presiding merchants split, with the local members siding with Musa and Mahmud and the Europeans siding with the Sardinian merchant. The court's president, who was authorized to break the tie, suggested a compromise, but none of the presiding merchants changed his opinion (*fa-lam yazal kull minhum musammim ʿala raʾiyih al-ʾawwal*). The president ultimately voted with the European members to uphold the contract—pending the verification of the quality at the hands of experts—since it did not specify a time for delivering the silk but rather a promise to do so "at the earliest possible time" (*fi aqrab waqt ʿala qadr al-imkan*).

We can only infer the reasons behind the uncommon situation where local and European merchants voted as blocs. A deadlock was a rare occurrence in the merchant court. Decisions were unanimous in the overwhelming majority of cases. Less often, a majority of presiding merchants issued a decision despite the different opinion of one or two of their peers. In the case above, the ambiguity of the contract—specifically, that the timeline was vague—created the space for different legal interpretations to emerge. Solidarity along national lines could have motivated members of the court as well. Additionally, material factors should also be considered. The merchants presiding over the court were major players within Cairo markets; otherwise, they would not have been elected. They also enjoyed political connections. The European consuls and Egyptian governors approved them as candidates for the leadership of the merchant courts. These merchants engaged in different economic activities, which influenced their views on how markets operated. They also inhabited different geographic domains where it must have been more common to deal with merchants or bureaucrats who were subjects or protégés of different states. The case above shows us a European merchant who made money importing goods from Europe to Egypt and did not want to be bound by a strict timeline because of the uncertainties characterizing that operation. His Egyptian peers whose business was to distribute these goods within Egypt were cognizant of different economic imperatives. Taken together, these factors offer clues as to why Musa al-'Aqqad—and his partner, Mahmud 'Abd al-Mu'ti, for that matter—would seek to join the Cairo Merchant Court in the following years. Court membership was not only associated with status and influence but was also a chance to fortify his position as a merchant within the market.

By 1862, Musa was elected as a member of the Cairo Merchant Court. He continued in that position until his death in 1867. During these years, Musa would hear and participate in adjudicating cases similar to the one he lost in 1854. For example, he heard a case in which an Italian broker sued a certain Ratib Pasha for not paying him a commission for an incomplete sale. The broker argued that Ratib Pasha's last-minute decision not to proceed with the deal was irrelevant to the fact that he had completed his job, which he corroborated with witnesses, including the Italian Consul General in Alexandria. The court voted unanimously in favor of Ratib Pasha.[62] In another case, an Austrian merchant accused the overseers of a *wikala* in Alexandria of moving commercial goods that belonged to him—tobacco and leather—within the *wikala's* premises without his knowledge, which led to them getting spoiled because of humidity. After studying the testimonies of the *wikala's* overseer, his assistant, and the brokers, the court unanimously decided that the claimant "could not prove [his version] with strong evidence."[63] In both of these cases, Musa heard disputes that emanated, like his own, from the contingencies of commerce. He also learned the situations where the merchants presiding over the state-organized merchant courts had the opportunity to define what was acceptable in day-to-day business practices and to interpret commercial law.

One of the privileges that he enjoyed during that period was timely access to information regarding the changing commercial-legal infrastructure. For example, in February 1862, *Majlis al-Ahkam* issued guidelines to the merchant courts of Cairo and Alexandria on how to deal with a backlog of cases. Musa and fellow members of the court were to reduce the number of questions that they could pose to each litigant to one and to close cases if claimants did not show up in court within a specified amount of time.[64] Musa was also gaining facility in the reading and interpretation of multiple codes of law. Later that same year, 1862, he was one of four members of the court who heard a case in which a merchant demanded his share of business profits that he was supposed to collect seventeen years earlier from what was, at that point, the estate of his now deceased partners. The decision that Musa signed his name under showed serious engagement with the legal codes underlying market governance:

> according to . . . article 41 of the [merchant court's] statute of procedural matters, the French Code of Commerce was consulted and article 64 was found relevant. Its interpretation is (*sharhuh ma yufid*) that partners could sue one another up to 30 years [from the date of the original dispute]. Article 40 of the Ottoman Code of Commerce specifies that partnership disputes are to be examined by auditors (*mumayyizin*).[65]

Eight years after losing a case in that same court because of an argument over dates, Musa had become responsible for applying a statute of limitations. He would also be responsible, along with his peers, for defining the boundaries of the merchant court's jurisdiction—a topic that will be discussed in detail in Chapter Five.

A revealing case from a few months later shows that during his membership of the merchant court, Musa continued to play a role as an arbiter outside of it. This is a particularly interesting case because it shows the friction between different sites of commercial dispute resolution. The Greek Yusuf Zarifa and his Egyptian partner, Butrus Jibara, had a fallout as they were about to settle their company's accounts. Yusuf was suspicious of his partner. He insisted that in advance of this settlement, Butrus would either surrender the company's entire stock of goods to him or otherwise issue him a security. Butrus refused claiming that Yusuf was already in possession of both his (Yusuf's) entire capital and profits so there was no point in handing anything else over to him at that point. He also objected to the security since he "could not guarantee something unknown." He wished to settle the accounts first, and only then, if it turned out that he owed his partner, he would pay him back. What ensued afterward is harder to explain. Two merchant assemblies (*jam'iyat al-tujjar*) were convened. The first supported Yusuf's condition, which it said was consistent with the tried and tested methods (*al-usul al-mutajarraba*). The second assembly contradicted that opinion and stated that since the account settlement was contentious it should proceed at the hands of auditors nominated by the litigants. The two merchant assemblies had a similar constitution with recognizable names of local and European merchants, some of whom were also members of the Cairo Merchant Court sitting on each—Musa al-'Aqqad was a part of the second assembly. Both were convened by the Cairo Governorate.[66] The relationship between them—whether they existed simultaneously, for example—is unclear from the record. The Cairo Merchant Court convened on Saturday, May 10, 1862. Those members of the court who did not participate in either assembly presided over it and discussed the two conflicting opinions. They voted unanimously to adopt the second opinion, of which Musa was one of the authors, citing its consistency with article 40 of the Ottoman Code of Commerce.[67] Just as Musa was acquiring the knowledge and authority to interpret the relevant commercial laws, he was also extending their influence beyond the walls of the court.

Membership in the merchant court did not prevent Musa and his peers from conducting their own private commercial businesses. Therefore, they were always subject to being dragged into suits that the court was considering. Musa faced this situation at least once. Two brokers, Aslan Musa and Musa Agri, brought up a business opportunity during a meeting with him: Muhammad Bey al-Amin was selling his "properties, ships and agricultural lands in Imbaba." Musa al-'Aqqad jumped at the opportunity, buying what was up for sale for the substantial amount of 11,000 British pounds. Before paying the brokers their 1 percent commission, he was instructed by the Cairo Police Department to hold off. Another broker, a Greek by the name of Leonida Sottiri, was claiming that he was exclusively authorized by the seller to find a buyer. Although he did not actually broker the deal between Muhammad al-Amin and Musa al-'Aqqad, he was still entitled to the commission because of the effort, time, and money he had spent in locating a buyer while the seller kept him in the dark about the deal with Musa (*nazaran li-sa'yih wa ta'abih wa daya' al-waqt wa tawajjuhih lil-iskandariyya li-i'rad qa'imat al-mazad 'ala al-raghibin wal-masarif alati nafadhat min yadih*). When Musa al-'Aqqad complied with the police's request, he was sued before the Cairo Merchant Court by Aslan Musa and Musa Agri for not paying them, but the case would not be decided on until the original dispute between the brokers was resolved. Ultimately, the court decided that Leonida was not entitled to a commission.[68] In this case, Musa was not the primary target of legal action and was not going to be meaningfully affected by the court's decision.

Within two years of his father's passing away, Hasan appeared on the list of Egyptian merchants serving on the Cairo Merchant Court. He would remain in this position from 1869 until the merchant courts ceased to operate in 1876. In certain ways, Hasan's merchant court was different from Musa's. In the 1870s, the court examined more disputes emanating from the sale of agricultural land, its mandate included more commerce-related administrative tasks (e.g., as a depository for monetary guarantees), and its operation became largely reliant on legal practitioners representing merchant litigants. The number of cases that the court was hearing increased exponentially because it acted as a court of appeals for cases decided on elsewhere, primarily in Alexandria. In the context of this intensity, Hasan did not only attend and participate in the proceedings but also, significantly, resorted to the merchant court to sue his former business associates. As merchants, the court members adjudicating these cases probably knew Hasan's legal adversaries. Yet his membership of the court, knowledge of its internal dynamics, and his familiarity with the corpus of applicable laws must have led both him and his adversaries to recognize that he held an advantage in the arena of commercial law.

The structure of merchant court membership allowed for any presiding merchant to miss some sessions. As explained in Chapter One, there were six main members (*a'da'*), but the quorum was set at four. Furthermore, there was an equal number of deputies (*nuwwab*), also merchants, who would step in to fill any empty seats below the quorum. For about one year between the autumn of 1871 and the summer of 1872, Hasan al-'Aqqad exploited that structure in a particular way. He appeared in the merchant court multiple times as a litigant, suing other merchants over unfulfilled financial promises. Significantly, he mostly attended in his capacity as a member of the court only in the days leading up to the hearing for his own cases. He missed all court sessions after September 27, 1871, reappeared to join other presiding members almost six weeks later on November 7 and 8, and sued Muhammad Ahmad al-Rifa'i the following day, November 9. On another occasion, he was in court on February 6, 1872 as a litigant in his ongoing case against Hasanayn Abu-Hamza. He did not attend court sessions for the following three weeks, only to reappear at the end of the month as a member of the court and, a few days later, as a litigant to resume his suit against Hasanayn. During the months of April, May, and June, he attended once as a litigant and twice to take on the responsibility of bankruptcy trustee in relation to bankruptcy cases being heard by the court. He returned as a member for one day on July 10, again to pursue his case as a litigant against Hasanayn on the following day, July 11.

To better appreciate Hasan's utilization of the court as a litigant, we need to first understand the extent of his knowledge of the workings of the merchant court. This is not knowledge acquired through formal legal education—a subject that will be discussed in the next chapter—but through membership of the court, which allowed him to interact with other merchants of different nationalities, state officials, and legal practitioners. From his position, he became acquainted with the administrative capacity of the merchant court. On one occasion, he participated in requesting relevant "original documents" (*asl al-awraq*) that were used by a council that was formed to settle the debts of a number of merchants. To enforce this administrative demand, the Cairo Merchant Court, functioning as a court of second instance, stopped the implementation (*tawqif nafadh*) of a ruling issued by the Alexandria Merchant Court.[69] On other occasions, the court demanded the police department to hand over contested amounts of money to be preserved at the merchant court while it was deciding on its rightful owners.[70] Hasan also took part in the court's notarization duties such as the certification (*al-tasdiq, al-i'timad*) of agreements (Ar. *kunkurdatu*; It. *concordato*) arrived at by creditors and debtors independently, outside of state-endorsed channels.[71] This firsthand experience offered Hasan a grip on the mechanisms through which a court decision would be put on hold, money could be sequestered or released, and unofficial agreements be made official.

Members of the merchant court did not only interpret and implement the law. They often stepped in to assume the trusteeship of bankruptcies or the representation of creditors whenever the litigants were unable to agree among themselves on who would fill these roles. During the first half of 1872, Hasan was appointed as bankruptcy trustee three times. Two of those appear to have been unproblematic cases. He assumed the position in relation to the bankruptcy case of Ahmad al-Bushi, who ultimately agreed with his creditors to pay a quarter of what he owed them over a period of one year.[72] In a different case, when the trustee of Ahmad al-Dijwi's bankruptcy passed away before the case was closed, the court asked Hasan to take his place, which he did.[73] The third case was more complicated and, therefore, more revealing of the authority of a court-appointed bankruptcy trustee. According to the proceedings, a group of creditors sought the court's help to reclaim outstanding debts from the estate of *al-hajj* Bura'i al-Hasiri, a recently deceased merchant. The court assigned two of its own members, Hasan al-'Aqqad and Mahmud 'Abd-al-Mu'ti (a business partner of Musa, Hasan's late father) to the key roles of bankruptcy trustee and creditors' representative, respectively. These appointments reveal that *al-hajj* Bura'i's inheritors were unable or unwilling to negotiate with his creditors. At the same time, the creditors could not agree on the best way forward—at least, they could not do so quickly enough. In his role as trustee, Hasan was now responsible for auctioning off five properties that belonged to the estate. He invited interested buyers to place their bids within thirty days. Of those, a house and an undeveloped lot (*kharaba*) became a subject of conflict. Salih Afandi Karara was leading the bid by the end of the designated period, but *al-mu'allim* Hasan 'Ali al-Muhandis outbid him by 1,000 *qurush* shortly after the deadline. At that moment, Hasan al-'Aqqad decided not to disqualify the highest bid on account of its lateness but rather to defer to the merchant court, which issued a unanimous decision to:

> instruct *al-sayyid* Hasan al-'Aqqad to accept the bid presented by *al-mu'allim* Hasan 'Ali al-Muhandis without regard to (*dun al-iltifat ila*) Salih Afandi Karara's objection. If the Afandi wishes to buy, he should present a higher offer.[74]

This was a surprising decision because the merchant court decided to disregard its own deadline, which was consequential for the bankruptcy and the prospective buyers. Hasan's decision to slow down the process and forfeit his decision-making authority in order to comply with the wishes of his merchant court peers could be read in several ways. It may have followed from an awareness of the court's flexibility with deadlines, the undue influence of the successful bidder, or Hasan's own wish to be on good terms with his peers at a time when he was suing others in the merchant court.

In addition to his status as a wealthy and well-connected merchant, his knowledge of commercial law, and his position on the merchant court, Hasan was also in close proximity to a notable historical development: the genesis of the modern legal profession. In 1857, the merchant courts of Cairo and Alexandria became the first forums to allow for legal representation within the Khedival judicial sphere. Despite its formal ban on "lawyers" (*avukatiyya*, sing. *avukatu*), the merchant court allowed for "deputies" (*wukala*, sing. *wakil*) to represent merchant-litigants. By the mid-1860s, a corps of specialized legal practitioners became a permanent fixture of the work of merchant courts.[75] Notable among them was Tito Figari, who is the subject of Chapter Four of this book and who was among Hasan's *wukala* in the suits he brought to the merchant court. Another was a legal practitioner by the name of Dimitri 'Abduh. What set Hasan al-'Aqqad apart as a client was that before hiring them he had had the chance to observe them in action, interact with them from a position of authority, and know what the merchants who presided over the court thought of them.

Hasan appeared in court as a litigant in relation to at least four cases. Two of those pertained to his ostensible right to commercial profits that were due to his father at the time of his death. The other two saw Hasan sue his own business partners. The information that survived from these disputes is uneven in terms of length and level of detail. Yet, collectively, they show us how Hasan's family background and his more recent status as a landowner were all intertwined with his position within the commercial-legal infrastructure. The appearance of a dispute over agricultural land is particularly significant because, as we will see in Chapter Five, land was supposed to be beyond the reach of commercial law. It is also important to note that Hasan was always the plaintiff in these court cases. There was no written rule against suing members of the court who were themselves merchants and must have been parties to commercial disputes all the time. In the absence of empirical evidence, we should consider the possibility that Hasan's position may have intimidated other merchants who were in conflict with him, and while they may have been willing to sue a business partner or a debtor, they may have deemed the official legal route futile in relation to him.

Material and social inheritance from Musa al-'Aqqad remained important to Hasan decades after his father died. During the official interrogations that followed the defeat of the ʿUrabists, Hasan was accused of having received "money from abroad to stir up the minds of Egyptians against the Khedive (*nuqud min al-kharij li-baththal-mafasid fi adhhan 'ahali al-qutr al-misri didd al-hadra al-khidiwiyya*)." Hasan refused to disclose the details of his wealth but, in response to the interrogator's insistence, he ultimately responded: "I have repeatedly clarified this matter before but since the Commission is repeating the question, I will say this . . . the existence of these [large] amounts of money is not strange and should not arouse suspicion. The wealth of our family is well known, particularly that I have received the inheritance of Musa Bey al-ʿAqqad sixteen years ago . . . ."[76] Hasan's statement was only partly accurate. As an active merchant, Musa's estate did not include money and assets that were easily enumerated at his death. He had ongoing business partnerships and loans that he had extended to other merchants, which would only be settled years after his death.

The incomplete record of one of those inheritance-related disputes is instructive of Hasan's utilization of his position on the merchant court to resolve some of these issues in his own favor. One of Musa al-ʿAqqad's business partners in Khartoum was a certain Ahmad al-Rifaʿi. By the spring of 1871, both Musa and Ahmad had passed away and it fell to their sons, Hasan Musa al-ʿAqqad and Muhammad Ahmad al-Rifaʿi, to decide on where to go from there. It appears that Hasan wanted to dissolve the partnership, believing that he would extract a certain amount of money as a result, and he may have tried to do so amicably at first. The archival record begins with a situation that shows Hasan enjoying a double advantage over Muhammad. He was thoroughly familiar with and involved in the operation of the judicial forum responsible for overseeing the dissolution of the partnership. He was also well-established in Cairo whereas his opponent resided in Khartoum, where the business was based. The initial ruling issued by the merchant court in May 1871 was in Hasan's favor, but its exact details are missing. It is possible that Muhammad did not get to present his case at that point because of being far from Cairo. Eventually, he did present a written contestation to the court, which decided to refer the matter to two auditors representing each of the litigants. Hasan had already named his own, and now the merchant court named Mahmud Bey al-ʿAttar, a colleague of Hasan on the court, to represent Muhammad.[77]

The court also telegraphed the Khartoum Governorate to convey two instructions to Muhammad, namely, to send the company's "ledgers and papers . . . within 60 days" and to be present personally or through a *wakil* before the auditors when summoned. The record ends here before a final resolution was reached but with Hasan well-positioned to achieve his goal, given his proximity to the site of settlement and his acquaintance with the auditors.

Approximately a year later, a similar dispute about another of Musa's business partnerships unfolded. This time, it pitted Hasan directly against his father's partner, Mustafa Afandi al-Hakim, a merchant based in al-Mahalla.[78] The contract signed in 1864 specified that Mustafa would supply 500 *quintals* (Ar. *qintar*) of cotton to Musa in installments (*shay' fi shay'*) over the course of two years. It detailed the specifications of the cotton as well as the methods of payment—half of the price would be paid upfront—and delivery—the first installment would be ready in al-Mahalla within sixty days of the first payment. When Hasan gained access to the paper trail of this deal after his father passed away in 1867, he discovered that his father had received only about 400 *quintals* of cotton even though he had paid the agreed-on price for 500 *quintals*. It may have taken him a while to make this discovery and he may have reached out to Mustafa informally first to collect the difference. Speculation aside, Hasan turned to the merchant court in early 1872 to sue Mustafa over the undelivered cotton. Mustafa defended himself, presenting the original contract, signed receipts, and a record of the cost of transporting the cotton by train to Alexandria. He also objected to Hasan's claim that one of the transactions was concluded without a paper trail, arguing that the merchant court "requires written evidence . . . otherwise [Hasan] has no right to demand the said amount." In the end, Mustafa admitted to owing a small amount to Musa's estate—less than 3,000 *ta'rifa* compared to the almost 18,000 that Hasan was asking for—which he was willing to pay.

Judging from the court record, Mustafa's defense seemed plausible. Particularly, his point about the necessity of a written document to establish debt was consistent with merchant court practices. Therefore, the way in which the case unfolded from that point onward is noteworthy. After studying the documents, the court decided on a date to hear the litigants' oral arguments and issue its ruling. Hasan hired a legal practitioner, Dimitri, who represented him in this session, but Mustafa did not show up. In his absence, Dimitri started with a technical point regarding the accounting. He explained several errors that Mustafa committed in calculating the total debt. Those alone would not have accounted for the significant difference in numbers between what he admitted to and what Hasan was demanding. Dimitri then claimed that transporting the cotton to Alexandria was not a part of the original agreement. Without written consent from the late Musa, it was possible that Mustafa was the one who needed to transport it for his own reasons (*li-darurat nafsihi*) and, therefore, there was no obligation to reimburse him for that expense. Moreover, Dimitri added, an implicit admission of the undocumented debt could be inferred from Mustafa's answers. The court unanimously concurred with each of Dimitri's arguments and decided in absentia that Mustafa was responsible for the entire amount that Hasan demanded. Like in his previous dispute with Muhammad al-Rifa'i, Hasan managed to utilize the commercial-legal infrastructure to his advantage. His claims may have been valid and his legal representative persuasive, but one cannot rule out the potential effect of a sympathetic court that was headed by Hasan and even Musa's peers and an anticipation of legal defeat that led Mustafa al-Hakim to give up before the case was decided.

His deep familiarity with the workings of the merchant court may have led Hasan to utilize it as part of a larger strategy to force debt repayment outside the official channels. The pressure he exerted on Ibrahim al-Amin al-Jallab, whom he claimed owed him 110,000 *ta'rifa*, is a case in point. On March 14, 1872, Ibrahim went to the merchant court to face Hasan's Italian lawyer, Tito Figari. No decision was reached at the end of that session, but the court ordered the appointment of inspectors to "search Ibrahim al-Amin's residence, seize whatever promissory notes and papers kept there and turn them in to the court."[79] Usually, in cases of debt-related disputes, the merchant court instructed merchants to present their ledgers for examination. In this case, it decided to use a heavier hand. The absence of an explanation for this measure in the court record opens the door for speculation: was Ibrahim known to be deceptive, or was Hasan's influence a factor? Two weeks later, the court met again to discuss the case—this time in the presence of Hasan al-'Aqqad. It decided to summon another merchant who it discovered had lent a smaller amount of money to Ibrahim and had not been paid yet.[80] As the amount of debt to be settled as a part of this case increased, Ibrahim was facing even more pressure.

Two days later, Ibrahim submitted a written statement in which he admitted to his debt to Hasan and explained that it had all been a misunderstanding. The court's summary of the statement is worth recounting here.

> The two promissory notes [proving] the debt, dated 19 Safar 1285 [June 10, 1868], had his [Ibrahim's] seal on them. *Al-sayyid* Hasan had demanded the repayment of the debt through government offices (*mahallat al-hukuma*) and the [merchant] court when they [i.e., him and Ibrahim] had a falling out (*hasil baynahu wa baynahu munafasa wa mukhasama*), and Ibrahim was objecting and complaining from *al-sayyid* Hasan. However, when they had a conversation and examined the documents and calculations, it became clear that the debt was legitimate and that the promissory notes were authentic . . .

Despite his unequivocal admission, Ibrahim was not in a position to pay his debt. Under pressure, he found another creditor, *al-Shaykh* Yusuf Muhammad al-Nur, who bought the debt from Hasan. In exchange, Hasan withdrew his lawsuit.[81] As Ibrahim's written account shows, when a disagreement ensued, Hasan's decision to escalate went through "government offices and the [merchant] court." While these official channels did not directly prompt a repayment, they constituted an effective instrument to force Ibrahim to search among his commercial network for an escape from Hasan's pressure.

A common thread in the previous examples is Hasan's deeper familiarity with the workings of the merchant court and potentially the impression that his rivals had about the court's readiness to support him. In a particularly interesting case, Hasan sued one of his debtors, a landowner named Hasanayn Abu-Hamza, to retrieve the significant amount of 3,100 Egyptian pounds. Commercial law and the established practices of the merchant courts distinguished between commercial and agricultural activities. As will be explained in more detail in Chapter Five, the agricultural land market was considered to be a noncommercial matter and was governed by separate laws. Hasan, however, was aware that the jurisdictional boundary between commerce and agriculture was porous in certain situations. Therefore, when he went to the merchant court to sue Hasanayn, he demanded that provisional sequestration (*al-hajz al-tahaffuzi*) be applied to Abu-Hamza's lands in al-Buhayra, south of Alexandria, and everything on it, including buildings and cattle. Hasanayn did not attend that session, and the merchant court granted Hasan his request, writing to the al-Buhayra Governorate to launch the sequestration process.[82] About a month later, and apparently with no progress on the sequestration front, Hasan reappeared in the merchant court to claim that Hasanayn owed him a substantially larger amount of money—7,080 Egyptian pounds.[83] This time, he requested the sequestration of more of Hasanayn's assets, including his residence in Cairo. Once again, Hasanayn did not attend the session, but the court, while accepting Hasan's claim about the larger debt, clarified the order of the sequestrations. First, it ordered the confiscation of agricultural goods in Hasanayn's possession and, second, to sequester agricultural lands, the value of which was equivalent to the remainder of the debt.

Most likely, because this case pertained to agricultural lands outside of Cairo, the merchant court could only act through the cooperation of the al-Buhayra Governorate. It was the latter that had the authority to sequester agricultural products and, more importantly, land. It was also the Governorate that was responsible for serving the summons from the Cairo Merchant Court. A few days after the revision of the debt's amount, the Governorate wrote back to the merchant court to confirm that Hasanayn had been notified of the date of the upcoming court session. However, it revealed a complication with regard to the court's debt settlement plan. Hasanayn's agricultural goods had already been sequestered to pay for debts that he "owed to the government (*lil-miri*)." In addition, Hasanayn's "lands (*atyan*) are scattered over many regions [within al-Buhayra] and there was no indication given regarding which plots were to be sequestered." The merchant court responded that it did not have a preference as long as the value of the sequestered lands equaled the value of the debt.[84] For several months afterward, Hasan repeatedly requested that the merchant court follow up with the al-Buhayra Governorate. The merchant court did, reminding the Governorate that Hasan's debt repayment would take place once the government's debts had been settled.[85] The archival record ends before the case was closed, but similar to the cases mentioned above, Hasan's utilization of the merchant court showed no sign of slowing down.

Commercial and Legal Activity After the Merchant Courts

The merchant courts closed their doors for the last time in 1876. Pending cases that were between local merchants were transferred to the government-enacted civil courts, while those that included "European interests" were sent to the newly inaugurated Mixed Courts. This judicial rearrangement took place in the context of a serious political and economic crisis, which Hasan al-'Aqqad was embroiled in. The year 1876 was a particularly critical time for Hasan. Not only did he lose access to the merchant court as a forum through which he pursued certain financial interests, but his future as a landowner was also in danger because of the government's first attempt to repeal the Muqabala Law. When the government ultimately succeeded in repealing the law in 1880, Hasan's public objections to the law would lead to his exile for about two years in Sudan.

After the closing of the merchant courts and before his exile, Hasan al-'Aqqad had his first encounter with the Mixed Courts in 1878. The case pertained to his peculiar partnership with the wealthy Alexandrian-Greek entrepreneur, and later Belgian subject, Menandro Zizinia, which had started almost a decade earlier.[86] In 1868, one year before the inauguration of the Suez Canal, Menandro Zizinia funded an exploratory project to establish the profitability of mining the quarries in the vicinity of Jabal Junayfah, north of Suez. The results convinced him that he should try to obtain a concession from Khedive Isma'il to extract "marble, gypsum, cement and other limestone." The Khedive was open to the idea but, according to Menandro's account, he would grant the concession only to a local subject. This political decision opened a path for Hasan to enter a new realm of entrepreneurship.

In April 1870, Khedive Isma'il's government awarded the concession that Menandro Zizinia had envisioned to Hasan al-'Aqqad. At the time, Hasan had wealth through commerce and landownership, official status through membership of the Cairo Merchant Court and Consultative Assembly, and pedigree through his recently deceased father. But Hasan's interest in this new opportunity was not at the expense of Menandro. It was in cooperation with him. Hasan, it seems, utilized his connections both within the government and private capitalist circles to facilitate this new mining operation. He would lend his name to Menandro Zizinia's concession in exchange for 10 percent of the profits. Once that major hurdle was cleared, the government and the concessionaire(s) turned to technical matters. Government-appointed surveyors determined the exact boundaries of the area of the concession, and engineers devised a plan for the extraction work given the conditions on the ground. This step was expected to be completed within a month. Instead, eight years later, the project had not taken off. Hasan al-'Aqqad, the nominal concessionaire, signed off on the government's surveys right away. Menandro Zizinia found them unacceptable and decided not to invest in the project, despite the existence of a concession.

Several years later, Egypt's economic conditions and judicial landscape had changed considerably. In 1878, the Mixed Courts existed as an authoritative judicial forum that was concerned with adjudicating disputes surrounding foreign interests specifically. Menandro used this newly established court to sue the government for the losses he accrued by not exploiting the minerals of Jabal Junayfah. The government responded that there was no case. The concessionaire, Hasan, had indeed signed off on the maps in 1870 and the fact that work never commenced was his responsibility. Menandro rebutted this argument, declaring that it was an open secret that he was the real concessionaire, whereas Hasan's involvement was only to appease the former Khedive. In fact, Hasan could not be located during the litigation and never showed up in court, despite his centrality to the dispute. Ultimately, the Mixed Court ruled in Menandro Zizinia's favor, accepting his claim that Hasan was, in effect, only his agent.

The period that immediately followed this Mixed Court case saw Hasan al-'Aqqad lend his name to the nascent nationalist movement. He was likely among the 330 signatories of the 1879 *al-La'iha al-Wataniyya*, which represented a wide array of social forces including landowners, merchants, senior bureaucrats, and army officers, who aimed to preempt the European control of government finances.[87] Contemporaneous calls for the establishment of a national bank did not include similarly broad lists of sponsors, but historians have generally considered those to be an expression of mercantile interests, which would have been pertinent to influential merchants like Hasan.[88] This political activism was only a beginning. Within a year, as recounted above, Hasan would be exiled to Sudan over his objections to the abolishment of the Muqabala Law—a direct threat to his land-based interests—play a significant role in the 'Urabist revolution, and be exiled once more in its aftermath, this time to Masawwa.

A decade later, in 1893, Hasan finally received a Khedival pardon. After his return to Cairo, his name continued to appear in the proceedings of the Mixed and National Courts in relation to financial disputes. Limitations on archival access make it difficult to recount the details of these disputes. It appears that a prolonged dispute—or a series of related disputes—between Hasan and his sister Fatima concerning their father's inheritance was a main reason for Hasan's continued interaction with the courts during the final phase of his life. The following synthesis of Hasan's final legal encounters shows the survival of the legacy of the merchant courts and the al-'Aqqads' involvement in them.

Fatima sued Hasan before the National Court in January 1883 as soon as he was sentenced to exile in Massawa. Probably, Fatima feared that Hasan's departure could mean the loss of assets that they had inherited when Musa al-'Aqqad died in 1867 and jointly owned since then. The National Court sent her back to a *shari'a* court since this was a dispute over inheritance. Just a few months before Hasan's unexpected return from exile in April 1893, Fatima went to the Mixed Court to argue against the seizure of a portion of this shared inheritance by the English-owned Egyptian Mineral Company Ltd. on account of the exiled Hasan's outstanding debts.[89] Next, Fatima sued Hasan in June 1898 and again in April 1901 before the National Courts. She was referred to in one of the French documents relating to this series of litigations as "Dame Fatma Epousé El Ezabi." Two men carrying the name of the family that Fatima had married into, Mahmud Bey al-'Izabi and Amin al-'Izabi, were also involved in lawsuits against either Hasan himself or Husayn and Muhammad al-'Aqqad, potentially Hasan's heirs since they jointly reacquired lands that had been expropriated from Hasan in exchange for unpaid debts.[90] The cases were litigated between 1894 and 1917. It is most likely that Hasan passed away sometime between 1910, the year when he was criticized publicly for political statements he had made against the National Party's call to increase taxation on the wealthy in order to create a social safety net for Egypt's impoverished peasants and workers,[91] and 1917 when a Mixed Court case referring to his land in al-Matariyya is mentioned in relation to his potential heirs, Husayn and Muhammad.

Some of these cases became references for a new wave of legal scholarship that aimed to distill the jurisprudence of the National Courts in the early twentieth century. The lawyer Ibrahim Jammal, founding editor of the journal *al-Huquq*, published a book in 1909 in which he attempted to engage with "what Europeans call 'La jurisprudence,' an art . . . the subject of which is to extract the opinions that the courts used to issue their judgements . . . . These opinions could be synthesized into legal principles [*fa-tata'allaf min tilk al-ara' qawa'id qanuniyya*] . . . that could become the foundation for new court rulings" in the future.[92] Of the principles he listed based on reading a case that Hasan had brought to the National Courts was one that evoked the language of the merchant courts that had ceased to exist more than thirty years earlier.

> No one is to be considered a merchant except if he has taken commerce as a vocation. As for the commercial activities that are conducted by a non-merchant [*ghayr al-tajir*], they are [also] to be litigated only under commercial law.[93]

The merchant courts, as will be explained in Chapter Five, defined commerce as the exclusive domain of merchants. It is possible that Hasan was repeating that older argument in the 1890s only to be rebuffed by a new generation of civil judges who were no longer knowledgeable of, or bound by, Ottoman law.

Concluding Remarks

The merchant courts were the state-organized judicial forums that merchants could resort to in order to resolve their commercial disputes. The Khedival state established those forums, defined their position in relation to itself and to the European consulates, and set the rules that ensured that their operation be in harmony with the larger bureaucracy. It also linked the merchant courts to the Ottoman legal domain. Still, the actual functioning of the merchant courts had to rely on the involvement and leadership of both local and European merchants. Musa al-'Aqqad was one of those merchants who stepped into this novel commercial legal realm in the mid-1850s, when he was at a high point in his career, operating a profitable business based in Khartoum and enjoying strong connections to the Khedival state. Like Butrus Tawil, whom we encountered in the previous chapter, Musa may have preferred not to settle his business disputes in court. Yet, when his Sardinian business partner sued him over a business deal gone sour and the panel of presiding merchants split along local-foreigner lines, Musa may have detected the potential of the new commercial-legal infrastructure.

With business interests spanning Khartoum, Cairo, and other regions within the expanding territory of the Khedival state, Musa was elected a member of the merchant court in 1862. He remained in that position until his death in 1867.

His son and heir Hasan al-ʿAqqad entered many of the same domains. He inherited commercial businesses and agricultural lands and, similar to Musa, joined the merchant court and strove to establish himself near the center of political power. In the face of rapidly changing political circumstances, Hasan took positions that set him apart from the legacy of his father. He used the merchant courts more cynically, suing former business partners and debtors from a clear position of power before the merchant court, aided by his institutional status and the expertise of some of the most effective legal practitioners around (including Tito Figari, who is the subject of the next chapter). His first foray into the world of national politics to defend the tax privilege of the *Muqabala* led to his exile to Sudan, where his father made a fortune twenty years earlier. A second, bolder involvement in the world of politics, as part of a wider coalition that coalesced around Ahmad ʿUrabi, sent Hasan back to exile in Massawa for ten years. When he returned, his attempts to resort to commercial law based on his deep familiarity with its pre-1883 iterations proved ineffective.

Hasan knew the commercial-legal infrastructure and was willing to use it to his own benefit. His commercial experience and position in the Cairo Merchant Court shed light on the growing importance of technical knowledge in engaging with commercial law. For a growing number of merchants in the second half of the nineteenth century, the ability to navigate the commercial-legal infrastructure depended on the help of specialized law practitioners. In the next chapter, we turn to one of those specialists, Tito Figari *al-avukatu*.

FOUR

Tito

THE "AVUKATU" WHO KNEW THE LAW

THE VICE PRESIDENT OF THE Institut d'Égypte asked to speak first during the board meeting on November 5, 1897. "Messieurs," he announced, "le commandeur Tito Figari vient de mourir."[1] The speaker was not an ordinary person. Onofrio Abbate (1824–1915) was a prominent Italian scientist who had lived in Egypt for over fifty years at this point. He was an ophthalmologist, a surgeon, a private doctor to several Khedives, an anthropologist, and a prolific writer. His leadership position within Egypt's longest surviving scientific institution, which was founded during the French expedition roughly a century earlier, was only one of several high-level appointments he held concurrently within the scientific community. But during that meeting, Onforio spoke as a friend and admirer:

> L'amitié sincère et fraternelle qui me liait avec Tito Figari, pourrait peut-étre faire supposer que les sentiments intimes rehaussent les mérites de celui dont on fait l'éloge . . . . Une grande facilité d'élocution, une parole nette et précise, une physionomie aux yeux vifs et francs, et l'art acquis qu'il avait développé dans les réunions et dans les tribunaux, a servi à en faire un orateur aimé . . . ce n'était pourtant pas une simple admiration d'esthétique oratoire, mais assurément une conviction profonde, un résultat de ses raisonnements solides et clairs.[2]

After he finished, another distinguished member of the Institut, Husayn Fakhri Pasha (1843–1920), took the floor. Husayn was a renowned statesman who had been a permanent feature of government cabinets since the British occupation of 1882 and who, in 1897, was holding two cabinet positions: education and public works. He was also a figure within Egypt's scientific societies. His elegy of Tito Figari was much more reserved: "un adversaire droit, loyal, correct, et malgré des discussions vives, amères quelquefois, les relations communes n'en furent jamais altérées."[3]

Over the following months, laudatory obituaries of Tito would be published in the bulletins of the Société Khédivale de Géographie[4] and the Società Africana d'Italia,[5] which described him as one with "d'ingegno eletissimo." Soon afterward, a leading Belgian freemason worried about the fragmentation of masonic bodies in Egypt, a danger that was exacerbated with the death of Tito Figari.[6]

Evidently, Tito was quite accomplished when he passed away, but his legacy was not a straightforward one. He was a member of Egypt's premier scientific circles, although he was not a scientist. He was well known to the top echelons of the Khedival state in various capacities, including as a leader within the large Italian community of Egypt. Yet, as a facilitator of Italian colonialism in sub-Saharan Africa, Tito spent a limited amount of time in Italy. He was not born there and his death near Naples may have been a coincidence—he was in Portici on the outskirts of Naples to seek medical treatment or recuperation. His family's hometown, where he would be buried, was in distant Genoa, in the north of the Italian peninsula.

At the moment of his death, the recorded memory of Tito Figari hinted at the complex identity that he had formed in relation to the rapidly changing world that he inhabited. An emphasis on his Italianness in these accounts was unsurprising. Not only was he genuinely committed to his expatriate community and to Italian imperialism more generally but also, especially under British rule, there existed an inter-European competition over presence and influence in the political and cultural spheres.[7] But Tito's sixty-year life overlapped with momentous political transformations that must have offered him multiple chances to redefine his place within Egypt and, from a distance, Italy. He was in his thirties when the Suez Canal was opened, Italian unification was completed, and the Egyptian Khedivate declared bankruptcy; in his forties when the 'Urabists took power in Cairo, the Mahdists did the same in Khartoum, and Britain occupied Egypt; and in his fifties when the Italian formal colonization of East Africa was on an upward trajectory.

The historical accident of him witnessing these large-scale events is significant for this study of market governance because of an overlooked, albeit important, detail in his life. Tito launched his professional career as a *wakil* in the Cairo Merchant Court during the early 1860s, when he was in his mid-twenties. He built a career and a reputation representing merchant litigants with reference to commercial laws before panels of merchant "judges." When the merchant courts closed their doors for the last time in 1876, Tito seamlessly joined the ranks of the first cohort of professional lawyers who practiced law before the newly established Mixed Courts. His engagement with the commercial-legal infrastructure was his entry point into Egyptian society: its local elite circles, its Italian community, its underground masonic lodges, its Khedival and colonial government centers, and its connections to sub-Saharan Africa. Understanding how Tito engaged with commercial law does not only teach us about the law as practiced in relation to commerce but also what being a commercial *wakil* and, later, professional lawyer allowed a European subject to be within Khedival and British-ruled Egypt.

I divide this chapter into three parts. The first is an attempt to sketch out the overall trajectory of Tito Figari's life. The second and third zoom in on his career first as a *wakil* in the Cairo Merchant Court and, after 1876, as a professional lawyer who appeared before the Cairo Mixed Court and undertook a range of non-adversarial lawyerly work.

His Life

The year of Tito's birth, 1838, was decisive in Ottoman imperial politics. The economic powerbase of Mehmed Ali was under immense pressure with the monopolies showing signs of disintegration domestically and being outlawed by international treaty.[8] The major Ottoman government reform program, known as the Tanzimat, would be launched the following year, partly in an effort to reconfigure imperial power in the provinces.[9] Damascus, the city of Tito's birth, had been under Egyptian rule for six years. As a newborn, he must have been surrounded by adults who talked anxiously about a new round of war that had begun in northern Syria when the Ottoman army invaded the province in an attempt to reclaim it from Egyptian control. As he turned three, Damascus had returned to the Ottoman fold. The Egyptian soldiers withdrew back to Egypt, while the Ottoman center recognized it as the dynastic domain of Mehmed Ali and his descendants. The era of Khedival Egypt had effectively begun.[10]

The exact date and circumstances of how Tito made his way from Damascus to Cairo are unknown. The fact that Tito became known only as a young man in Cairo, where another famous Figari—Antonio Figari (1804–1870), a pharmacist and botanist—had lived since the 1820s, has created some confusion over his ancestry as well. The British orientalist James Heyworth-Dunne has mistakenly referred to Tito as the "[s]on of Dr. Figari, a colleague of Clot Bey."[11] Based on multiple obituaries, Tito Figari was born in Damascus to a Genoese father and only later relocated to Cairo, where his uncle, Antonio, was leading a remarkable career as a scientist and government official and was well established within the circles of political power in Mehmed Ali's Egypt. By the late 1830s when his nephew was born, Antonio had served in multiple prestigious government posts, including as overseer of Cairo's military hospital, director of the medical school's laboratories, and inspector of pharmacies. He would lead scientific expeditions in Anatolia, Arabia, and Egypt itself in the 1840s and would continue his relationship with Egypt's dynastic governors until the end of his life, sitting on Khedive Isma'il's committee for the 1867 Exposition Universelle at Paris.

The connection between Antonio and Tito was clear to their contemporaries who inhabited the same social circles. For example, the museum of the Société Khédivale de Géographie, which opened in December 1898, featured two traces of Antonio Figari. The first, appropriately, was a geological map that he had produced during his work as a scientist and was now on display in one of the museum's halls. The second was a portrait of his that was gifted to the Société by the family of his recently deceased nephew, "Commandeur Tito Figari," who had passed away just one year earlier. Antonio's portrait would join those of prominent Egyptian and European scientists such as Mahmud al-Falaki (1815–1885), 'Ali Mubarak (1823–1893), and Georg August Schweinfurth (1836–1925).[12] The Société Khédivale de Géographie had been established in 1875, five years after the death of Antonio Figari. While not a scientist, his nephew Tito served as its first "secrétaire adjoint." Despite his presence at the moment of its founding, Tito would be mentioned in relation to his famous uncle after both had passed away. Additionally, Tito's obituaries would inform readers that he was a member of a family that is well-known in Syria and Egypt and a relative of "Antonio Figari Bey, illustrious naturalist."[13]

This familial connection was not insignificant. It is likely that Antonio Figari's stature had a lot to do with Tito's pursuit of a legal education. Throughout the first half of the nineteenth century, but especially starting in 1826, Mehmed Ali sent several education missions to Europe to prepare a new cadre of graduates who would lead his burgeoning state structure. The extant information about these students is incomplete, but it seems that they were generally Arabic-speaking Egyptians who showed promise in primary education and Ottomans of diverse backgrounds—for example, Armenians and Circassians. A significant number of them studied military sciences.[14] Had students of similar backgrounds and courses of study continued to dominate these education missions, someone of Tito Figari's profile would not have been eligible for a government-sponsored scholarship. Yet the constitution and purpose of these missions changed with time. In the mid-1840s, after Mehmed Ali had moved on from his military approach to Ottoman politics and received an imperial investiture for hereditary rule in Egypt, he sent a final student mission to Europe, which had a different character. This one would include four of his descendants, including his grandson Isma'il who would become Khedive of Egypt two decades later, as well as the close relatives of a number of top government officials. A growing portion of these students focused on non-military courses such as civil administration and engineering.[15] Under Sa'id Pasha (r. 1854–1863), this orientation would resume. A larger percentage of the students joining the missions focused on medicine and other non-military sciences, and a significant portion of them were close relatives of the top echelons of the state, including Europeans (as opposed to Egyptians or Ottoman subjects). The first group of students that was sent to Europe under Sa'id included two nephews of Nubar Pasha (1825–1899), the son of Sa'id's interpreter, one of Sa'id's *mamluks*, and the sons or nephews of at least three top medical officials. One of those was Tito Figari, the Damascus-born nephew of the Italian inspector of pharmacies, Antonio Bey Figari.

Thus, in 1855, at the age of seventeen, Tito was on his way to France on scholarship from the government of Egypt. For the first time, over half of his cohort—twelve out of twenty-two students—were Europeans like himself. About half of the students received funding for five or six years. Upon their return, only one, a nephew of Nubar Pasha, does not seem to have received a government appointment. More typically, five returned to join the military and four to join the civil government in various capacities, including one who studied medicine but ended up working for the Khedival household as the *wakil* of the estate of Sa'id Pasha's wife, Inji Hanim (d. 1890).[16] Two of the three students who studied law followed a similar path. Ahmad Afandi Shukri and Wasif Afandi 'Azmi, both Egyptians, joined the civil administration—the latter was awarded the honorary presidency of the Mixed Courts in 1883. The third, Tito Figari, was the exception. When his government funding ran out, he remained in France at the expense of his family, and when he returned eventually, he started a private practice.

Tito's decision was probably unusual. Legal representation was practiced in particular ways in Egypt at the time.[17] In *shari'a* courts, business associates or relatives represented absent litigants on the grounds that they were related to them and not based on their legal credentials.[18] *'Ardhaljis* who wrote petitions and coached litigants outside of courthouses earned their reputation because of their literacy and practical experience, not because they went to law school. Consular courts may have been an exception in that respect, but they were limited to protecting the interests of their own subjects and protégés and were not necessarily restricted to upholding a particular legal code.[19] Furthermore, in 1857, two years after Tito left for France, the merchant courts of Alexandria and Cairo explicitly banned lawyers (*al-avukatiyya*) from entering the courtroom. In short, there was practically no space for a private lawyer within the judiciary.

At twenty-four or twenty-five, Tito returned to Cairo, qualified for a vocation that did not exist. His credentials and his well-connected uncle, Antonio, could probably have secured a government job for him. Yet Tito chose a different path that was consistent with his academic training. In 1863, his name appeared for the first time in the records of the Cairo Merchant Court, not as an *avukatu*—a title that he must have felt entitled to after years of study and one that he would proudly hold onto for the rest of his life—but as a *wakil* of an Italian creditor. Tito's first client was Ilario al-Hakim, a physician, who was suing a certain Idris Afandi over an unpaid debt.[20] The circumstances of Tito's entry into the realm of legal practice can only be speculated. Given what we know, Tito must have known, possibly through his former colleagues in law school who returned before him and had by then assumed positions within the civil government, that his best chance was in commercial law. Venues for private legal representation were extremely limited with the exception of the merchant courts, which would accept written arguments on behalf of litigants. As an Italian and a physician, Ilario must have known Antonio Figari, a high-ranking member of the medical establishment and, by extension, a well-known figure within the Italian community in Egypt. It was he who was in a position to help an acquaintance find a highly qualified, if inexperienced, legal counsel, while promoting his nephew's budding private legal career.

Within a year of Tito's first case, the statute of the merchant courts was revised to allow for in-person legal representation, while reaffirming that only *wakils*, and not *avukatus*, were allowed inside the courtroom. The *wakil* would be a deputy or an agent of the litigant who would stand in for him when absent, but the *avukatu* was a legal specialist who deployed technical knowledge on behalf of any client. Tito was a law school-educated *avukatu*, but if he refrained from using the title during court sessions, he could finally begin practicing law. Indeed, over the following twelve years between 1864 and 1876, Tito Figari would become a well-known name in the world of commercial law. As a *wakil*, he represented numerous litigants of different nationalities in a wide range of commercial disputes. Eventually, he would occupy an office at the heart of Cairo's modern city and in one of its most prominent buildings, Maison Matatia at "3 sharia El-Teatro," overlooking al-'Ataba Square and al-Azbakiyya garden and, after 1876, a stone's throw from the Public Debt Commission and the Mixed Court.[21] Jamal-al-Din al-Afghani had turned the café occupying Maison Matatia's ground floor into a platform for preaching anti-imperialism until his arrest and exile in 1879. The Matatia Café would continue to serve as a popular meeting place for 'Urabists over the following few years. The location must have harbored so many possibilities for Tito, who would meet Ahmad 'Urabi himself in the summer of 1881 and on a separate occasion appear before the Mixed Court in a matter related to the Public Debt Commission in 1884.

The 1860s, which witnessed Tito's career rise as a *wakil* before the Cairo Merchant Court, also saw him enthusiastically embrace his

Italian identity. Freemasonry provided an important path for him to engage in all matters Italian within his immediate community in Egypt as well as in his family's original homeland. In 1867, under the umbrella of freemasonry, he contributed to the creation of a mutual aid association for workers and a chamber of commerce within the Italian community in Egypt, as well as in raising money and donating ambulance equipment to "General Garibaldi," himself a committed freemason.[22] The following year, he began a commitment to Italian education that he held onto until the end of his life. At the same moment that Garibaldi was leading a campaign to abolish the papacy in Italy, Tito was laying the foundation of a secular Italian school in Cairo that practically rejected religious control and promoted the love of country and humanity.[23] Freemasonry continued to be a presence in his life, but over the next decade, he cultivated a public profile that exceeded what the secret society, with its continuous contests over leadership, could have allowed him to achieve. In 1871, during the second Italian Census, Tito was one of eight Italians who were commissioned by the Italian consulate to carry out a census of Italians in Cairo.[24] Shortly afterward, and although not a scientist himself, he joined multiple scientific associations, most prominently the Società Geografica Italiana,[25] the Institut d'Égypte, and the Société Khédivale de Géographie. In each of these, he played a formal institutional role, serving as a representative for the Società in Egypt and receiving a medal for his services in 1874,[26] as assistant secretary of the Société Khédivale de Géographie at its founding in 1875, and as a "membre résidant" of the Institut in January 1878.[27]

The second half of the 1870s was a period of intense change in Egypt and within its broader Ottoman context. An economic depression saw Egypt default on its debts to European creditors, and its ruler, Khedive Isma'il, under tremendous European pressure, established the Public Debt Commission, thus effectively surrendering control over the state's finances in 1876. Three years later, facing an acute political crisis that culminated in the first national-scale anti-imperialist political movement led by Ahmad 'Urabi, Isma'il was forced to step down, opening the way for a direct confrontation between the 'Urabists and the British army and ultimately the British occupation of Egypt. Simultaneously, the Ottoman Empire also defaulted on its sovereign debts, witnessed a short-lived constitutional era that ended with significant territorial losses in the context of the Russo-Ottoman War (1877–1878), and saw the inauguration of a distinctive era of modern autocratic rule under a new sultan, Abdul Hamid II (r. 1876–1909). These changes were not only experienced on the level of state elites and the wealthiest investors. For Tito Figari, a well-to-do professional with a growing presence within a European community resident in Egypt, these changes presented new opportunities for work and social positioning.

As a lawyer, Tito had built a twelve-year career in the merchant courts. In 1876, when he was thirty-eight, the merchant courts were to close their doors for the last time, with pending cases that included European interests to be transferred to the newly established Mixed Courts. Most *wakils* who had practiced law before the merchant courts since the 1840s would be disqualified from following these cases or, more importantly, taking new ones in the context of the Mixed Courts because of their lack of formal qualifications. Tito's French legal education on a Khedival government-sponsored scholarship got him across this institutional hurdle. The prospects of professional success, not shared by many of his peers, probably also confirmed his status within the Italian community in Egypt. Yet Egypt's gradual passing from Khedival political control with its distinctive Ottoman background toward the British political realm must have also brought to the Italian community in Egypt a sense of uncertainty about its future. Communal leaders such as Tito must have wondered in those turbulent years what the future of Europeans would be when the 'Urabists seized control of the country and raised the slogan "Egypt for the Egyptians." A different kind of anxiety must have also been expressed at their social gatherings about whether Italians, among other continental Europeans, would face an unequal competition in the cultural and economic arenas to the benefit of Egypt's British colonizers and their subjects and protégés.

On a certain level, Tito Figari appears to have entered the 1880s unscathed by these political and social earthquakes. In the realm of legal practice, Tito's name soon appeared as a legal adviser in a discussion cited in the Report on the Work of the Egyptian Public Debt Commission.[28] It also appeared in the proceedings of the Mixed Courts, where, expectedly, he took on cases with a clear economic dimension. For example, in the initial months of its operation, Tito appeared in the Mixed Court of Cairo to represent the insolvent owners of the Société Anonyme des Eaux de Suez.[29] He would return time and again to the Mixed Court in his capacity as legal counsel to various litigants, aided not only by his professional credentials and years of practice before the merchant courts but also with the help of his now expanded law practice at the Matatia Building, in which he employed at least four others: "Rossano Augusto, 1° clerc à l'étude de M° Tito Figari [,] Ciampini G. B., avocat à la Cour d'Appel, (étude M° Tito Figari)," whose names suggest Italian origins, as well as Marqus al-Kabis, a "Catholic Copt," and Habib Bulad.[30] Tito's professional reputation grew significantly in the 1880s and 1890s. His professional services would be sought by both the Italian consulate as well as by local Egyptian elites in high-profile cases into the 1890s. He would even lead the Mixed Bar Association briefly, despite being based in Cairo when the position was monopolized by Alexandria-based lawyers.[31] Given all that, it is not surprising that his practice would be included among "prominent" lawyers operating "in foreign cities," who are worthy of the trust of "attorneys, bankers, merchants, manufacturers, and business men generally" in a Philadelphia-issued directory "of lawyers and bankers" at the turn of the twentieth century.[32]

Tito's professional successes were evident. His politics were ambiguous. On June 26, 1882, less than three weeks before the British military campaign to occupy Egypt commenced, Tito met with Ahmad 'Urabi, then Minister of War. Shortly afterward, 'Urabi would become Prime Minister and leader of the anti-colonial war of resistance against the British invasion. This was a tense summer. Successive governments were falling in Cairo roughly every two months since 'Urabi had assumed control of the army and demonstrated against the Khedive in the fall of 1881. British warships were stationed off the coast of Alexandria since May in anticipation of a military invasion. On June 11 and 12, intercommunal riots and mob violence in the city had left dozens of Egyptian and European casualties, and large numbers of Europeans were fleeing Alexandria ahead of what seemed like an imminent British-led attack. Yet, in the middle of the widespread tension and preparations for war, 'Urabi accepted Tito Figari's invitation to be a guest of honor at the annual celebration of the Italian school that Tito had co-founded in 1868. The Egyptian leader spoke, as he always did, in Arabic, and Tito translated the speech into Italian. The content of the speech was fitting for a politician in a time of crisis. He emphasized to his Italian audience that Jews, Christians, and Muslims were brothers, thus implying that the context for the recent violence in Alexandria was political rather than sectarian. He reminded them that their school memorialized the name of Vittorio Emanuele II (r. 1861–1878),[33] the King who achieved Italy's freedom, and lamented the passing of Garibaldi three weeks earlier, thus indirectly alluding to the parallels between the hero of Italian unification and himself—both of them would go to war to liberate their countries.[34]

'Urabi's quest ultimately failed, and his leadership of the anticolonial resistance ended with his surrender and exile in British-ruled Ceylon later in 1882. That Tito offered 'Urabi a platform to speak to a European community on the eve of the British invasion of Egypt is not sufficient evidence of a principled position on colonialism. When 'Urabi's archrival Khedive Tawfiq passed away, Tito, in his capacity as governor of the masonic Grand Order of Cairo, eulogized him as "[a]n honest sovereign, gentleman, of an affable and good disposition, a husband and father of untarnished morality, greatest of heart, [who] leaves this classic land overwhelmed with grief, beloved by all those who have had the good fortune to approach him."[35] Moreover, during the 1880s and 1890s, Tito became increasingly the go-to person for Italian colonial explorers on their way to and from East and Central Africa. British-ruled Egypt was often a stopping point for such figures as Romolo Gessi (1831–1881), Gaetano Cassati (1838–1902), Guiseppe Cuzzi (1843–1923), and Gustavo Bianchi (1845–1884). Tito welcomed them to Cairo, arranged for them to meet with members of the Italian community, and offered them his legal services when needed. He was generous with his support, hosting naturalists at his own residence in Shubra, where they recorded seeing a recently identified lizard species.[36] As will become apparent below, he was also trusted by them, serving as a will executor and being approached by the Italian government to represent the families of Italians who never returned from their expeditions. The scientific aspect of these explorers' work was, in certain respects, a continuation of his involvement with the established scientific institutions of Cairo. Thus, in addition to his membership of the Società Geografica Italiana, he eventually joined the Società Africana d'Italia as a corresponding member.[37]

We do not know how much time Tito actually spent in Italy. During the last decade of his life, the intensity of his professional and social activities in Egypt, especially among Italians, showed no sign of abating. He founded and presided over a social club for the Italians of Cairo located at "sharia El-Manakh."[38] In his fifties, the Damascus-born Italian was likely a recognized face in that central and busy part of modern Cairo, centered around al-'Ataba and al-Isma'iliyya squares, where he was moving tirelessly between his office, the courthouse, and the Risotto Society before returning to his villa in the quiet suburb of Shubra to the north. He ventured outside of the city to fulfill social obligations related to his position within the Italian community, such as when he showed up at the Italian consulate in Alexandria to serve as a witness at the marriage of Mosè and Gabriella Tilche in 1894.[39] But few of those who recognized him as a lawyer and a community leader would have known about his embattled leadership of the Italian freemasons in Cairo, an ongoing unresolved matter that must have occupied him during these years.[40] Even fewer people would have recognized his professional and social prominence as a continuation of his early career in the then-defunct merchant courts. He was fifty-eight or fifty-nine when he became sick and left Cairo, not to his father's hometown of Genoa, but to Naples. The circumstances of his death, similar to those of his birth, are not known in detail. His passing, it was reported, was a painful and prolonged affair.[41] His remains would ultimately be placed in an ossuary in 1901, four years after his death, in the vicinity of Genoa.

Tito's rich life provides a fascinating window into that moment of Egypt's history, in which a novel commercial-legal infrastructure was created in the 1830s and 1840s, populated and utilized from the 1850s to the 1870s, and ultimately absorbed and recast in the 1880s and 1890s. The following two sections, which form the remainder of this chapter, shed light on Tito's career as a legal practitioner: first as a *wakil* in the merchant court and, after their closure, as an *avukatu* before its successor, the Mixed Court.

Wakil in Commercial Cases

The merchant courts, where Tito Figari would make his career, had been in operation for a decade when he left for Paris in 1855 to study law. At that time, these courts emphasized the necessity of merchant litigants directly making their case before the court, without mediation. Only in specific circumstances were they allowed to be represented by someone else. The statute of the merchant courts did not explain what these circumstances were but referred to "excuses that are acceptable under the established norms (*al-a'dhar allati tuqbal bi-muqtada al-usul*)."[42] Recorded court practices suggest that the norms included physical disability (due to illness) or absence (due to travel). In these cases, legal representatives were, most likely, business associates or relatives.[43] The most obvious explanation for this rule is that there existed only a very small number of individuals who trained in law or practiced it as a profession. Those who, similar to Tito, studied law as part of government-sponsored student missions up until that point all went into government service upon their return.

Another explanation, in conjunction with the first, is also likely. French commercial law was suspicious of lawyers and keen on excluding them from merchant litigation. Amalia Kessler has argued that the mission of the Parisian Merchant Court was not simply to apply the law but, more importantly, to reestablish trust between disputing merchants, who, by definition, belonged to one commercial community characterized by fraternal relations. Strict application of the law could lead to the confiscation of goods and imprisonment, which might ultimately result in the final exclusion of a merchant from that commercial community and mark his accuser as someone who was dangerous to conduct business with. Therefore, the court wanted to ensure that "merchant litigants . . . speak the simple truth, instead of relying on lawyers to couch their claims in complex legal fictions and technicalities."[44] As the Khedival legal system continued to absorb French legal ideas and forms in the nineteenth century—either directly or through its adoption of Ottoman laws—this concern with lawyers became manifest in 1857, when the merchant court statute was revised to include the following provision:

> [when] dealing with claims in the merchant court, lawyers [*avukatiyya*] are not permitted to enter [the courtroom]. The litigants submit their [written] claims in person or via a *wakil* who holds a [written] authorization [*sanad tawkil*].[45]

This rule, allowing representation in writing through a deputy, such as a business associate or a relative, but banning lawyers from appearing before the merchant court was in effect when Tito—now Tito *al-Avukatu*—returned to Egypt at some point between 1861 and 1863, having studied law in France for at least five years.

Tito's first client was an Italian physician named Ilario al-Hakim. He had loaned a certain Idris Afandi, a former clerk (*mustakhdim*) at one of Cairo's *shari'a* courts, a sum of money. When the agreed-on payment date passed, the physician decided to sue his debtor. Ilario may have become familiar with Tito's recently launched private law practice through the Italian community or through Tito's uncle, Antonio Figari, who was among the top officials of the medical establishment in the country. The case appeared to be straightforward because Ilario held an authentic promissory note (Ar. *kambiyala*, It. *cambiale*). All Tito had to do—and all that he did—was present the note to the court and ask for it to summon Idris and ensure his payment of the debt. Idris showed up in court, confirmed the validity of the debt and his intention to pay it back, and asked for an additional fifteen days to find the money. Tito agreed on the condition that Idris pay the entire amount of the loan in addition to interest and all related fees by that date. When fifteen days later Idris failed to fulfill his promise, Tito asked the court to imprison him and to sequester all of his current and future possessions to force debt repayment. At this point, what seemed like an assured success for Tito on his debut as *wakil* turned into a failure. The merchant court decided unanimously that, upon reexamining the documents of the case, it was a civil rather than a commercial debt and, accordingly, was outside the jurisdiction of the merchant court.[46] Thus, Tito, with years of French legal study under his belt and a pool of potential clients available through familial and communal connections, failed in his first test because of a procedural matter—one that was raised not by an adversary, for the defendant did not have legal representation, but by the court itself.

This first foray into commercial law may have been frustrating—embarrassing, even—for Tito, especially at the beginning of his career. Fortunately for him, the conditions under which he practiced law would soon change, presenting him with the opportunity to do his job in a profoundly different way. A year after representing Ilario in writing, the merchant court got a new statute that reemphasized the ban on lawyers' participation in legal proceedings but allowed *wakils* to take part in court hearings. The ability to argue against other *wakils* before the panel of distinguished merchants that presided over the merchant court presented a new opportunity for Tito. He was fluent in the three languages that the court used: Arabic, Italian, and French. Unlike other litigants and their *wakils*, who may have relied on translators, including a court-appointed clerk who was authorized to act in this capacity when needed,[47] Tito spoke for himself and avoided such interruptions. Being trilingual must have also made him an appealing option for potential clients of different nationalities. In addition, the new rule allowing oral arguments was instituted in 1864, right before the end of the American Civil War (and the global depression of 1873), which would have a profound effect on cotton prices and witness the steady rise in the number of indebted and insolvent merchants Egypt.[48] Tito Figari would now be bombarded with requests for legal representation before the merchant court in bankruptcy cases. The archival record shows that within the span of one year starting in September 1871, Tito served as *wakil* for twenty-eight different clients who were subjects or protégés of at least six different states, including the wider Ottoman Empire. He represented them in thirty different lawsuits, which amounts to about one-tenth of all the cases that were heard by the Cairo Merchant Court during the same period.[49]

There is strong evidence of Tito's facility for public speaking later in his life. In journalistic reports on the Italian community in Egypt from the 1880s, and in his obituaries from the late 1890s, he was praised for his oratorical skills. The general impression about lawyers was that they were eloquent orators. That Tito spoke and served as master of ceremonies in public events that were organized by the Italian community and charitable societies that he headed, such as when he hosted Ahmad 'Urabi at the Italian school's celebration, must have been expected by his audience.[50] A telling moment took place in December 1881, involving Charles P. Stone Pasha (1824–1887), the American Chief of Staff of the Egyptian Army and President of the Société Khédivale de Géographie. While reading an elegy of his compatriot and comrade in the Union Army during the American Civil War, Erasmus Sparrow Purdy Pasha (1838–1881), Stone became emotional and could not continue reading, so Tito Figari stepped in, completed reading the elegy, and asked everyone in the hall to rise to honor the late Purdy Pasha.[51]

These moments, in which Tito demonstrated confidence in public, had their precedents in the Cairo Merchant Court years earlier. For example, in November 1873, Tito showed up in the merchant court to represent Musa Hazan, a local tobacco merchant, in his case against his debtor 'Ali Afandi al-Jabalawi. The dispute had emerged two years earlier, when 'Ali suggested that Musa collect his debt from another person named Ahmad al-'Inani, who was due to pay back a loan to 'Ali.

This transfer of debt (Ar. *hiwala*), however, seems to have gone awry. Musa claimed to have collected only a portion of his debt, and ʿAli insisted that he had made up for the deficit in kind. Ultimately, Musa and ʿAli authorized their *wakils*, Tito Figari and Dimitri Afandi ʿAbduh, to take the case to the merchant court. The *wakils* submitted a range of documents to the court, but their oral arguments were what shaped the outcome of the case. Dimitri asked for witnesses who would verify that the debt was settled, while Tito objected, prompting the court to postpone the hearing to a later date, in which the *wakils* would be expected to discuss substantive rather than procedural points. When they reconvened, Dimitri asked the court to reconsider his request, and when it was denied, he refused to present his argument. Tito seized the opportunity, arguing that if Dimitri refused to engage in a legal argument, he should, legally speaking, be considered absent from the proceedings, and a ruling against his client should be issued "in absentia (*al-hukm bil-ghiyab*)." The court concurred, granting Tito and his client Musa a victory and judging that ʿAli was still responsible for paying his debt as well as the court fees.[52]

Paying attention to legal definitions and distinctions was part of the culture of the merchant courts. Tito was always referred to as *al-avukatu* in social functions organized by the Italian community, in the correspondences of his masonic lodge, and in the meetings of the scientific associations he belonged to. Inside the courthouse, where the title should have been most relevant, he was always *al-wakil*. The merchants presiding over the court and the clerks who recorded the proceedings in writing were careful to uphold the letter of the ban on lawyers that was issued in 1857 and confirmed in 1864. Tito, like his peers, cooperated with the court in order to be permitted to provide legal counsel. None of these parties were ignorant of this dynamic, therefore merchant court case summaries would occasionally include a reference to "lawyers (*al-avukatiyya*)" as a matter of course.

A telling example is that of a certain Leonel, who represented the creditors of Yaʿqub Jurj as *wakil* in a successful lawsuit before the appellate court of Alexandria but was denied his fee of 75 English pounds when he asked for it. Therefore, Leonel decided to sue the creditors (i.e., his clients) before the Cairo Merchant Court. He hired Tito Figari, who brought the case to the merchant court, referring to his client as Leonel "*al-Avukatu*." Neither his adversaries in the case nor the merchants presiding over the court stopped at the use of the term. At the end of the day, Tito was an authorized *wakil*, and Leonel had offered his service to the creditors while using the same term. In his capacity as a litigant, Leonel could be referred to as *al-avukatu* since he was not appearing in this capacity on behalf of clients. In the end, the court found the 75 English pounds to be excessive and ruled that two-thirds of that amount would be sufficient.[53] Tito's success may have been incomplete in this case, but his work, unwittingly, provides the reader with an insight into the politics of language surrounding the formal ban on lawyers in the merchant courts.

Consistent with this ban was the absence of an association for legal practitioners during the years of operation of the merchant courts. Tito's relationships with other *wakils* (or *avukatus*) are worth nothing because they shed light on how these individuals associated with one another in the absence of a permanent forum, one where they could define the boundaries of legal practice and undertake collective bargaining strategies. Tito's collaboration on merchant court cases with the Egyptian Marqus al-Kabis in particular is illustrative in this regard. In December of 1875, Marqus served as one of two representatives of the creditors (*wukala al-dayyana*) of 'Ali Hasan Salam, who had at that point already been held in debtors' prison. Alongside the other representative, *al-shaykh* Ibrahim Khalil, Marqus hired Tito to serve as his *wakil* while negotiating a debt settlement in the merchant court. In this context, Tito rejected the legality of a proposed settlement that would have included the payment of two-thirds of the amount of the original debt and excluded other expenses like "lawyer fees" ("'*ujrat al-avukatiyya*)." The court ruled unanimously that the part of the settlement that included repayment of two-thirds of the debt was valid but that the disagreement over related "official and unofficial expenses" would have to be taken up in a separate lawsuit.[54] While the court was non-committal in relation to the legitimacy of the lawyers' right to collect their fees, it did not dismiss it as illegal out of hand.

The work relationship between Marqus and Tito extended beyond this case, in which the first hired the latter. Four years earlier, Tito had hired Marqus in the context of a rather unusual commercial dispute. Tito had agreed to represent an Italian printer, Moïse Castelli, in his case against the prominent Azhari scholar Hasan al-'Idwi.[55] The two litigants had had a falling out over the discrepancy between the projected and actual costs of printing a number of books at Moïse's publishing house.[56] To his surprise, Moïse lost two rounds of litigation before the merchant courts. In each, he was represented by an Italian lawyer: Tito Figari at the merchant court of first instance in Cairo, and Domenico Gatteschi in the appellate court in Alexandria. His legal defeat and associated financial loss occurred despite what he deemed to be fine legal representation and the fact that he enjoyed extraterritorial privileges as an Italian subject. In the aftermath of this fiasco, Moïse commissioned the Alexandria-based Gatteschi to write a treatise in which he exposed the structural flaws of the entire Khedival legal regime, especially what he deemed to be its bias against Europeans like himself. The Italian lawyer wrote the treatise, but Moïse wanted to publish it in Arabic, partly to ensure that his clientele of Azhari scholars—Hasan al-ʻIdwi's peers—would read it. This is when Tito recommended "Marqus bin Qiryaqus al-Kabis" as translator. This was a notable choice because, as Marqus himself explained in the Arabic version of the treatise, he was asked to "translate it, although I do not claim for myself some of what is necessary to enter this field [of translation]. However, I agreed because I was in the office of *khawaja* Figari and had examined all the papers of the case."[57] Thus, Tito was not only a private legal practitioner but he also cooperated with other lawyers on cases that required two rounds of litigation, reached out to his connections to offer related services such as translation, and took advantage of his office to facilitate this complex operation.

An Italian diplomatic document from around the same time, 1870, offers us a clue as to why Marqus may have frequented Tito's office. It refers to Marqus as a lawyer and a "Catholic Copt" who cared about the Italian "politico-religious cause." The reference is interesting given Tito's own masonic affiliation and repudiation of religion. Marqus's Catholicism may have offered him grounds for tying his career fortunes to Italian interests. He was not entirely reliant on this connection, however. Over the next few years, he appeared in multiple cases as an independent *wakil* for local and European litigants in the Cairo Merchant Court. The alternation between working together and working separately, and the changing capacities in which collaboration occurred (e.g., Marqus as *wakil dayyana* and as translator), suggests that the existence of a field of legal practice, rather than a series of anomalies, predated the creation of a formal association of lawyers in the context of the Mixed Courts in 1878 by several years. It also shows that the appeal of hiring Tito as a *wakil*, by both merchant litigants and legal practitioners, did not simply follow from a good record of winning cases, for the examples cited here show that he also lost, but from his embeddedness within this field of legal practice—he had a permanent office, was able to utilize his connections within the field to facilitate related services such as translation or to recruit a peer to pursue a second round of litigation in a different city, and was himself available in a similar way to assist others within the field.

In light of his central position within the field, it should come as no surprise that some of his clients were influential members of Cairene society, such as Moïse Castelli, who owned the first license for a private Arabic press in the city. Tito was also hired in 1872 by Hasan al-'Aqqad, one of the merchants who presided over the merchant court, who was well-positioned to assess Tito's work (Hasan al-'Aqqad is the subject of Chapter Three).[58] In 1874, he represented the Ottoman Bank, which was being sued by Carlo Costa, who accused the bank of cheating him in a sale of a used steam locomotive. The buyer, Carlo, stated that the horsepower of the vehicle was smaller than advertised and that he had insisted that the sale would only become formalized five days after acquiring it because the only way to confirm its specifications would be through usage. Tito's case rested on the validity of the paperwork, and he won the case for the bank.[59] Similarly, Tito also had the confidence to stand against litigants who wielded power. For example, in the fall of 1875, he won two similar cases for two Austrian merchants against 'Ali Pasha Sharif over a number of unpaid promissory notes.[60] 'Ali Pasha was a member of the ruling elite in Khedival Egypt. His father served in leadership roles under Mehmed Ali Pasha. 'Ali Pasha Sharif himself had preceded Tito in studying in France as part of a government student mission in 1844 before returning to join the army. He would be remembered later for being president of the Legislative Assembly under the British occupation, a famous horse breeder, and for his arrest and trial for illegally buying enslaved Sudanese women in 1894.[61] Tito also represented clients who sued government agencies such as the Railway Traffic Department[62] and even the Greek Orthodox Patriarchate in Alexandria.[63]

Reputation and social connections may account for Tito's popularity as a legal practitioner. Yet the fact that he was hired by peers like Leonel and by merchant court authorities like Hasan al-ʿAqqad suggests that his strategies as a *wakil* in the courtroom were also significant. After all, Leonel and Hasan had the opportunity to observe Tito in action before hiring him. Tito, like others with similar credentials or work experiences, emphasized procedural points and based his own legal arguments on links between specific legal codes and articles. These tactics set him and his peers apart from other legal representatives who held the same title—*wakil*—but were business associates or relatives of the litigant and who made no claim about possessing technical legal knowledge through formal education.

Readiness to demonstrate mastery of procedures and legal codes was not unique to Tito, nor did it always translate into legal victories. In fact, just as he pursued these strategies, they were often deployed against him. At times, Tito seems to have been careless or to have exhibited excessive self-confidence, neglecting simple but essential tasks such as holding a written authorization to represent a litigant. In November 1871, for instance, his obligation to present such authorization came up three times in the merchant court. The first time, Tito had his papers in order but had a hearing postponed for ten days because his rival, Muhammad Bey Rustum, who represented the estate (*tarika*) of his deceased wife, *al-sitt* Fatima, could not find the written authorization to represent her legally, which she had left him during her lifetime (*hal hayatiha*).[64] The next day, Tito was back in court in relation to a different case involving his client, the estate (*da'ira*) of Ahmad Pasha, and a Greek merchant named Dimitri Makri. At the beginning of the session, Tito raised a procedural point in which he argued that it was impossible to ascertain that Dimitri's *wakil* was indeed who he claimed to be since the authorization he held was written in Greek, a language that the court did not admit. When asked to present his authorization from the estate of Ahmad Pasha, it turned out that he did not have one. Again, the hearing was postponed.[65] When the litigants returned to court eleven days later, Dimitri's *wakil* produced an authorization that the court accepted but Tito could not, and his case was dismissed as a result.[66]

Procedural points were not limited to this basic issue. Merchant court records abound with references to "secondary questions" (Ar. sing. *mas'ala far'iyya*), in which typically a *wakil* tried to quash a case before it had been discussed over such matters as the legibility of the signatures, the jurisdiction of the court, or the statute of limitations. In one case, Tito persuaded the appellate court to drop a case against his client because the financial amount in dispute was less than 5,000 *qurush*, and so fell below the threshold required to re-adjudicate the case.[67] He achieved a similar result in a more complicated case in which Antun Hanna, a Tanta-based merchant, sued Solomon Kramer, a subject of Austria-Hungary, for failing to pay the full amount of grain sold to him on account of a disputed claim that the grain had gone bad. Antun had lost the first round of litigation and had taken his grievance to the appellate level. Tito argued that Antun missed the deadline for submitting an appeal and failed to pay the surety required for the case to be reconsidered. Thus, without getting into the details of the grievance, the court dropped the case.[68] In yet another case, ʿAbduh Afandi, on behalf of ʿAli ʿUkasha, objected to the way that the merchant court calculated his client's debt—specifically, that it relied only on his ledgers and refused to consider separate receipts. Representing the creditor Muhammad al-Shafiʿi, Tito insisted that the receipts should not be included because they were only introduced after the ledgers were examined. His argument persuaded a majority of the merchants presiding over the court.[69] These examples show how far the ideal of merchants speaking the truth in the absence of lawyers was from the reality.

The same *wakils* who tried to secure legal victories based on procedural points were also ready to persuade the court using references to specific articles of Ottoman and French legal codes. On that front too, Tito resorted to this tactic with mixed results. Again, just as he adopted it, others directed it against him. Consider the case mentioned above in which Tito served as *wakil* for the representatives of the creditors of ʿAli Hasan Salam during the negotiations to reach a debt settlement that allowed them to claim a portion of their debt and resulted in freeing ʿAli from debtors' prison. ʿAli claimed not to possess the money to pay back even a portion of his debt. Tito argued in opposition that ʿAli made a mistake by paying another debt while imprisoned and urged the court to reclaim this money and make it a part of the settlement. His argument went as follows:

> . . . the payment was inappropriate and not legally binding (*fi ghayr mahalihi wa ghayr nafidh*) to [ʿAli] Salam and his bankruptcy . . . according to articles 153 and 156 of the Ottoman Code of Commerce, which state that the entire amount paid by a debtor, or through a representative of

> his, and all contracts that he makes while incarcerated (*ba'd wuqu'ihi fi halat al-tawqif*) could be invalidated.[70]

Similar to his deployment of Ottoman law in this specific way, he seized opportunities to demonstrate his knowledge of French codes. In a different case about the same debtor, Tito's adversary referenced "articles 1603, 1625, 1641, 1643 and 1644 of the French Civil Code" to establish that a seller was liable for any unapparent defects in the goods sold even if he was unaware of them at the time of the sale and that, accordingly, the buyer had a right to be compensated even if these defects were discovered after the sale. In his rebuttal, Tito wanted to achieve two goals: demonstrate that he was equally knowledgeable about the technicalities of French civil law and use this knowledge in such a way as to nullify his adversary's tactic. He, therefore, acknowledged the validity of the aforementioned legal articles but qualified their validity based on an explicit reference to another article from the same code and to the prevalent custom in Egypt.

> The opposition did not apply what is stated in article 1648 of the French Civil Code to the current matter. I mean that he had to (*kan wajib 'alayh*) make this argument sooner than now but did not. The aforementioned article [1648] requires that appeals need to be raised within a short period of time but this [duration] depends on the kind of commodity that was sold and the current custom in the town where the sale was contracted (*jins al-shay' al-muba' wa ittiba'an lil-'ada al-jariya bil-balda allati sar biha tawqi' al-mubaya'a*).

Thus, Tito communicated to the merchants presiding over the court both his technical knowledge of the law's letter and his ability to match it with actual commercial practice.

Tito Figari was trained in French law and well-versed in its nineteenth-century Ottoman counterpart. He also knew the Khedival legal system. The court proceedings in which he participated show that this knowledge was not limited to commercial law but included more generally civil and procedural laws. His command of Arabic, French, and Italian gave him direct access to clients and to the merchants presiding over the court, who were split along linguistic lines. This particular set of competencies allowed him not only to appear in court as a *wakil* but to also be called on to serve as an expert, such as in a case that required verifying the signature of a deceased debtor. The latter had signed his name on two promissory notes in Latin letters but in a non-metal (*ghayr al-hadid*) pen that was "not commonly used in writing in French." A relative of his could not verify the handwriting because he could only read in Arabic. The court was at pains to verify the signatures so it located more samples of the deceased's signature and brought in three experts (*ahl al-khibra*), including Tito Figari, who decided that the signatures were authentic and persuaded the relative of their conclusion (*iqtana' bi-dhalik*).[71]

In his study of "the rise of Western-oriented lawyers in Egypt," the late Farhat Ziadeh found that "not a single Arabic name figured among the seventy-nine members present" at the election meeting of the Mixed Bar Association in 1877.[72] To him, this was evidence of the organization's exclusive European membership.[73] Ziadeh's finding is significant to telling the story of anti-colonial nationalism—the Egyptians who joined the profession in subsequent decades became the leaders of Egyptian nationalism until the mid-twentieth century. Yet his argument also harbors a misleading assumption, which is that Egyptians and Europeans, or those who knew the law in Arabic and those who knew it in French, constituted distinct categories. The inauguration of the Mixed Court and Bar Association in 1876, his argument goes, was *the* beginning of modern legal practice in Egypt, and Arabic speakers joined this effort at a later point. The example of Tito Figari defies this neat binary—here was a Damascus-born, tri-lingual lawyer who studied in France at the expense of the Khedival government and whose career spanned the years before and after the creation of the Mixed Courts.

Professional Lawyer

During the last months of the operation of the merchant courts, two lawyers, Tito Figari and Philippe Rocaserra, were preoccupied with simultaneous lawsuits about the sale and distribution of water. They were adversaries. In the first case, Philippe's client complained that the Cairo Water Company (*Qumbaniyyat Miyah Misr*), represented by Tito Figari, had failed to fulfill its contractual obligation toward him. The company had agreed to supply him with a certain amount of ice every day, which he, in turn, parceled out to a number of consumers within the city. When it abruptly stopped the supply, the client fell into debt. Philippe Rocaserra referred to article 65 of the appendix to the Ottoman Code of Commerce as the basis of a financial compensation that included not only the debts that resulted from the company's actions but also an estimate of the profits he would have made had it fulfilled the contract and his work overhead costs during the same period, such as the rent of stores and salaries of employees. Tito Figari explained that the company's failure was due to mechanical problems in the relevant machines. Such problems "were not borne out of negligence but because of *force majeure* (*lam yakun nashi' bi-wasitat ihmaliha bal inahu min 'arid qahri*.)" Tito added that the contract stated that the company would supply its production of ice to the project, without specifying a set amount. The merchant court did not accept either argument fully. It ordered the compensation of Philippe's client but accepted Tito's point that the amount of ice exchanged was expected to fluctuate according to the contract.[74] While this case was being adjudicated, another dispute about a different water company, *Qumbaniyyat Miyah al-Suways*, was unfolding before the same court, pitting the same two lawyers, Tito and Philippe, against each other. This second case, however, would still be unresolved in 1876, when the merchant court closed its doors for the last time.

In 1866, while the construction of the Suez Canal was ongoing, Khedive Isma'il authorized a concession for water distribution in the city of Suez, which two Europeans by the names of Lasseron and Marini acquired. Subsequently, they formed a joint-stock company. Lasseron moved to Egypt and took over the responsibility of directing the effort to establish the company and physical infrastructure. His partner, Marini, maintained a nominal title as co-director but was mostly based in his residence in rue d'Amsterdam in Paris. In early 1869, less than a year before the canal's inauguration, the company began its operation. The partners had a falling out soon afterward, and Lasseron convinced the general assembly of stockholders to amend the company's charter to enable him to be the sole director. Marini hired Philippe Rocaserra to help him contest Lasseron's course of action. Ultimately, in July 1874, the court ruled that the company must compensate Marini because it fired him from his position before his term ended.[75] This burden only added to the financial difficulties that the company was facing. In April of the following year, it defaulted on its debts, and the Cairo Merchant Court declared its bankruptcy and recognized the same Philippe Rocaserra, alongside Dimitri 'Abduh, as bankruptcy trustees.[76] Philippe, representing Marini, was now in a position to liquidate the company in order to pay the creditors, but before he could arrange for a sale in early 1877, the merchant courts had expired and were replaced by the new Mixed Courts. Tito Figari, until recently a *wakil* before the merchant courts, appeared for the first time as a lawyer representing Lasseron before the Mixed Court of Cairo to oppose the sale of the company. The Mixed Court reaffirmed the decision of its predecessor, the merchant court, handing Tito a new defeat—his first as an *avukatu*. Its outcome notwithstanding, the case shows an ongoing litigation beginning in the Khedival legal system and continuing in the Mixed Courts and, with it, three *wakils*, including Tito Figari, transitioning to the professionalized world of legal practice in the second half of the 1870s.

These early cases were only a beginning for Tito, who continued to be involved in legal cases in the Mixed Courts during the 1880s and 1890s (see Figure 4.1). His legal work in these years brought him in close contact with the politics of the British occupation. In the summer and fall of 1884, for example, the British Consul-General Evelyn Baring (later to be known as Lord Cromer) was still unsure whether a quick British evacuation from Egypt was a viable option, or if he should preside over a colonial administration that would reform government over a period of several years. As he contemplated his options, he determined that crucial to his decision would be the extent to which the British could oversee Egyptian finances independent of the inter-European Public Debt Commission. Therefore, Baring and the British advisor at the Egyptian Ministry of Finance, Edgar Vincent (later to be known as Lord D'Aberon), convinced the Khedival government to limit its payments to the Public Debt Commission and to use its money differently according to a British-devised plan for financial reform.[77] This decision prompted the Commission to sue the Khedival government before the Mixed Courts. Tito emerged in this court case as one of the lawyers of the Commission. It was "en l'étude de M. Tito Figari, avocat à la Cour d'appel" that they prepared for the case, which they won in December of that year.[78] Tito's involvement in the case was a precursor for his participation in other lawsuits against the Khedival government. In 1887, alongside a few Europeans, Tito protested the property tax rates for certain Cairo neighborhoods where they resided. In this case, Tito was involved in his personal capacity as well. A swift political response to the petition was sufficient, and no legal action ensued from the petition.[79]

As a continuation of non-adversarial lawyerly work, Tito also found himself in a position to negotiate or accept agreements on behalf of members of the Khedival family in their relationships with the government. Early in the reign of Khedive 'Abbas II (r. 1892–1914), his minister of finance, 'Abd-al-Rahman Rushdi Pasha, negotiated a settlement regarding the allowance and land that three granddaughters of Khedive Isma'il (then in exile in Constantinople) were entitled to after the death of their mother, Tevhide Hanim, in 1888. The three princesses were under the guardianship of their father, Mansur Yakan Pasha, who hired Tito Figari to communicate with the government. In the spring and summer of 1893, Tito received the final acceptance of his proposal on behalf of Mansur and the princesses from the minister of finance. The settlement included the reduction of the allowance they received as members of the Khedival family. At the same time, it allocated to them equal lots of land from the *al-Da'ira al-Saniyya*, the body which managed Khedival estates, as a family *waqf* and extended a line of credit, for example, to allow for the purchase of livestock. The kind of negotiation that Tito engaged in in this case is not different in its logic from the work that he conducted in the merchant courts two decades earlier, but it was tied to land, and it did not involve merchants but government officials and members of the Khedival family. Khedive 'Abbas personally signed off on the agreement.[80]

A particularly interesting category of legal work that Tito engaged in during these years, when he was a senior figure within the Italian community and an established lawyer, was his work with Italians who took part in colonization efforts in sub-Saharan Africa. The case of Guiseppe Cuzzi shows Tito, the lawyer, taking on the function of *negotiorum gestor*—a manager of the business of an absent Italian subject. Guiseppe was a merchant who Gordon Pasha, the British governor of Sudan, appointed as a British consular agent in Berber, north of Khartoum, weeks before the city fell to the Mahdists. Guiseppe himself was captured by the Mahdists as he attempted to escape to Egypt and remained a prisoner until the defeat of the Mahdist state fifteen years later.[81] Tito's appearance is, unsurprisingly, related to a legal matter, which is the official capacity of Guiseppe at the time of his capture: was he a British consular agent only, or did Gordon also appoint him as the assistant (*mu'awin*) to the Governor of Berber? Clarifying the matter was legally consequential. Egypt was the colonial power in control of

Sudan, but Egypt itself was under British occupation.[82] When the Khedival government established a commission to consider the requests made for pensions or severance pay by government employees who were prisoners of the Mahdist state, Tito, acting as *negotiorum gestor*, applied on behalf of his fellow Italian. Specifically, he demanded late salary payments as well as an annual pension for his absent client. The government commission, however, rejected the request on the grounds that there was no documentary evidence of Guiseppe Cuzzi's appointment in an official position in the Khedival colonial administration of Sudan and that, in any case, he would not have worked for enough years to qualify for a government pension. Being appointed as a British consular agent was, of course, besides the point. This rejection led to a lawsuit before the Mixed Courts, which was still being heard when Tito passed away in September 1897. Four years later, the Mixed Court validated Tito's position and obligated the Khedival government to grant Guiseppe, who was then represented by another lawyer, severance pay.[83]

In the legal documents, there is no definitive explanation for why Tito acted on behalf of Guiseppe. By definition, a *negotiorum gestor* is not hired by the person he is representing but rather steps in out of a sense of duty. Tito may have done just that because Guiseppe was a friend or compatriot, or he may have acted out of a sense of obligation as a leader of the Italian community in Cairo at the instigation of an affected family member, or even at the urging of an Italian official. Some of these possibilities are evident in two instances that occurred nearly at the same time and that included Tito conducting lawyerly work on behalf of Italian explorers in sub-Saharan Africa. Romolo Gessi was a former Italian solider under Garibaldi, who later refashioned himself as a Nile explorer and who was later chosen by Gordon Pasha to serve as the governor of the Bahr al-Ghazal province in the Egyptian-ruled Sudan. When Romolo fell sick in the spring of 1881, he traveled back to Egypt, where he died upon arrival in Suez. Tito, apparently a long-time associate of Romolo, was entrusted by the late explorer to be the executor of his will.[84] Tito traveled to Suez upon hearing the news, from where he took possession of his papers to deliver what was private among them to Romolo Gessi's widow and the rest to a fellow Italian explorer, Manfredo Camperio, who he had commissioned to edit and publish his memoir, which was later translated into English under the title *Seven Years in the Soudan*.[85]

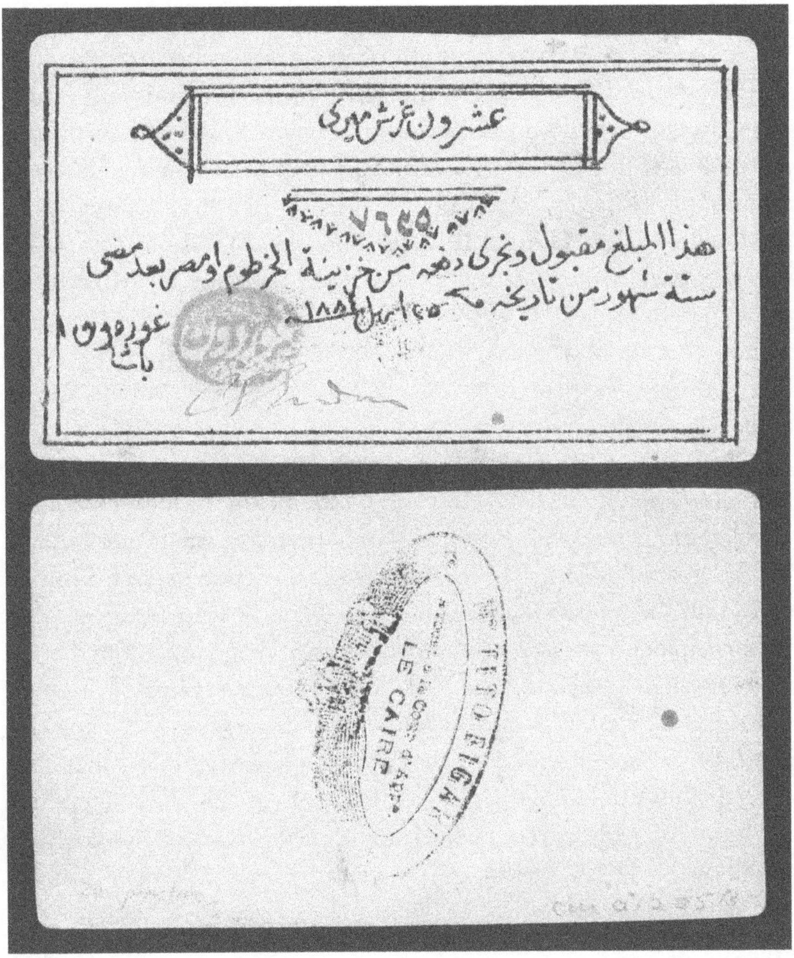

Figure 4.1. Promissory note issued during the 1884 Mahdist siege of Khartoum, with Tito's seal on the back: "Tito Figari. Avocat à la Cour d'Appel. Le Caire." Source: National Numismatic Collection, National Museum of American History. Reproduced from Wikimedia Commons.

Incidentally, as Tito was sorting out Romolo Gessi's legacy, a group from the Danakil tribe, local to the Afar region in East Africa, confronted and killed an armed Italian contingent led by Giuseppe Maria Giulietti. The confrontation took place near Lake Afrera (in the northeast of modern-day Ethiopia), about 200 miles south of the Egyptian fort in Massawa on the Red Sea. The Khedival government claimed to have taken into custody individuals guilty of the murder of Giuseppe Maria Giulietti and his contingent. After communication with the Italian government, Sharif Pasha, the Egyptian prime minister, decided to send them to Cairo to be put on trial before a regular court (*tribunali oridinari*), rather than a special tribunal or to be punished through an administrative decision. Upon learning of Sharif Pasha's decision, the Italian foreign minister, Pasquale Stanislao Mancini, wrote to the Italian Consul General in Egypt to request that Tito Figari be hired to represent the families of the slain Italians, because of his "ingenuity . . . and patriotic spirit."[86] The consul replied that, even though he could not locate Tito immediately, he was confident that he would accept this request.[87]

Apparently, Tito's reputation as trustworthy was not only shared by Italian imperialists like Cuzzi and Gessi but also by anti-imperialist Europeans. The English poet and 'Urabi supporter Wilfrid Blunt had left Egypt after the defeat of the 'Urabists at the hands of the British. In early 1887, he returned to what was now British-occupied Egypt. The Italian captain of the ship he boarded to Egypt suggested to him that he reached out to Tito Figari who "would do my business honestly . . . as he is a friend of Arabi."[88] Blunt accepted the advice and met with Tito, who agreed to become his lawyer. The professional legal services that Tito offered Wilfrid and his wife, Lady Anne, was to help them figure out the future of their "garden," which was "thirty-three acres enclosed in a wall, with eighteen outside" that included a famous farm of Arabian horses.[89] The Blunts wanted to rent it out as a way of keeping it without having to bear the burden of its expenses. Tito, well-connected and with decades-long legal experience, found an experienced gardener to assess the property.[90] He then helped broker a deal to rent the Blunts' garden out for nine years while they retained the right to live on it.[91] Tito earned Wilfrid Blunt's trust, not only professionally but also politically. According to Blunt, Tito shared with him some of his interactions with 'Urabi, claiming to have informally advised 'Urabi's legal counsel and expressing his wish to have defended him. He also opened up to Blunt, commenting on how people think of 'Urabi today and stating his preference for Turkish over English control. He went as far as stating that Khedive Tawfiq had lost legitimacy and may better be substituted by his heir-presumptive, Halim Pasha.[92] (Tito, of course, would mourn Tawfiq in 1892 in masonic circles, describing him in positive terms.)

For his part, when he feared arrest by the Egyptian police, Blunt deposited his diary in Tito's office "for security."[93]

Concluding Remarks

Tito Figari belonged to a generation that lived through two periods that often appear in historiography as antithetical to one another. In the first, the Khedives presided over a modern state and ruled through a sophisticated bureaucratic apparatus and an expansive network of judicial forums. In the second, the British Empire seized control from the Khedives, and its agents made it their mission to reinvent the state. There are obvious political reasons to periodize modern Egyptian history around the date of the British occupation in 1882. This periodization, however, is less effective when we use other categories of analysis. The focus on law—on legal practice, to be specific—through tracking down one individual uncovered a different analytical plane where historical erasures reappeared. The same individual who made his career mingling with local and European merchants, and reading and deploying Ottoman commercial law, forged close personal and professional relationships with imperialists like Cuzzi and Gessi and anti-imperialists like 'Urabi and Blunt. Throughout his professional formation in the commercial legal sphere, he remained influential—just as his early days in the merchant courts were filled with arguments over the validity of promissory notes issued by private merchants, his seal would mark similar notes that were issued by the besieged colonial ruler of Khartoum, Gordon Pasha, when Tito had established himself as a seasoned lawyer.

Born to an Italian father in Damascus, Tito Figari lived most of his life in Egypt. His uncle, a senior official in Mehmed Ali's state, probably used his influence to help Tito study French law in Paris at the expense of the Egyptian government. Upon his return, Tito took a different path than most graduates of the educational missions. He opted to begin a private legal practice in the early 1860s at a time when the institutional space available for lawyering was hard to negotiate, when it was at all possible. Within a few years, Tito had built connections within the resident Italian community and among local and European merchants, and by the 1870s he had established himself as a well-known *wakil* in the Cairo Merchant Court and as an able *avukatu* within his circles in Cairene society. A centrally located office and a team of assistants, a growing social role among the Italian community, and cordial relationships with Italian government officials all entrenched Tito in Egypt. When the merchant courts closed their doors in 1876, Tito made the transition to the Mixed Courts, appearing as a lawyer in a wide range of cases, a portion of which had a financial angle. He also conducted non-adversarial lawyerly work such as facilitating sales and serving as an executor. His prestige also granted him a spot on the boards of several scientific institutions. But this continuity is to be contrasted to what, from a retrospective standpoint, appears a confusing engagement with politics: traces of anti-imperialist ('Urabi) and pro-imperialist (Italian colonialism) sentiments.

Tito's later prominence in British-ruled Egypt as a communal leader and professional lawyer overshadowed his earlier formative experiences in the Cairo Merchant Court. The jurisdiction of the merchant courts is the subject of the next chapter. The texts of the commercial laws that were applied within these courts are not sufficient on their own for understanding how commerce was legally regulated. Legal texts were interpreted by merchants like Musa and Hasan al-'Aqqad in response to arguments that were articulated by merchant litigants who were represented by law practitioners like Tito Figari. These interactions culminated in the demarcation of a law-defined realm of commerce. It is to this act of demarcation that we now turn.

FIVE

Concepts

THE LAW-DEFINED REALM OF COMMERCE

ISMA'IL BEY WAS EIGHTEEN YEARS of age in October 1859 when he borrowed a sum of money and signed a promissory note in exchange. When the payment date arrived, about a year later, Isma'il seemed impossible to pin down. Spiridione Zangarus, the British subject who held the note, went to the police station (*al-dabtiyya*) and the Cairo Governorate to reclaim his money, but on both occasions, he was told that only the merchant court had the authority to help him. It took another year before, in July 1862, the merchant court issued a decision: Isma'il was a legal minor, which rendered the promissory note he signed void. Having run out of options, Spiridione petitioned the British consulate for intervention with the Khedival government to collect his money. The petition, which was penned by his attorney, contained three intertwined claims. First, Isma'il was not necessarily a legal minor. He was indeed three years below the age of legal majority set in the Ottoman Code of Commerce (i.e., twenty-one) but, at the same time, he was three years above the normative age of legal majority that was recognized by both the "civil government and *shari'a*" (*al-hukuma al-madaniyya wal-shari'a al-muhammadiyya*) (i.e., fifteen). By one definition at least, he was legally responsible for paying back the debt. Second, the loan in question was not commercial because Isma'il did not use the borrowed money to "buy goods for commerce" (*bida'a akhadhaha luzum al-tijara*) but to buy clothes for "his and his women's [personal] use" *(asnaf malbusat . . . luzum isti'malihi wa-isti'mal harimihi)*. Since the promissory note was valid, non-commercial, and uncontested by the debtor, it followed that, third, the police or the governorate were authorized to enforce the debt repayment without resorting to the merchant court.[1]

These arguments hint at the concomitance of dissimilar concepts surrounding what constituted commerce legally in the middle decades of the nineteenth century. They suggest that far from being a self-evident category that encompassed all market exchanges, "commerce" was a legally-bounded sphere of activity within which certain individuals and activities were included. At the same time, because the law was evolving and its interpretation and authority were being contested, the boundaries of that commercial sphere were not absolutely fixed. Spiridione and Isma'il's dispute is telling in that regard. Evidently, a level of uncertainty existed surrounding the appropriate age at which it became lawful for an individual to engage in commerce. Those who did buy and sell, or extend and receive loans, found themselves in situations in which the ultimate usage to which they put the goods or money they exchanged led them down different bureaucratic and juridical paths. The simple incorporation of "civil government" and "*shari'a*" within a single coherent statement also raises substantive questions: did *shari'a*, which seems to have been excluded from commercial dispute resolution by the 1840s, contribute to defining the commercial sphere? And did the same range of dissimilar concepts about the legal constitution of commerce influence market exchanges that were conducted outside of the state-organized infrastructure of law?

In Chapter One, I reconstructed the commercial-legal infrastructure and placed it within the larger state and imperial bureaucracies. I explained how its structure, corpus of laws, and geographical spread prepared it to play a certain role in market governance, one that aimed to circumvent the multiplicity of jurisdictions, make market exchanges legible to state officials, and enable the speedy and seamless collection of debts, especially those owed to foreign merchants in urban areas. In this chapter, I ask whether the intended objectives of this mode of market governance materialized and explore the existence of other logics of governance outside of the state-organized commercial-legal infrastructure. I raise these questions in relation to the estates of deceased merchants, forms of legal evidence, auxiliary commercial activities, and the legal uncertainties that surrounded the sale of agricultural lands and crops in the middle decades of the nineteenth century. The first step toward attempting to answer these questions is to examine the paper trails that were produced inside and outside of the state-organized commercial-legal infrastructure.

Paper Trails

The nineteenth century witnessed extensive state efforts to revise and reorganize its laws, with the goal of consolidating the legal regime and extending its reach. From the standpoint of Islamic law, that meant the culmination of a general tendency observable throughout Ottoman history to not only elevate a particular school of Islamic law, *Hanafism*, but also to enforce certain *Hanafi* opinions and not others within the *shari'a* court system.[2] Starting in 1802, probably in an attempt to resuscitate Egypt's provincial government at the moment of practical power vacuum and civil war that followed the end of the French occupation, the Ottoman sultan issued a decree making *Hanafi* law the exclusive law of the land in Egypt at the expense of coexistent schools of Islamic jurisprudence. In the mid-1830s, Mehmed Ali ordered Egyptian *muftis* to refer to *Hanafi* law exclusively when issuing *fatwas*.[3] These official state decisions were meant to create "a uniform legal doctrine and a predictable administration of the law."[4] Yet, as Ahmed Fekry Ibrahim has argued, "eclectic pragmatism" through the methods such as *talfiq*, which characterized pre-modern legal practices, persisted.[5] In other words, while Hanafization led to uniformity, that uniformity itself was not necessarily formulaic or inevitable. Rather, it entailed the generation of new rules that were based on, and consistent with, Islamic legal concepts.

At the same time that the Khedival state was compressing all of Islamic law into an Ottoman brand of *Hanafism*, its increasingly intricate network of state-organized judicial forums preserved specific elements of Islamic law within its own procedures, especially in relation to criminal law.[6] As importantly, *Hanafi muftis* became omnipresent in the state bureaucracy, sitting on committees that were tasked with legislation as well as on new judicial forums, such as *Majlis al-Ahkam*.[7] The merchant courts constituted an exception to this trend. They were presided over by merchants, with a state-appointed bureaucrat as president, but neither did *muftis* play a role in their operation nor was Islamic law considered a reference in their rulings.[8] However, the two general developments, namely, the compression of Islamic law and its survival, in subtle forms, within the new Khedival law regime at large left paper trails that also shed light on market governance during the middle decades of the nineteenth century.

This chapter is based on reading two sets of archival paper trails: case summaries from Cairo's merchant court and the *fatwa* collection of Egypt's Grand Mufti for most of the nineteenth-century, Muhammad al-'Abbasi al-Mahdi (d. 1897). Like its counterpart in Alexandria, the Cairo Merchant Court functioned continuously from the mid-1840s to the mid-1870s. It heard cases that originated in the city of Cairo and, in its capacity as an appellate court, Alexandria. It also adjudicated cases that took place in different Egyptian, and occasionally Sudanese, towns. This extended period and geographical reach distinguished it from the remainder of the merchant court network that included Dumyat and Asyut, which opened at least a decade later, and most probably ruled on disputes that occurred regionally. The records of the Cairo Merchant Court, therefore, contain a wealth of information on commercial disputes in the middle decades of the nineteenth century from throughout Egypt. By reading summaries of cases while focusing on how the court defined its own jurisdiction, we can learn how the boundaries of commerce were constituted legally. To put it differently, by documenting the cases that the merchant court refused to hear because it deemed outside of its scope, we will discover, inversely, what activities and which individuals belonged within a legally-defined commercial sphere. Locating those boundaries is significant because the merchant court was a judicial forum in which merchants heard and decided on disputes that emerged among their own peers. This legal definition of commerce then was not only one that was dictated by the upper echelons of the Khedival state but one that was also enacted by the merchant community.

Merchant court documents alone, however, constitute an insufficient basis for answering the question of how markets were governed. Disputes, commercial and otherwise, were frequently resolved outside of direct state control, within communities and vocational associations.[9] *Fatwas* are particularly useful in capturing some of those instances and the resolution attempts that they triggered, especially where Muslims were involved. From the point of view of Islamic legal theory, they are non-binding legal opinions. However, in practice, *fatwas* were more influential than what a strict reading of state-enforced law would suggest, both historically and in the specific context of nineteenth-century Egypt. First, the historical trend was that disputants who wanted to improve their chances of winning legal disputes or less formal community-based settlements commonly sought to acquire *fatwas*. A favorable *fatwa* would, it was hoped, provide the judge or unofficial mediator with a ready answer that he could adopt in his ruling. A *fatwa*, therefore, may contain a fairly detailed account of a dispute between merchants, in addition to a learned Islamic opinion regarding the validity of the disputants' respective positions. Moreover, the fact that *shari'a* courts were no longer authorized to adjudicate on commercial disputes in the main cities meant that *fatwas* became the only medium in which actual commercial disputes were considered from the perspective of Islamic law. Therefore, from an Islamic legal standpoint, *fatwas* could be understood as complementary to court rulings.[10] Within our particular historical context, *muftis* became directly involved in implementing Islamic law in the state, serving in government committees, and issuing official orders to judges.[11] Reading a major *fatwa* collection systematically in relation to commercial questions, then, complements the view from the merchant courts and the French-inspired state-enacted laws that it applied.

In light of this reality, it would be wrong to treat *al-Fatawa al-Mahdiyya*, which is the major *fatwa* collection consulted here, as a body of unofficial legal opinions that were issued independently of state authority. Ottoman government policy since the sixteenth century stipulated the appointment of an official Grand Mufti whose opinion was to be considered in top-level state decision-making, and who also fulfilled the more typical function of answering questions from the general public.[12] Khedival Egypt adhered to this tradition. Its longest-serving Grand Mufti was Muhammad al-'Abbasi al-Mahdi, who assumed the position in 1848 at the unusually young age of twenty-one during the short reign of Ibrahim Pasha (and during the lifetime of Mehmed Ali) and held it until his death in 1897, fifteen years after the British occupation of Egypt.[13] In other words, he was the most influential Muslim jurisconsult from a few years after the establishment of the merchant courts until two decades after their dissolution. Al-'Abbasi al-Mahdi's unparalleled longevity in office is reflective of the strong ties he enjoyed with successive Khedives, who, at different moments, charged him with bold and politically controversial undertakings. He was to ensure the uniform application of *shari'a* in government affairs, according to the official *Hanafi* school of law, and was even authorized to issue legally-binding *fatwas* in certain situations.[14] Al-'Abbasi al-Mahdi's *fatwa* collection is therefore the ideal site where we would find state-enforceable *shari'a* opinions, including on matters that fell outside the jurisdiction of *shari'a* courts, such as commerce. The same could not be said of contemporaneous collections by his contemporaries, such as the *Maliki mufti* Muhammad 'Ilaysh (1802–1882), whose *Fath al-'Ali al-Malik* may have been innovative from an Islamic legal point of view but whose work was not of clear relevance to state affairs such as market governance.[15]

In the remainder of this chapter, I read merchant court records and the *fatwas* of al-'Abbasi al-Mahdi together in order to empirically reconstruct the *conceptual* boundaries of market governance that were upheld by state officials, merchants, and Muslim jurists. This collective reading will sometimes reveal parallel but similar concepts of commerce that were widely upheld across the judicial landscape.[16] At other times, especially when reading al-'Abbasi al-Mahdi's *fatwas*, questions emanating from the *shari'a* court system or government departments will shed light on the continued relevance of Islamic law to questions of market exchange. The next section on the estates of deceased merchants introduces the first set of tensions among coexisting concepts of market governance in mid-nineteenth-century Egypt.

Death

Unlike other areas of social activity, questions of inheritance, which constitute a sub-category of what legal scholars refer to as "family law," never left the domain of *shari'a*. These perennial questions were among the reasons for the persistence of an extensive network of *shari'a* courts, albeit with a reduced jurisdiction, during the decades that witnessed the invention of a novel legal infrastructure with a previously unfamiliar set of procedures—one that was intended to not contradict *shari'a* principles but that existed outside of the *shari'a* court system. Books on jurisprudence contained long chapters on inheritance that explained how the normative calculus of inheritance distribution would be properly applied to complicated familial arrangements.[17] Along the same lines, *muftis* provided answers on how common properties were to be divided, how guardians of minors were to be compensated, and how the constantly shifting asset values were to be established. The *fatwas* articulated widely accepted principles, which *shari'a* court judges translated into workable action plans. A general principle that is of particular importance to our discussion was that outstanding debts had to be settled before the distribution of the inheritance to entitled family members. To put it differently, the right of the creditor to reclaim his or her money took precedence over the right or actual need of the deceased's family. *Shari'a* courts enforced this order of priorities, and *fatwas* consistently affirmed the soundness of that position.

However, this seemingly straightforward rule that placed a creditor's financial claim ahead of the family's right to inheritance was difficult to apply whenever merchants were involved. If the creditor or the deceased debtor were merchants, the debt in question needed to be classified either as a familial or a commercial matter. If the first, debt repayment would be overseen by the *shari'a* court, and if the latter, it would be administered by the merchant court. The decisive criterion in determining whether the debt was part of a familial or commercial process was counterintuitive: the nationality of the creditor. Therefore, regardless of the specifics of the debt, local merchants appeared before *shari'a* courts to claim money that was owed to them by deceased debtors, while foreign merchants had to seek the help of the merchant courts to collect their money. This division of responsibilities between different courts seemingly contradicts the overarching objective of legal reform that characterized the nineteenth century, namely, the consolidation of the legal regime. Yet a careful examination of the actual processes of debt resolution according to the *shari'a*-based opinions expressed in *al-Fatawa al-Mahdiyya*, and the legal regulations recorded in the proceedings of the state-organized merchant courts, reveal quite similar logics at play.

To clarify this point, let us turn to what appears at first to be a complicated legal dispute but one that sheds light on how the appropriate judicial forum for facilitating the settlement of an outstanding debt, in the case of the debtor's death, was determined. In 1867, Sa'd Qurra, an Alexandria-based merchant, passed away and was survived by several wives, each of whom was entitled to a share of his estate, which included money and assets. The inheritance could have been divided seamlessly, according to established *shari'a* norms, had it not been for claims made by two creditors, *al-sayyid* Muhammad al-'Awwad and 'Ali al-Qahwaji. In refusing to pay the creditors, Sa'd's widows coordinated poorly. They approached the Alexandria Merchant Court to nullify the debts but failed to show up in court on the day their case was to be heard. The court confirmed the validity of the debts in their absence and notified them that they were legally obligated to pay them back. Faced with this unfavorable court decision, the widows collectively hired an attorney, ʿAbduh Afandi, who appealed the decision before the Cairo Merchant Court. While their debts were separate, the creditors, *al-sayyid* Muhammad and ʿAli, hired one attorney to represent them on the appellate level, Marqus al-Kabis. ʿAbduh and Marqus had an intense debate in court. They each raised multiple procedural points that were meant to undermine their adversary's position. The most surprising of those maneuvers came from ʿAbduh, who argued that his clients, the widows, should not have reached out to a merchant court in the first place. He explained that since the main issue was inheritance, and since all the parties to the dispute were "subjects of the local government," the *shariʿa* court was the appropriate judicial forum to consider the case. To substantiate his statement, he referred to a Khedival edict issued by Saʿid Pasha in 1862/63, which stipulated that "only the claims of Europeans [on the estates of deceased local merchants] are to be heard by the merchant courts *by way of exception* (*bi-tariq al-istithna*)." The reactions in the courtroom to this specific reference from ʿAbduh contain the clue to understanding how nationality was an essential factor in determining the nature of the debt (i.e., civil/familial or commercial) and, accordingly, the court that was authorized to rule on its validity.

Marqus did not comment on the content of the Khedival edict. His lack of response is revealing because during the exchange he had spoken over ʿAbduh more than once to the extent that the latter walked out of the session at one point in protest. Marqus's silence amounts to an implicit acceptance of the validity of the reference, which is noteworthy given his status as an experienced attorney who frequented the merchant courts to represent clients of different nationalities.[18] The merchants presiding over the court must have also been familiar with the content of the edict because they did not contest its validity. They did, however, object to its relevance to ʿAbduh's request to close the case due to the court's lack of jurisdiction (*ʿadam ikhtisas*). The court explained that the request was "unwarranted (*la haqq lahu fiha*) because the claimant was a merchant and the deceased was a merchant and *disputes between merchants are the domain (min khasa'is) of the merchant court.*"[19] The court's decision to elevate the disputants' vocational identity above their nationality requires further clarification.

It is evident that a Khedival edict was circulated in the early 1860s within the relevant departments of the state bureaucracy ordering them to treat all Europeans' claims on local merchants' estates as commercial matters. In other words, the established practice in the Khedival state from the 1860s onward was to litigate such questions under commercial law, within the commercial-legal infrastructure. The timing of the edict is consistent with the longstanding view of Sa'id Pasha's political orientation as sympathetic if not outright susceptible to the demands of European consuls.[20] It also anticipates a similar, if more reserved, decision by the Ottoman sultan in 1869, whereby he granted creditors the right to collect outstanding debts from the estates of *insolvent* debtors before the *shari'a* court could consider any inheritance-related disputes.[21]

Yet what the merchants presiding over the court in this case relied on was a different set of considerations. It is true that the disputants, as well as the deceased, were all "subjects of the local government," but the commercial dispute under consideration was ongoing during the life of the debtor, Sa'd Qurra. In such circumstances, the commercial character of the debt/dispute would not change with the death of the debtor, and the merchant court would continue to enjoy jurisdiction over the matter, regardless of the nationalities of the disputants. Had the creditor been a local and the debt been uncontested during the lifetime of the debtor, the latter's passing would automatically grant the *shari'a* court the authority to facilitate the collection of the debt. This rather convoluted set of procedures becomes clearer when examined in light of straightforward cases that pit local and foreign merchants/creditors against local merchants/debtors, including in the years preceding Sa'id Pasha's reign.

Significantly, it seems that Sa'id's edict formalized an already common practice. In a rather clear case that was heard by Cairo's merchant court in 1850, a Copt by the name Mikha'il al-Biblawi embarked on a new business venture through which he would buy a range of goods in Cairo and sell them in Khartoum. Short on cash, he bought a quantity of goods on credit from Yusuf Ya'qub, a subject of Portugal, and Sulayman Salamah, a subject of Iran. He agreed to split the profits with his creditors but had not done so yet by the time he passed away in Khartoum several years later. When Mikha'il's son and inheritor denied any knowledge of the outstanding commercial debts, Yusuf and Sulayman resorted to the merchant court, which decided unanimously to treat the case as a matter of partnership (*maddat sharikah*) and to rule on it "according to article 40 of the Ottoman Code of Commerce, [which deals with] disputes between partners."[22] In this example, because the claimants were subjects of foreign states, the only appropriate judicial forum they could use was the merchant court. The fact that they may not have tried to collect their debts during the lifetime of the local debtor was irrelevant.

Nationality, it must be noted, should not be confused with religious affiliation. This factor was not similarly decisive in other parts of the Ottoman Empire, where in 1856 the second Tanzimat edict stipulated that commercial disputes between Ottoman subjects who belonged to different religious or denominational groups would be referred to "mixed tribunals."[23] Outside of the Ottoman domain, Morocco, as late as 1872, had witnessed a short-lived experiment in which foreign ambassadors verified the unfulfilled credit claims of their compatriots prior to allowing them to make a case for collecting their money before a panel of Muslim jurists, who were to reach a decision based on *shari'a*.[24] In these cases, religion played an important role in determining how a commercial debt would be proven or reclaimed. By contrast, in the previous example, Mikha'il al-Biblawi was a non-Muslim Ottoman. His creditors may or may not have been Muslim, but they were non-Ottomans—their names were insufficient to indicate a particular religious affiliation. The court did not ask for this information. Their nationalities—that is, whether they carried Ottoman/local or foreign papers—were the only decisive factors in determining where and according to what laws the dispute would be litigated.

Over a decade after Mikha'il al-Biblawi borrowed the money, another Copt, *khawaja* Mansur Mansur, turned to the merchant court to reclaim 14,000 *qurush* that he had lent to yet another Copt, 'Abd-Rab-al-Masih, who had just passed away before paying back his debt. Since both the creditor and deceased debtor were subjects of the Ottoman Empire, and since the outstanding debt was not the subject of a dispute during the debtor's lifetime, the court decided to treat this claim as a matter of inheritance rather than commerce. Accordingly, the case was to be referred to the relevant confessional authority. The court explained in its decision that "since [the parties to the dispute] are subjects [*min atba'*] of the Coptic Patriarchate, the case should be heard in the Patriarchate, which is the center of their legal authority (*mahal shari'atihim*)."[25]

Uncontested debts that involved local Muslim merchants followed the same trajectory. They were transformed from a commercial to an inheritance matter as soon as the debtor passed away. Fatima bint Muhammad, a meat seller (*tajirat jizara*), owed a debt to Mahmud Dawud, a sheep merchant. Although she was unable to pay her debt according to their original agreement, Fatima never denied that she was indebted to Mahmud and even "admitted [this fact] in the police department." Aware of her financial difficulties, Mahmud agreed to reschedule her debt payment. As soon as Fatima passed away, Mahmud sought the help of the merchant court, asking them to inquire whether the inheritors intended to pay the remaining installments of the outstanding debt. When approached, the inheritors replied that the merchant court ceased to be the appropriate forum for settling the debt since it had become part of a larger arrangement, which is the inheritance. The court agreed to their argument unanimously.[26] To clarify, the debt was recognized by the relevant parties and was in the process of being paid during the lifetime of the debtor. While it was still outstanding at the moment of her death, Fatima was never involved in a legal dispute until she died. Similarly, when Ahmad Khalifah resorted to the merchant court to enable him to reclaim the remaining value of a promissory note owed to him by two brothers, Muhammad and 'Ali Isma'il, the court replied that that was not possible. Regarding Muhammad's share, who had passed away, Ahmad was instructed to seek the help of the *shari'a* court, which enjoyed jurisdiction over questions of inheritance. As for the other debtor, who was still alive, the court reaffirmed Ahmad's "right to sue [the other defendant] 'Ali Isma'il in a separate case."[27] Hence, a single uncontested debt that was owed jointly by two brothers could be the subject of litigation under different laws and in different sites within the judicial landscape of the nineteenth-century Khedival state.

Questions of jurisdiction that arose from the death of a debtor were not uncommon in the merchant court. The answers to those questions mattered because once the court decided that it had jurisdiction, it was obligated to consider and eventually issue a ruling on the case. A *mufti's* situation was different because he answered any question that the *shari'a* literature in its entirety had considered without being responsible for actualizing his viewpoint. Expectedly, then, *al-Fatawa al-Mahdiyya* contains numerous questions related to deceased debtors but does not address matters of jurisdiction. In order to understand how the merchant court and the Grand Mufti's office were linked, it is useful to consider the appearance of a single name in the paper trails of both of these institutions.

Sulayman Agha al-Silahdar was a wealthy army officer and government official who was among the group that Mehmed Ali brought from his hometown of Kavala to form his trusted entourage as governor of Egypt. To further solidify his position within that circle, he married *al-sayyida* Wasila, a former slave of the Pasha. When he passed away in 1846, Sulayman left behind an impressive architectural legacy in the form of *waqf* at the heart of Cairo and a large number of slaves, some of whom were emancipated upon his death.[28] His name appeared sixteen years later in *al-Fatawa al-Mahdiyya*, when his widow, Wasila, passed away.[29] A number of Wasila's emancipated slaves (*ma'atiq*) had petitioned before *Bayt al-Mal* against what they considered to be the irregular disposition of her estate, which included adding a house she owned to her existing *waqf* in Cairo, establishing a new *waqf* out of her agricultural landholdings north of the city, and a diamond ring, the value of which she intended to use to pay for her coffin. *Bayt al-Mal* forwarded these concerns to al-'Abbasi al-Mahdi to inquire about their validity from a *shari'a* perspective. What we learn from this *fatwa* is that the Grand Mufti had the authority to shape the ownership status of property that, until that moment, had belonged to the domestic circle of Sulayman Agha. The questions at hand included ownership (of land and urban property) and exchange (i.e., the sale of a diamond ring), which, technically speaking, were not commercial matters.

A decade later, in 1873, Sulayman Agha al-Silahdar's name appeared in the Cairo Merchant Court records. This time, it was Sulayman's *waqf* that was being sued for failing to pay back a debt to al-Sayyid Pasha Abaza. Sulayman had been long dead at that point, and the debt was acquired by the overseers of his massive *waqf*. Yet the court considered the *waqf* to be the late Sulayman's estate (*tarika*) and decided to dismiss the case because the debt was a civil rather than a commercial one, and because "cases against estates (*al-tada'i 'ala al-tarikat*) are not within the jurisdiction of the [merchant] court *if both the plaintiff and the defendant are subjects of the Sublime State* [i.e., the Ottoman Empire] (*al-dawla al-'aliyya*)."[30] Unlike the earlier instance in which the fate of Sulayman's wife's property, including her *waqfs*, was going to be decided according to *shari'a*, the financial dealings of his own *waqf* were briefly considered within the commercial-legal infrastructure before being passed on to the realm of state-enacted civil law. In this indirect way, commercial law and *shari'a* could potentially influence the same pool of wealth years after its owners have passed away. This tenuous connection appears much more clearly when considering forms of admissible evidence in relation to commercial questions.

Handwriting

Unlike the question of jurisdiction, which has to be settled before the process of dispute resolution begins, the question of evidence is answered only during that resolution process. Therefore, determining the validity of the evidence under the merchant court system, which is part of the state-organized commercial-legal infrastructure, and in *al-Fatawa al-Mahdiyya*, for which the frame of reference is *shari'a*, should shed light on the extent to which the Khedival legal system was consolidated or fractured in relation to commerce. Recent historical scholarship has revised long-held views about the legal reforms of the nineteenth century as constituting a process of secularization.[31] It considers such reforms more correctly as attempts to facilitate a more effective implementation of the logic of *shari'a*, using modern evidentiary technologies and modern "productive" punishments, rather than as measures meant to diminish the role of *shari'a* in government affairs.[32] The term used for these state measures, "*siyasa*," itself derives from the *shari'a* term "*siyasa shar'iyya*," a term that encompasses state-initiated measures that are neither detailed in *shari'a* literature nor contradictory with it but that enable the implementation of the objectives of *shari'a* in contexts where the *shari'a*-stipulated forms of evidence or punishment are unachievable.[33] The bottom line of this revisionist argument is that *shari'a* and *siyasa* shared the same goal but that they achieved it through different means. This section will show, however, that forms of evidence that emanate from *shari'a* and *siyasa*, with regard to commercial litigation, were actually strikingly similar, although not identical.

In the first two chapters, I showed that the commercial-legal infrastructure privileged standardized recordkeeping. A merchant's ability to record their transactions in ways that resembled the recordkeeping practices of state employees, and by extension that was legible to them, was directly related to their ability to access and benefit from that legal infrastructure. This dual role of standardized recordkeeping—as financial accounting in the moment and as potential legal evidence in the case of a future dispute—would seem at first to be foreign to *shari'a*. Classical Islamic jurisprudence favored reputable witnesses and set the appropriate number of testimonies needed to prove that a particular instance of legal transgression had occurred. More broadly, however, Islamic jurisprudence counted three forms of legal evidence: witness testimony (*al-bayyina*); admission (*al-iqrar*), by which a litigant admits to having done something unlawful; and the refusal to take an oath (*al-nukul*), which amounts to an implicit admission of guilt. The limitations of these forms of evidence provided the context for the Ottoman state's reliance on *siyasa* measures on a wide scale. In the early modern period, for example, Ottoman courts often failed to prove instances of adultery using the established *shari'a* methods and, accordingly, did not apply the *shari'a*-sanctioned punishment in these cases, namely, stoning. To alleviate the social tensions that arose from such legally unresolvable disputes, judges often resorted to banishing the accused.[34] A clear example of this dynamic in Khedival Egypt was the decision to institute forensic medicine as a form a legal evidence that carried more weight than witness testimony and to outlaw torture, a method of interrogation that was allowed under *shari'a*, and replace it with imprisonment.[35]

The examples of adultery and torture shed light on the ways in which the early modern Ottoman state and the modern Khedival state deployed *shari'a* and *siyasa* conjointly. The logic at work in these and other comparable "criminal" issues was distinct from that which informed matters of law and commerce. The *shari'a* courts' status as "imperial courts" under the Ottomans[36] meant that they served as the major registries for deeds and commercial contracts.[37] They were not necessarily, however, the merchant community's most desirable forums for litigation. Merchant-run guilds may have been as influential as *shari'a* courts in settling commercial disputes. The co-existence of two institutionalized paths to dispute resolution among merchants until the early decades of the nineteenth century suggests that *shari'a* was deployed in the commercial sphere in two overlapping ways. First, contracts and deeds followed customary and legal *shari'a* formulas, since they were deposited at the *shari'a* court. Second, the disputes emerging from the enactment of these *shari'a*-conforming agreements were often resolved with an eye to power relations and business interests embedded in the appropriate guild's hierarchy. This dynamic, which is evident in eighteenth-century Egypt,[38] was also reproduced in a variety of forms within the Indian Ocean's economy, well into the twentieth century.[39]

Yet, as Pascale Ghazaleh has shown, the merchant guilds' ability to survive as major forums for commercial arbitration received devastating blows at the hands of Napoleon's colonial administration (1798–1801) and, in a more sustained and ultimately decisive way, Mehmed Ali's burgeoning state in the 1810s.[40] The state's co-optation of guilds and the shrinking jurisdiction of the *shari'a* courts paved the way for the rise of other forums of dispute resolution. *Fatwas* continued to play a role because they were versatile tools that could be deployed in a wide range of unofficial resolution efforts. In the case of al-'Abbasi al-Mahdi, his opinions also carried weight in official circles, including overriding the opinions of other *muftis* anywhere in Egypt. At the same time, merchant courts that were established in the 1840s became the official forums to resolve inter-merchant disputes, with the notable exception of cases that included a foreign merchant defendant. It is to these two sources, *al-Fatawa al-Mahdiyya* and the proceedings of the merchant courts, that we need to turn in order to understand the practical differences between *shari'a* and *siyasa*-based resolutions of commercial disputes.

From its inception in 1845, the merchant courts emphasized that a standardized form of recordkeeping was essential. All merchants were instructed to keep records according to government-specified rules, in bound and sealed ledgers, as contiguous entries with no blank spaces in between. Doing so constituted a necessary but insufficient requirement for having recourse to and standing a chance to win in the merchant courts. In spite of the unambiguous legal language, the merchant courts' centrality to the commercial sphere fluctuated during the first decade of its operation, until two new statutes issued in 1856 and 1857 revised its *modus operandi* and prepared it to function more effectively during the following two decades. It is noteworthy that as early as 1849, when the merchant courts' ability to promote such recordkeeping practices among merchants was uncertain, al-'Abassi al-Mahdi was consistently issuing *fatwas* that validated the use of merchants' accounting ledgers as *shari'a*-sanctioned evidence in legal disputes at the expense of the established forms of testimony and oath.[41] These *fatwas* demonstrate that state agents within both the bureaucracy and its more specialized *shari'a* branch, represented here by the office of the Grand Mufti, propagated standardized recordkeeping practices in the commercial sphere during the second half of the 1840s. The resultant records would become an integral part of the evidentiary regime under both the merchant court system and, somewhat unexpectedly, under *shari'a*-informed unofficial commercial settlements.

Through examining hundreds of merchant court case summaries and al-'Abbasi al-Mahdi's *fatwas*, it becomes evident that there are two types of writing that could potentially count as evidence in a commercial dispute: the contract (or similar standalone documents) and the ledger. For a merchant court to request such documents was part of its routine, since the court expected merchants to be keeping records regularly—the commercial-legal infrastructure propagated the *standardization* of such recordkeeping practices rather than introducing the concept. Therefore, it was not uncommon for a defendant, like the widow of Hasan Agha Hulwa in her dispute with *khawaja* Musa Hiri, to state as part of making her case in court that "if the claimant is [indeed] a merchant, he must have registers [that record] his buying and selling and [lists] his credits and debits."[42] By contrast, the Grand Mufti was not in a position to request such records but would express an unequivocal opinion on the validity of relying on them as evidence during a commercial dispute resolution. As the examples below will show, the merchant courts and the Grand Mufti both agreed in principle that ledgers, if properly compiled, constituted sufficient evidence of the existence of a commercial debt, without the need for additional corroboration. They also agreed to request further corroboration whenever the written evidence in question consisted of a detached piece of paper, typically in the form of a contract. Their disagreements were limited to the legal weight that they assigned to those standalone commercial papers.

Whenever the resolution of a case hinged on the existence of a ledger, the merchant court had to verify two aspects of that ledger before proceeding. First, the court asked whether the ledger was used to prove the existence of a debt or of money owed. The rule was to use ledgers as evidence only if they contained a record of a debt that the ledger's owner had to pay back. A ledger that showed that its owner was owed money by others was of no value to the court. Therefore, when a French woman by the name of Basha Berkovitch sued the estate of Yusuf Bey Tahir over an unpaid debt, her claim did not convince the Cairo Merchant Court.[43] Basha brought her business ledger to the courthouse to show the members of the court and her contestant, Yusuf Bey's son, that the deceased had bought clothes from her on credit. In response, Yusuf Bey's son denied any knowledge of that debt and stated that "if [Basha] held a written note and if it was verified that it was sealed with [my] father's seal, there would be no objection to taking the necessary steps [of debt repayment]." The court accepted the argument of Yusuf Bey's son and decided that the case "lacked foundation" since Basha "has no evidence (*lam yujad 'indaha dalil*) that would prove her claim." Had Basha located a record of that transaction in a ledger of the late Yusuf Bey, she would have won the case.[44]

It is worth noting that Yusuf Bey's son did not only make debt repayment contingent upon the existence of a note but also of a verified seal of his deceased father. His second condition marks the other aspect of a ledger that the merchant court considered before admitting it as evidence, namely, the verification of the seal or signature of the ledger's owner. Fulfilling this condition was a standard request by inheritors who were facing claims on the estates that had recently come into their ownership. It was not uncommon for those inheritors to clearly state that they would pay the debt in question as soon as a seal or a signature was verified. This was what the widow and inheritor of 'Ali Bey Raghib did during the last months of the merchant court's tenure; she agreed to pay Topologlou Zigarah the price of goods that her late husband might have bought from him on credit after she ascertained the authenticity of his seal.[45] Oftentimes, this verification process was rather straightforward, as was the case with the estate of 'Abduh al-Halawani. Upon 'Abduh's death, two Germans, Schazman and Walter, presented his inheritors with four promissory notes worth 3,650 *qurush*. The notes had 'Abduh's seal imprinted on them, but the inheritors could not verify its authenticity. Hence, the merchant court solicited the help of *Bayt al-Mal*, which compared 'Abduh's seal on the notes to the one preserved in its own records and, ultimately, confirmed its authenticity. Only then did 'Abduh's estate become responsible for paying the borrowed amount to the creditors.[46]

At other times, recovering a seal or, as in the following case, a signature was a complicated bureaucratic and technical matter. In March 1874, the representative of Coleman and McKinsey Limited Company of Alexandria, an English company, complained to the merchant court that the guardian of the late Bahjat Pasha's estate denied knowledge of a debt of 32,725 *qurush*. The guardian explained that he could not read French and therefore was unable to confirm whether the promissory notes written in that language, including Bahjat Pasha's signature, were authentic. To overcome this hurdle, the court forwarded the notes to the Department of Public Works, where documents signed by Bahjat Pasha were stored and where the signatures could be compared. Yet the relevant official at the Department of Public Works at that department failed to verify Bahjat Pasha's signature. As he explained, "the signature is written using a pen [that is commonly used] for Arabic writing and not the metal pen used for French writing. Therefore, it is impossible to ascertain the authenticity of the signature." Still determined to confirm the signature, the court sent to the Ministry of War requesting some samples of documents that contained Bahjat's signature and received six sample letters in response. To examine the signatures, the court brought in three experts (*ahl khibra*) who, after taking the oath, compared the signatures in the Ministry of War's letters to the ones in the promissory notes. In conclusion, they submitted a written report in which they confirmed that "the [written] forms to be found under the statement of acceptance are no doubt written in the hand of the late Bahjat."[47] For Coleman and McKinsey Limited to collect their debt, the merchant court reached out to two different departments within the state bureaucracy and relied on the assessments of no less than three independent experts.

The same question surrounding the validity of using ledgers as evidence in the course of dispute resolution recurred in *al-Fatawa al-Mahdiyya*. In an especially revealing example from 1859, al-'Abbasi al-Mahdi received an elaborate question regarding a business partnership, which could be summarized as follows: Two merchants agreed to do business together and, since they lived in different places, at some point one of them sent a copy of their transactions as recorded in his ledger to the other to confirm that he had an identical list in his own ledger. The latter compared the entries and found them "absolutely correct" (*fi ghayat al-sihha*). On his deathbed, the first merchant informed a group of Muslim witnesses that the ongoing transactions recorded in his ledger were current. The question to the Grand Mufti was whether the content of the deceased's ledger, which was verified by both partners and named witnesses, could suffice as evidence of an outstanding debt. Al-'Abbasi al-Mahdi's opinion is worth citing in full.

> There are three forms of evidence that are accepted by *shari'a*: witness testimony, admission, and refusal to take the oath. Handwriting (*al-khatt*) is not to be relied upon. The only exceptions are those whom the late [*Hanafi*] jurists (*al-muta'akhkhirun*) have exempted, namely, the handwriting of a broker (*simsar*), a seller (*bayya'*) and a moneylender (*sarraf*). [This exception applies] Only to what they owe and not to what they are owed. [As for] Where it is recorded, the handwriting of [any of] the aforementioned is to be relied on [when recorded] in his preserved ledger in relation to what he owed, and it takes the place of witness testimony on that [debt]. And, God, may He be exalted, is the most knowledgeable."[48]

In this *fatwa*, al-'Abbasi al-Mahdi establishes handwriting as a potentially acceptable form of evidence but makes that statement conditional upon three requirements: that the handwriting belongs to somebody who is engaged in some kind of market or monetary exchange, that it is preserved in a ledger, and that it is used to prove only debts owed to others. His justification for taking this position follows an established convention of the *fatwa* literature, which is to rely on the opinions of former jurists.[49] Al-'Abbasi al-Mahdi offered similar versions of the same opinion in response to comparable questions.

Compared to merchant court decisions, the previous *fatwa* might appear to offer an identical path to commercial dispute resolution. Both court decisions and *fatwas* refer to ledgers, and to debts owed. Yet a closer look reveals three differences. The *fatwa* refers generally to individuals who engage in market or monetary exchanges. This difference means effectively that the utility of the ledger as evidence could potentially apply in situations which were not commercial, by the strict definition of the merchant courts. For example, a "seller" who traded goods for the purpose of direct consumption rather than circulation or a "moneylender" who extended loans that were not going to be turned into commercial investment were still subject to their ledgers being used against them as evidence of debts they owed to others, according to *shari'a*. Moreover, al-'Abbasi al-Mahdi left the burden of verifying the handwriting of the debtor to the community to which he or she belonged. Unlike the merchant court, which took the responsibility upon itself to contact bureaucratic departments and to hire experts, al-'Abbasi al-Mahdi explained that for a ledger to be considered as evidence, the handwriting of the ledger's owner must be "recognizable among the merchants and townsmen (*ma'luman bayn al-tujjar wa-'ahl al-balad*). It comes into effect [as evidence] . . . if the people recognized (*idha 'arif al-nass*) that the handwriting is that of the deceased."[50] Lastly, al-'Abbasi al-Mahdi, citing the influential late *Hanafi* jurist Ibn 'Abidin (d. 1836), makes a further exception to the anomalous status of the ledger, stating that only the moneylender's handwriting could be used as evidence "even if it existed outside of his ledger."[51] These differences serve as reminders that the logic underlying the merchant courts' and the Grand Mufti's conclusions on what constitutes evidence in relation to commercial disputes, as well as the tools of implementation available to them, were not identical, despite the strong similarities between the final court decisions and *fatwas*.

Likewise, when the form of evidence in question was a standalone document, the assessment of the merchant courts and the Grand Mufti were quite similar. Specifically, they agreed that such documents carried less evidentiary weight when compared to the bound ledger and that further authentication was needed before taking them into account. However, like with the ledgers, merchant court decisions and *al-Fatawa al-Mahdiyya* usually arrived at similar conclusions based on different logic. A merchant court case that spanned most of 1855 illustrates the evidentiary status of the standalone document in the merchant courts clearly. Early that year, two French subjects, Costandi Filiu and Livore Soteri, sold "eleven boxes of European mirrors" to a Cairo-based "*khurdaji*" by the name of Ahmad Yusuf al-Numrusi.[52] They agreed that Ahmad would pay the price of these mirrors in six equal installments over the course of twelve months and wrote a promissory note to that effect, which Ahmad added his seal to. Similar to other cases cited earlier, when Ahmad passed away, his inheritors stated that they would not pay back any alleged outstanding debts until a state court verified that claim. Yet, unlike those earlier examples, the merchant court did not search the debtor's ledgers for the relevant entry or bring in experts to authenticate his handwriting or seal. Instead, the court asked for witness testimonies. Two brokers, Muhammad Bayumi and Mustafa al-Tunisi, who may have had a hand in initiating the mirror sale in the first place, and one of whom at least had witnessed the transaction, were summoned. They independently testified that they knew this promissory note to be legitimate. At that point, the trustee of Ahmad's estate affirmed that the witnesses were "upright (*madhbutin*) and their testimony is acceptable to us" and agreed to pay the debt. Analytically, the standalone document did not contain the evidence. It only determined the elements of the debt agreement—the amount, the mode of payment, and the identities of creditor, debtor, and witness—that the court needed to verify. The verification was realized through the testimony of witnesses, and not through the written record.

Al-Fatawa al-Mahdiyya includes multiple direct comparisons between the ledger and the standalone commercial document. When a group of villagers wrote to the Grand Mufti to ask about the legal soundness of the village's mayor's claim that he was owed a debt by a deceased member of their community based on "a promissory note written in [the deceased's] hand and [displaying] his seal" and on his ability to produce witnesses, al-'Abbasi al-Mahdi found the mayor's claim baseless. He explained that the handwriting and the seal were to be used as evidence in a limited number of texts, not including the promissory note—namely, imperial certificates and the "*ledger* of a seller, a moneylender or a broker."[53] When asked about the evidentiary weight of a wide range of standalone documents, such as the deed (*sakk*)[54] and account list (*qa'imat hisab*),[55] al-'Abbasi al-Mahdi consistently answered that they had none without the *shari'a*-specified methods of establishing legal proof—testimony and oath. In response to a specific question about the prevalence of using signed or sealed promissory notes as proofs of debt as a matter of societal custom (*al-'urf jariyan bayn al-nas*), the Mufti insisted that the written document had no evidentiary value on its own, regardless of social practice.[56] Al-'Abbasi Al-Mahdi's strict position was based on the separation between the established documentary forms of commercial mechanisms and the evidentiary weight of these forms in the absence of the appropriate testimonies and oaths recognized by *shari'a* courts. The fact that such courts no longer enjoyed jurisdiction over commercial cases in Egypt—at least not in its major urban centers—was beside the point. In his view, the commercial arrangement itself, like any other lawful agreement, could be the subject of legal proof and was to be protected from unwarranted violation. Yet documentary evidence was secondary to the arrangement itself. Therefore, if a contract was not notarized,[57] included an incorrect detail,[58] or was not sufficiently detailed,[59] the commercial arrangement that contract represented was valid as long as the involved parties, including the witnesses, agreed that it was in effect. By extension, if those parties agreed that a commercial partnership was ended verbally without generating a documentary trail, their agreement would be valid.[60] Accordingly, it becomes clear that while both the merchant court decisions and the *al-Fatawa al-Mahdiyya* treated standalone documents as insufficient evidence of the existence of commercial agreements, they arrived at that similar general conclusion following a dissimilar logic.

Actors

Thus far, we have established two facts about the conceptual boundaries of the commercial sphere: that the nationality of the merchant could determine their ability to access the commercial-legal infrastructure, and that certain forms of written records could be deployed as evidence in both state-organized courts and *shari'a*-based forums. Building on these findings, we now turn to the vocational identities of those historical actors who were positioned to benefit from the legal recognition of nationality and of documentary evidence. I use the term "actor" rather than "individual" or "merchant" for two reasons. First, under Ottoman commercial law, companies held an independent legal personality. Merchant courts treated such companies in the same way they treated individual merchants. In a case that spanned over a year between September 1874 and December 1875, *khawaja* Tial sued the Cairo Water Company for failing to supply him with the daily amount of ice they had agreed upon. Tial was a retailer. According to his contract with the water company, he expected to regularly receive specified amounts of ice, which he would then sell for profit. In the merchant court, Tial and the company's representative argued over whether or not the company's delays were justified. Specifically, they debated if the mechanical malfunctioning that affected the company's ice production constituted an inadvertent and unavoidable reason for discontinuing supplies. Furthermore, they disagreed over how to calculate the suitable compensation for this breach of contract.[61] Throughout the proceedings, however, none of the parties involved questioned the company's legal personality as a merchant.

Second, *shari'a* and Ottoman commercial law alike often included those non-merchants who facilitated commercial transactions, such as brokers and freighter captains, within the same vocational category as merchants. As I show below, the apparent overlap between how the merchant courts and the office of the Grand Mufti defined those vocational identities belied dissimilar logic. The merchant courts' identification of merchants and their associates was conditional upon the roles they played in recording and executing commercial operations. By contrast, al-'Abbasi al-Mahdi understood those vocational identities to be self-evident—he did not link a merchant's identity to a particular practice. Yet he extended the procedural exemptions allowed for merchants and their associates to encompass their non-commercial transactional activities. To explicate these logics, let us examine concrete examples of how the vocational—in this case, commercial—identities of buyers and sellers, and their associates, entered the purview of the merchants presiding over the merchant courts, of the Grand Mufti, and by extension, of the range of laws that governed commercial activity.

The central actor within the commercial sphere is the merchant. The merchant court, as the state-organized forum led by merchants and specialized in handling commercial disputes, did not take any litigant's vocational identity for granted. It made it its mission to always ascertain that all parties to a dispute were merchants before it looked into their case. No manual exists within the courts' archives that determined the distinguishing features of a merchant's identity. Yet following the merchant courts' practices over time reveals consistently recognized signifiers of that identity. If those signifiers were absent from either the plaintiff or the defendant, the merchant court would dismiss the case on the grounds that one of the litigants was not a merchant. So, what were those essential signifiers?

A merchant needed to engage in commerce continuously—as opposed to occasionally, when taking a break from another form of employment, or when buying or selling as part of a non-commercial occupation. When Lumbra Avram sued Qilfa Zanub over an unpaid debt that resulted from the sale of marble (*rukham*), Qilfa defended himself by stating that he was not a merchant (*lam yakun min zumrat al-tujjar*) but rather an architect (*muhandis mi'mari*) who was employed as the director of purchases at the Khedival department of buildings (*da'irat al-'imarat al-saniyya*). He had bought the marble on behalf of his employer to use it in construction. Neither him nor the Khedival department of buildings was engaged in commerce. The court accepted his argument, and the case was dismissed.[62] In a similar case that the court heard a few months later, Khalil al-Qash'ami sued Ibrahim Afandi Hasan over an unpaid promissory note. Ibrahim had not borrowed this money himself but had agreed to serve as a guarantor for a loan taken out by his brother. When the brother defaulted, Ibrahim became responsible for paying back the debt in addition to the accrued interest. Yet, without contesting the facts of the debt, Ibrahim argued that he was not a merchant but a military officer (*min dhubbat al-jihadiyya*). The court accepted his argument, stating that it enjoyed no jurisdiction over him and that it was inappropriate (*la yasihh*) for him in the first place to guarantee a commercial loan.[63] In dismissing the case, the court effectively made the creditor and plaintiff, Khalil, bear the consequences of involving somebody who was not a merchant in a commercial operation.

It was not uncommon for the court to list two reasons in tandem for deciding that a case fell outside of its jurisdiction. In these cases, it was not always clear which of the specified dimensions of the case weighed more in the court's decision to dismiss it. For example, we do not know the circumstances in which Muhammad Afandi 'Asif, a clerk (*mu'awin*) at the municipal council in Bani Swayf, borrowed a sum of money from several people in the town of al-Zaqaziq, 150 miles north. What we do know is that his creditors presented multiple promissory notes as evidence of debts he owed them, and which he did not fulfill on time, in the course of suing him in the Cairo Merchant Court in the summer of 1863. The court dismissed the case on two grounds: Muhammad was not a merchant, and the debts in question constituted a personal loan (*sulfa*), not a commercial one. Muhammad, it appears, had borrowed the money to alleviate a personal financial hardship, such as paying rent or alimony, rather than to invest it in some market transaction.

About a decade later, Casimir Olivier, a French subject who was a hotel owner, sued his landlords, the inheritors of Husayn Bey al-Jamashiri. He had rented a house from them and converted it into a hotel. While the rental contract was in effect, Casimir noticed that the building needed some repairs so he contacted his landlords, who either ignored his request or otherwise indicated their unwillingness to help him out with the renovation. Be that as it may, he held the landlords responsible for a substantial financial loss that resulted from their dereliction of duty and sued them before the merchant court. Like with the previous example, the court dismissed the case on two grounds: "since the claim of *khawaja* Casimir Olivier does not contain any notes or contracts (*mujarrad 'an al-sanadat wal-kunturatat*) and is not related to a commercial matter, this case does not fall within the jurisdiction of the merchant court."[64] Yet, unlike Muhammad's case, in which the identity of the litigant and the nature of the debt (being a clerk and taking out a personal loan) could not be ranked in terms of their importance, the court's logic in Casimir's case could be gleaned from comparable instances. Two Greek subjects, Dimitri Vassili and Manoli Papazaki, had sued Ghattas 'Abd-al-Masih, who had invited them to partner with him in his Khartoum-based business. Upon arriving in Sudan, they discovered that there was nothing for them to do there and failed to convince Ghattas to sign a document stating that they had traveled to Khartoum according to his invitation. The merchant court dismissed the case because "the documents or contracts, upon which a case could have been built, are absent. Therefore, the case will not be heard in this court."[65] The court's explicit reasoning could be applied by extension to Casimir's case—because he had no documentary evidence to show, the court would not recognize the dispute as commercial. In other words, the existence of the documentary evidence could determine the commercial character of the dispute.

In the merchant court, the combination of the commercial identity of the litigant—as merchant or commercial company—with the existence of particular documentary evidence was usually taken as a proxy for the existence of a commercial transaction. In some cases, however, the court judged the intentions of the buyer in order to ascertain the commercial character of the dispute at hand. To put it differently, the court tried to establish why a certain exchange had taken place in order to determine whether it enjoyed jurisdiction over the case. In one instance, Niqula Wasili rented clothes from Rashid Agha and did not pay for the exchange. When Rashid solicited the help of the merchant court to collect his money, he was turned down. The court explained that it was not authorized to pass a legal opinion on the dispute because Niqula was "not a merchant" and because the clothes were "not [rented] for a commercial purpose (*laysa 'ala sabil al-tijara*)." It is worth noting that the court decided to dismiss the case without either of the concerned parties contesting its jurisdiction over the dispute.[66] In an earlier example, the court reached a similar conclusion in relation to the government architect Qilfa Zanub, who bought marble for the government agency he worked at with the intention of using it as construction material. Taken together, these two examples show that not every exchange with a monetary value was necessarily considered to be commercial within the state-organized legal infrastructure. Legally speaking, commerce included exchanges of commodities or of money that would lead to further circulation—buying a good in order to sell it, or borrowing money in order to invest it. It did not include lending to alleviate financial hardship or retail sales, be they for a productive activity (e.g., marble) or private consumption (e.g., rental, clothes).

The *shari'a* literature did not share these technical concerns because it covered all areas of social activity, and not only commerce. Therefore, al-'Abbasi al-Mahdi aimed to answer questions about all sorts of exchange—for example, their soundness, fairness, or revocability—without dwelling on their particular purposes, be they circulation or immediate consumption. His attention in arriving at an answer to these questions on exchange was often set on determining whether the person involved in the query was entitled to use handwriting as legal evidence, as we have seen in the previous section. In the course of doing so, *al-Fatawa al-Mahdiyya* reveals a difference between state-organized commercial law and *shari'a*. Whereas the former examined the written record to uncover the purpose of the transaction it represented, *shari'a* looked beyond the written record to its author. Within the span of a few months in the early 1850s, al-'Abbasi al-Mahdi received two separate questions, both of which described outstanding debts that were recorded in writing, with one of them relating a sale of wheat that appeared in the ledgers of both the creditor and the debtor. In both cases, he answered, the paper trail notwithstanding, that if the parties involved were not merchants, their documentary record was worthless from a legal point of view.[67] Unlike the merchant court, which would have considered the identity of the merchant, the fact of the recordkeeping, and the character of the transaction to establish whether the case at hand was commercial, the Grand Mufti needed only to verify that the parties to the exchange identified, and were identified by others, as merchants, brokers, or moneylenders.

It must be noted that the merchant court's interest in locating merchants among potential litigants was related to their central role in commercial undertakings. Therefore, an individual who was not, by the court's strict definition, a merchant, but who facilitated commercial activities through his knowledge or endeavors, was able to access the commercial-legal infrastructure and appear in the merchant court when certain conditions were fulfilled. For example, in 1862, a group of Yemeni merchants based in Cairo sued a boat captain by the name of Muhammad Muhsin. They had contracted him to transport 250 parcels of goods from Jedda to Suez. They claimed that upon receiving the parcels in Suez, they discovered them to be "wet and eroded" and held Muhammad responsible for not taking sufficient precautions to keep the goods dry and for recklessly choosing to travel at night. In the merchant court, Muhammad defended himself, saying that he could not have kept the parcels dry because the weather had been rainy for eleven consecutive days, and all the boats that traveled the same Red Sea route received unusually large amounts of rain. After further investigation, the court discovered that the water residue in the goods was seawater rather than rain and concluded that Muhammad had not told the truth. Remarkably, however, it acquitted him because the Yemeni merchants had signed an invoice confirming that they received the parcels in good condition.[68] The court decided that, despite their claims, the plaintiffs had failed to examine their goods thoroughly as soon as they received them, which meant that they had effectively given up their right to compensation. For his part, the boat captain, Muhammad, was not only accorded access into the merchant court but was able to prevail, using the tools of commercial law, against the merchants who had implicitly enabled him to participate in the commercial sphere.

Whereas captains who otherwise would use their boats for fishing or transporting people may enter the commercial sphere temporarily to aid merchants with their task of circulating goods, brokers worked exclusively with merchants. It is not surprising, then, that the merchant court understood its purview to not only include brokers as litigants but to also monitor the organization of their associations, namely, the guilds (*tawa'if*; sing. *ta'ifa*). A revealing incident took place in the summer of 1863, when the head of the brokers' association (*ta'ifat al-samasira*) embarked on reorganizing the association in light of recurring fights between the brokers of the neighborhoods of Sahil Misr al-Qadima and Bulaq, where Cairo's two riverine ports were located. Accordingly, he created a new organizational structure, appointing new deputies, while expelling fourteen brokers and banning them from offering brokerage services. He also emphasized to all members of the association the necessity of recording all the deals that they broker. Finally, he solicited the help of the police department in enforcing these decisions. Upon learning of the issue, the Cairo Merchant Court contacted the police department requesting that it immediately send all the papers related to this incident to the court. In an official correspondence, the merchant court reminded the police department that "legal cases related to brokers are within the jurisdiction of the [merchant] court and not the police department . . . even if the expelled brokers acted in unauthorized ways, the investigation and subsequent decisions regarding these actions are the [exclusive] right of the merchant court."[69]

The merchant court's assertiveness in relation to supervising the brokers' guild is meaningful. It sheds light on the often-hidden dynamic of the Khedival's state's co-optation of the guilds, revealing potential competition among bureaucratic departments over who gets to oversee corporatist interests.[70] At the same time, it hints at the merchant court's embeddedness within the state structure, which enables it to perform an investigative role in certain circumstances. For example, in 1856, Zaynab Khatun turned to the police department for help while she was trying to tie some loose ends from her business partnership with her recently deceased husband Salih al-Barrad. "She was not comfortable" (*lam hasal laha raha*) with the way that the guardian of Salih's estate was handling the posthumous business dealings. He seemed, to her, to not recognize her business ties to her late husband. To establish the truth, the police department asked the merchant court to look into the matter. In turn, the merchant court asked to see the estate's records from *Bayt al-Mal*, the financial authority authorized to store these documents.[71] That the police department did not contact *Bayt al-Mal* directly is significant. Technically, there was no case against the estate. What was at stake was determining whether Zaynab was indeed Salih's business partner during his lifetime. It was within the merchant court's purview to offer its expert knowledge on the question of partnership—to use a contemporary idiom: Salih's business history. For Zaynab to collect any dues from the estate, however, was a different question that had not been raised at this point.

The merchant court's strategy of inextricably linking a merchant's identity to commercial practices led, in certain circumstances as we have seen, to the inclusion of other agents of commerce, such as the ship captain and the broker, into the law-defined realm of commerce. By contrast, the *shari'a* outlook, which equated the merchant with the broker and the moneylender from the start, did not change the number of legally recognizable agents of commerce. Rather, it treated the documentary trail produced by those three as legally valuable in relation to all legal questions and not only commercial ones. For example, al-'Abbasi al-Mahdi affirmed that a will that was recorded by a merchant in his own business ledger was valid without the presence of witnesses. If the *fatwa* he issued in July 1849 was implemented, it would have enabled the former slaves of a deceased merchant to share his estate with his offspring on the grounds that, as a merchant, his handwriting carried legal value on its own, regardless of whether the content of the writing was related to commerce or not.[72] The exception that al-'Abbasi al-Mahdi made to this expansive recognition of the documentary trail produced by commercial actors was if it seemed to allow a self-serving result. When asked about the validity of a broker's testimony in court, he answered that a reputable broker was as good a witness as any other, except if he served as a witness of a commercial transaction in which he was involved and from which he may have benefitted.[73] To put it differently, in a *shari'a* context, the handwriting of a broker could influence the outcome of a non-commercial settlement, but his oral testimony, if related to his own business, was worthless.

Agriculture

No discussion of the legal regulation of commercial activity could claim to be complete without addressing its intersections with the agricultural economy. During the second half of the nineteenth century, land was the primary source of wealth, and the largest part of commercial activity was based on the circulation of this rurally generated value. The production and circulation of cotton, in its raw and processed forms, occupied much of Egypt's landowners, peasants, merchants, and state officials. Yet, as I will show below, the merchant courts were constantly trying to mark a conceptual and legal boundary between activities that it considered commercial and would rule on and often similar or clearly related activities that it deemed to be "matters of agricultural land" (*mawad al-atyan*) that fell outside of its jurisdiction. This rather surprising, and sometimes seemingly arbitrary, legal distinction between otherwise continuous agricultural and commercial market operations did not emanate in commercial law but rather in a parallel attempt to protect the land ownership regime from the mid-nineteenth century onward. The Khedival state's orientation in that regard strongly resembled Ottoman imperial policy during the same time period.

In his seminal study *The Pasha's Peasants: Land, Society, and Economy in Lower Egypt, 1740–1858*, Kenneth Cuno reconstructed the dynamic of commercial agriculture in the eighteenth century. In his account, credit-based agricultural activity, through which urban-based merchants extended loans to peasants in the countryside, was a permanent feature of urban-rural relations. This dynamic was codified through a series of land laws in 1847, 1855, and 1858. These legislations were meant "to establish firmly the state's regulatory control over land," through ensuring that the peasants in possession of land were managing it profitably (to be able to generate tax revenue for the state), that inheritance practices would not lead to the uneconomic fragmentation of landownership (to maintain economies of scale), and to ensure that the state-organized legal infrastructure was the only medium through which landownership was documented, usufruct rights were transferred, and disputes surrounding land were regulated.[74] The Khedival state's orientation on these questions was informed by a long history of Ottoman land policies written from Constantinople, the most recent of which was a Land Code implemented in April 1858, a mere four months before Sa'id Pasha approved a similar Khedival Land Law in August of the same year.[75] Eight years later, in 1866, when Khedive Isma'il (r. 1863–1879) established a consultative assembly (*Majlis Shura al-Nuwwab*), he appointed to it rural notables, thus marking the rise of prominent landed interests in the political and legislative spheres. Soon afterward, in 1871, Isma'il created a legal path for transforming usufruct rights into absolute private ownership rights, although there are indications that that path became functional on a wide scale only in 1874.[76]

As I discussed in the introductory chapter, studies of modern state formation in Egypt have focused on the final decades of the nineteenth century, building on this history of land. For example, Timothy Mitchell, whose work has informed numerous studies of this subject, historized the property regime in the Egyptian countryside.[77] More recently, Aaron Jakes uncovered the connection between the organizing of land ownership under British rule and European financial capital.[78] The centrality of landownership to these important accounts leaves no space for merchants, who are assumed to be the co-opted elites of a bygone era and who, therefore, do not contribute to modern state formation. However, already in the mid-nineteenth century, specifically between the mid-1840s to the mid-1870s, the rapid development of the landownership regime paralleled the state's efforts to govern the commercial sphere. The first land law of 1847 was issued only two years after the establishment of the first merchant court in Alexandria in 1845. The second and third land laws of 1855 and 1858 came into effect immediately before and immediately after the major reorganizations of the merchant court system in 1856 and 1857. Significantly, the heightened legislative activity in relation to both agriculture and commerce had the effect of legally distinguishing between these two economic spheres. Commercial agriculture that relied on merchant financing had been widespread for at least a century. In the nineteenth century, Egypt's incorporation into the world economy, and the large-scale reorientation of agricultural activity toward the cultivation and exportation of cotton, led to the amplification of these urban-rural credit relations. Significantly, however, in the 1870s, as the privatization of agricultural land on a wide scale was becoming a legal and political reality, the merchant courts were emphasizing that questions relating to agriculture were by definition not commercial, and would not be litigated under commercial law. The clearest articulation of this logic could be seen in an 1874 court case (an important date for establishing private land ownership), in which Hasan Afandi Ghanim, a French subject and landowner, sued the estate of Hasan Afandi Husni, a local tenant who was renting from him 26 *feddans* at the time of his death. The landowner resorted to the merchant court because he understood the unpaid rent to be a debt owed by a local to a European. The court, however, cited a Khedival order (*amr ʿali*) that specified that European merchants could sue the estates of local individuals before the merchant courts only "if the [matter] . . . was related to their commercial business but not to issues of agriculture or properties (*al-mawad al-mukhtassa bil-atyan wal-ʿaqarat*)."[79]

By the early 1870s, then, a clear Khedival order that was sent specifically to the merchant court[80] was meant to guarantee that land-related disputes were to be settled under a specialized set of laws outside of the commercial-legal infrastructure (see Figure 5.1). At least two decades later, widely circulating state law compendia were still reproducing those nineteenth-century legal demarcations between commerce and agriculture. For example, in Filib Jallad's *General Encyclopedia of the Administration and the Judiciary*, the entry for commerce (*tijara*) states that "according to the law, the following is considered a matter of commerce (*'amalan tijariyan*)—the purchase of [goods] . . . in order to sell them in their original form or in an altered form . . . ." The list that follows includes other activities, most of which include references to contracts and promissory notes, before making a notable exception toward the end of the entry: "If the owner or cultivator of a land sells the produce of this land . . . [then] this operation is not considered commercial."[81] The format of Jallad's entry is noteworthy. Rather than producing an abstract definition of commerce that revolves around exchange, it lists a finite number of exchanges and highlights the indispensability of certain written forms to these commercial exchanges. Seventeen years later, in 1909, an important work of jurisprudence that distilled the principles underlying the rulings of the National Courts included the principle that "for farmers, to promise supplying a portion of the cotton they cultivated . . . makes the [relevant] lawsuit civil rather than commercial, even if the person being supplied were a merchant."[82] Evidently, the legal separation of commerce from agriculture survived the commercial-legal infrastructure of the mid-nineteenth century and into the period of British rule.

Expectedly, the specialized laws and Khedival orders that were intended to distinguish between the commercial and agricultural spheres

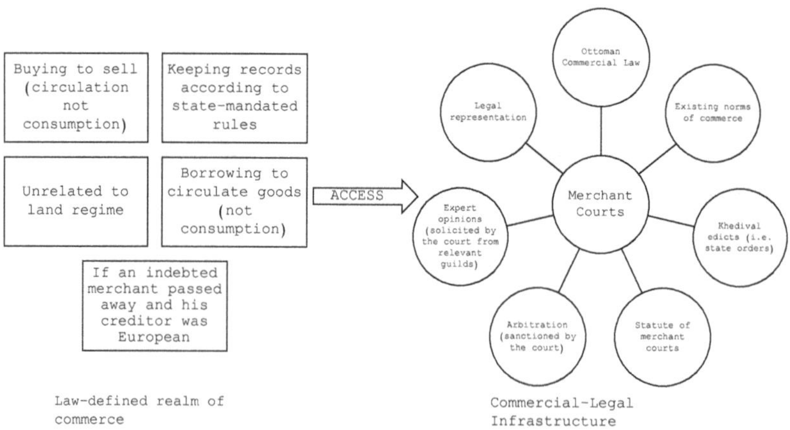

Figure 5.1. Conditions for accessing the commercial-legal infrastructure.

were often the source of confusion for state administrators as well as for potential litigants. To better understand the significance of ambiguous cases, let us first consider briefly a court case in which the merchant court was able to decisively determine where its jurisdiction ended. In March 1874, Muhammad Yusuf Wahba requested that the merchant court sequester the goods in possession of his debtor, Khalil Abu-Shanab. The court summarily rejected Muhammad's request. It did not ask to hear the defendant, nor did it, as was customary, recount the outline of the dispute. Instead, it issued a firm one-line statement: "disputes over land and agriculture (*al-munaza'at allati tahduth min ajl al-atyan wal-zira'a*) lie within the mandate of civil judicial councils."[83] Reading the statement against the grain, it becomes clear that Khalil's debt was related to the sale or rental of agricultural land or produce, and that it was absolutely clear to the court that such a case was outside of its purview. It was an open-and-shut case.

If Muhammad and Khalil's case is an example of the unproblematic legal separation between the commercial and agricultural spheres, the merchant court archives contain other disputes that occur at the overlap of these two spheres of economic activity. Scrutinizing these cases reveals two facts about the law in practice: one, that the legal boundary between commerce and agriculture was seldom clear, and two, that the courts had to resort to a seemingly counterintuitive line of reasoning in order to maintain this boundary. To be specific, the merchant courts declined to hear cases that revolved around the exchange of agricultural land or crops. Yet, at the same time, in the course of resolving commercial disputes, they claimed the right to sequester or confiscate agricultural land and crops belonging to a merchant debtor, in order to compensate a creditor for an unpaid debt. In other words, despite their insistence on their exclusive commercial specialization, they could influence agricultural exchanges. Moreover, the merchant courts claimed jurisdiction over all brokerage activities, regardless of the substance of the transactions being brokered. Interestingly, this last point marks an overlap between commercial law and *shari'a*, since both legal corpora treat merchants and brokers similarly, regardless of the specific exchanges they facilitated.

It should be clear by now that the merchant courts consistently affirmed the commercial character of a dispute and the occupational identity of the litigants before actually scrutinizing its details, hearing the competing arguments, and issuing a ruling. With the privatization of landownership in the early 1870s, more litigants defied the merchant courts' strict definitions. In the city, they were merchants, who profited from market exchanges and extended or solicited loans. Simultaneously, in the countryside, they were absentee landlords. This dual economic identity meant that if the merchant court ruled against them, the assets it would have recourse to in order to compensate the prevailing party would be agricultural land or crops. By seizing those assets, the merchant court would be in effect a participant in the land market and the commercial agricultural market, a role which contradicts one of its core missions, which is preserving the boundary between the commercial and agricultural spheres. The following two examples will shed light on this paradox.

In August 1875, *khawaja* Sophocle Akupolo, a subject of Austria-Hungary, had probably lost hope that 'Ali Pasha Sharif was going to pay him 17,786 *liras*, the value of ten promissory notes that he held. After asking for the money repeatedly in a friendly way (*bi-tariq al-mahabba*), Sophocle decided to go to the merchant court and ask for the temporary sequestration of 'Ali Pasha's lands (*ab'adiyya*), which were located in the governorate of al-Gharbiyya, north of Cairo. The merchant court decided that Sophocle's request was legitimate and did order the sequestration of some of the mentioned lands in addition to an amount of cotton stored in 'Ali Pasha's name in depots in Alexandria and Cairo.[84] In court, 'Ali Pasha's agricultural land was dealt with as a regular object of sequestration. It followed a general rule that the merchant courts abided by, which stipulated that "unmovable assets" (*al-a'yan al-ghayr manqula*) were legitimate objects of sequestration. In this case, 'Ali Pasha could reclaim control over his assets if he paid his debt to Sophocle. Hence, the court becomes a potential participant in the agricultural economy pending the action of the losing party, who is an actual landowner. Yet there were other examples where the court assumed an active role in the agricultural economy directly. In a case that spanned 1872 and 1873, Mirza 'Abd-al-Jawwad convinced the court that Muhammad Hasan al-Isfahani had stopped paying the installments he owed regarding indigo (*nila*) that he had bought on credit. The court issued a temporary sequestration order for a range of Muhammad's possessions, including his residence in the town of Fuwwa about fifty miles east of Alexandria, his shop, and his crops (*mazru'at*).

The sequestration did not compel Muhammad to reach a settlement with his creditor. As a result, the court decided to sell the sequestered assets in order to repay Mirza. Soon afterward, Muhammad appeared before the court to appeal this decision. He maintained that he did not breach his agreement with Mirza, and so his assets should not have been sequestered in the first place. After several court sessions, in which partners were called in and new documents presented and verified, Muhammad was able to prove his case. The court reversed its earlier decision and directed the revenue that resulted from the sale of his possessions toward paying for the indigo.[85] This second example shows the court taking concrete steps toward liquidating agricultural assets through the direct sale of crops.

Brokerage activities constitute another point of intersection between commerce and agriculture that the merchant courts oversaw. In two cases that the court heard in late 1873, brokers who had facilitated the sale of agricultural land resorted to the Cairo Merchant Court, and their cases were considered on substantive grounds. In September, *khawaja* Wita Abul-'Afiyah, a broker, sued two fellow brokers, *khawajas* Aslan Musa and Haim Susniu, for not paying him his rightful share from brokering the sale of a tract of agricultural land. The court did not express concern about the object of the sale, which is typically the initial obstacle to considering a case. It did, however, dismiss Wita's claim as it was not supported by the appropriate documentary evidence. The exact language of the court's decision reflects the applied legal reasoning.

> Since *khawaja* Wita . . . did not prove in a legally sanctioned way that he has participated with . . . Aslan . . . and Haim . . . in brokering the sale of the . . . agricultural land . . . and since, in accordance with the law, his testimony could not be relied upon . . . and since there was no [written] contract . . . regarding the sale . . .[86]

A couple of months later, Muhammad Abu-Jahin al-Dallal went to court to complain that Khalil Afandi al-Ibriqji sought his help to sell his agricultural land but did not pay him his fees. Muhammad was not the only broker to help Khalil Afandi with the sale. Another broker, Ahmad al-Khayyat, worked with Muhammad on finding a buyer for Khalil's land. After the sale was concluded, Khalil disregarded Muhammad but paid Ahmad the complete fee. Khalil Afandi ignored the merchant court summons to attend the session that was set to discuss

Muhammad's claim. Therefore, in his absence, the court ruled that Khalil was to pay Muhammad Abu-Jahin the brokerage fee he was owed.[87] Like with the earlier case of Wita Abul-'Afiyah, the court considered brokerage to be in and of itself a commercial activity, regardless of the character of the asset that was actually exchanged, including agricultural land.

The treatment of brokerage as necessarily a commercial activity was a fact of *shari'a* too, as is clear in al-'Abbasi al-Mahdi's consistent assignment of equal evidentiary weight to the documentary trail produced by "merchant, broker and money-lender" in the course of doing their jobs. What sets al-'Abbasi al-Mahdi's opinions apart from merchant court rulings is that he did not treat transactions of commercial agriculture as essentially outside of the commercial sphere. For example, when asked about a man who lived with his two brothers and who invested their collective inheritance from their father to buy agricultural land, al-'Abbasi al-Mahdi stated that the landownership was by default shared equally by each of the siblings. When the man who bought the land produced a deed that listed him as the sole buyer and owner, al-'Abbasi al-Mahdi answered that the deed on its own, without further *shari'a*-sanctioned evidence, was not sufficient to exclude his brothers from equally co-owning the land.[88] His *fatwa* is identical to others he had issued in relation to the sale of non-agricultural assets, which the merchant court would have defined strictly as commercial. Similarly, when he received a question from the judge of the *shari'a* court in Giza regarding an unprofitable sale of onions, al-'Abbasi al-Mahdi paid no particular attention to the detail that the traded good was an agricultural crop. The question was in reference to a *mudaraba* agreement. It included a woman who owned the capital and who would claim a third of the profit and a merchant who would buy goods in Giza, resell them in the towns of the Nile Delta, and claim the remaining two-thirds. As it happened, the merchant did not return to his partner with a profit but with a substantial loss on account of the onions rotting (*hasal lil-basal 'ufuna*) during his business trip—the woman had invested 1,250 *qurush*, but the man sold the onions for only 400. The woman could not resort to the commercial-legal infrastructure because the exchange was of an agricultural crop, so she sued her partner at the *shari'a* court. Had the agreement and subsequent dealings been written down in a recognizable way, the *shari'a* court would have relied on that documentary evidence. Since the only information that the *shari'a* court judge was presented with was the partners' verbal claims, he applied the general *shari'a* principle, namely, that the burden of proof was on the claimant. To be absolutely sure, he wrote to the office of the Grand Mufti to seek his opinion. The latter confirmed that if no *shari'a*-backed proof was presented, the denial of responsibility by the defendant under oath was to be believed.[89] In other words, when a merchant failed to access the commercial-legal infrastructure because she undertook a market exchange that it defined as non-commercial, she resorted to the more universalistic legal field of *shari'a*, where the exchange would be judged irrespective of the presumed dichotomy between commerce and agriculture.

Concluding Remarks

In this chapter, I used a wider lens to capture how commerce was defined legally both inside and outside the state-organized commercial-legal infrastructure. To capture the conceptual boundaries of this law-defined realm of commerce, I read two sets of sources: the proceedings of the Cairo Merchant Court, which enabled me to empirically reconstruct the state-mandated jurisdictional borders of commercial law, and *al-Fatawa al-Mahdiyya*, which provided me with a view of *shari'a* reasoning in practice, especially how it understood legal evidence and how it informed the operation of the *shari'a* court system, both in relation to questions of exchange. Looking at these two historical sources in tandem revealed a complicated intertwining of legal logic that sometimes overlapped, and at other times, diverged. If historians understand the overall objective of judicial reorganization and legislative revision as the consolidation of the Khedival legal regime, then the incongruence of coexisting legal logics in relation to commerce should be recognized as a sign of inherent tensions within this process of legal streamlining.

The consolidation of the legal regime was predicated on the creation of specialized law and forums—in this case, commercial law and the merchant courts—and on neutralizing exceptions to the law, most importantly extraterritorial privileges—hence, creating the merchant courts as mixed tribunals. In practice, however, the boundaries of that legal specialization were bound to be incomplete. When merchants passed away with outstanding debts, a common scenario, the nationalities of the creditors and the now-deceased debtors determined whether the debts would be treated as family matters to be adjudicated under *shari'a* or other confession-based laws or as commercial matters that would be resolved under commercial law. The documentary trail that merchants and their associates produced in the course of conducting business was accorded legal weight that superseded oral testimony under oath, which was the more common form of legal evidence—a fact that parallels the increased importance of forensic science in the field of criminal law. Yet that reliance on writing which was introduced in relation to commercial contracts spilled over into the sphere of civil disputes under *shari'a*, whenever merchants or their associates were involved. Furthermore, in setting rather exclusive standards when defining who a merchant was, commercial law prevented occasional buyers and sellers in the marketplace from accessing the commercial-legal infrastructure while enabling others who aided them, such as ship captains and brokers, to be treated as merchants for legal purposes. And, in protecting the legal regime of landownership, Khedival state legislators pushed disputes around commercial agriculture and the sale of private lands outside the purview of commercial law and into the domains of civil law and *shari'a*. Yet, especially starting in the 1870s, the merchant courts enjoyed the authority to intervene in the agricultural economy through the direct sale of agricultural land and crops in the case of sequestering assets as part of commercial dispute resolution.

EPILOGUE

"There Was No Special Law for Commercial Activities"

FOR THOSE WHO LIVED THROUGH the 1880s, Egypt must have appeared as a transformed place. The 'Urabi revolt that aimed to establish national control over the government was defeated decisively in battle. Its leaders, including Hasan Musa al-'Aqqad, were sent into exile. In the course of invading the country, the British navy bombarded Alexandria. The city that Butrus Tawil had lived in, and from which he managed his international commercial business, was in ruins. Khedive Tawfiq (r. 1879–1892), whose position depended on direct British protection, would have less autonomy than any of his predecessors. During that decade, the political defeats of the nationalists and the material destruction that paralleled it paved the way for Egypt's new British rulers to redefine government and politics. Spearheading this process was the British Consul-General of Egypt, Evelyn Baring (r. 1883–1907), better known as Lord Cromer.[1]

In 1885, Baring was living through a defining moment in what would become the seventy-two-year-long British occupation of Egypt, a third of which he was the country's effective ruler. Egypt's government had defaulted on its debts a decade earlier, and his main task was to manage its budget to ensure the payment of interest on longstanding debts while keeping the government running. He decided that to be able to do so necessitated the continued British occupation of Egypt. The possibility of a swift military victory followed by evacuation and indirect imperial domination was dead at that point. Instead, Egypt would become a British imperial domain for the foreseeable future.[2] With that realization, those whose fortunes were tied to the commercial-legal infrastructure of the mid-nineteenth century would quickly learn to navigate the new government arrangements. Butrus Tawil and Tito Figari appeared in the Mixed Courts, the first as a litigant in land-related disputes and the second as an *avukatu*. Because of his involvement in the ʿUrabi revolt, Hasan Musa al-ʿAqqad spent ten years in exile in Massawa. Following his return to Egypt in 1893, his name too appeared in the new court system in disputes over land and inheritance.

The experiences of Butrus, Hasan, and Tito, who we met in Chapters Two, Three, and Four, were not entirely unique. They were embedded in larger networks that tied merchants to legal expertise and market governance. When the commercial-legal infrastructure that existed from the mid-1840s to the mid-1870s was dismantled and replaced by the Mixed Courts and the National Courts in 1876 and 1883, respectively, they adapted to the new reality. However, if they, along with their peers, moved on from the old legal regime to the new, why did their reorientation go unnoticed by their contemporaries? Was the move self-evident that it did not invite any comment, or was there a substantive reason for forgetting—or erasing—that move? The year 1885 might hold a part of the answer.

The merchant courts closed their doors for the last time in 1876. Pending cases that included foreign interests were transferred to the newly inaugurated Mixed Courts, while those pertaining to locals, a category that included Ottoman subjects in general, were handed over to the existing state-organized judicial councils.[3] Several years later, in 1883, these councils were absorbed into the new National Courts.[4] The latter were to apply new criminal, civil, commercial, and procedural laws.[5] Despite the appearance of a complete rupture with the Khedival past, the new laws had much in common with their Ottoman predecessors, most importantly, their commitment to synthesize French law with *Hanafism*.[6] On November 13, 1883, Egypt's first *national* commercial law was issued, signed by Minister of Justice Husayn Fakhri Pasha[7]—the same Husayn Fakhri who would be present at the memorial held for Tito Figari upon his death almost fifteen years later.

The National Court system would become the institutional home of a growing corps of law-educated professionals. One of them, ʻAziz Kahil, deserves attention for being the first to write a systematic study of the new commercial law in 1885, within two years of its issuance.[8] He was born around 1860 into a Syrian family and had traveled to Europe on a scholarship from the Khedival government in 1877 to pursue legal education.[9] Upon his return, he was appointed as the secretary of the Criminal Investigation Commission (*qumisyun tahqiq al-jinayat*).[10] When the National Courts were finally opened in 1883, he joined them as a prosecutor before the Court of Appeals (*wakil al-niyaba al-ʻumumiyya bi-mahkamat al-istiʻnaf al-ahliyya*).[11] Over the following decades, he rose within the judiciary, serving as the deputy to the head of the Alexandria Criminal Court (*wakil mahkamat jinayat al-iskandariyya*) in the 1890s[12] and presiding over the Alexandria Court of First Instance (*ra'is mahkamat al-iskandariyya al-ibtida'iyya*) at the turn of the twentieth century.[13] For almost two decades after that, until 1920, ʻAziz Kahil occupied various senior positions within the judiciary, most prominently heading the civil and commercial circuit of the Court of Appeals (*al-da'ira al-madaniyya wal-tijariiya*)[14] and serving as a judicial adviser at the Court of Cassation (*mustashar mahkamat al-naqd*).[15] When he reached the government-mandated age of retirement, he was appointed as a senior judge in the Mixed Court of Appeal.[16]

ʻAziz Kahil's judicial career opened for him other opportunities for eminence among his immediate community and well-known intellectual circles. Like Butrus Tawil, ʻAziz was a Greek Catholic, a denomination that historically consisted of Syrian immigrants and their descendants and that had been under clerical control since the 1830s. When ʻAziz was embarking on his career in law in the 1880s, he was among a new generation of professional and/or wealthy Greek Catholics who established themselves as a lay leadership of the community. At first, they did so by establishing a communal welfare organization outside of the church. With the increasing popularity of ideas of constitutionalism and representative government in Egypt, they expanded their claims over communal affairs more generally. ʻAziz sat on the five-member committee that drafted the community's constitution at the turn of the twentieth century, which secured the position of laymen like himself in running the community's affairs.[17]

Outside this Syrian context, ʿAziz was a well-known name in intellectual and elite circles. Naturally, he was an acquaintance of leading lawyers who occupied prominent positions in the public sphere like Saʿd Zaghlul (1859–1927)[18] and Ibrahim al-Hilbawi (1858–1940).[19] But he was not limited to these professional connections. For example, his presence was noted in the funerals of figures such as Muhammad ʿAbduh (1849–1905)[20] and Jurji Zaydan (1861–1914)[21] and a celebration of Najib Mitri (1865–1928).[22] As one of the translators of ʿAbd-al-Rahman al-Jabarti's chronicle, *ʿAja'ib al-Athar*, into French, it should come as no surprise that he was careful to attend social events related to the country's most prominent (Syrian) publishers.[23]

Combining a career in law and a presence in intellectual circles, ʿAziz Kahil's most important legacy today is his legal scholarship. The generational difference between him and Tito Figari sheds light on why ʿAziz should be considered a pioneer in that regard. Tito studied law in Europe and practiced it in Egypt before the professionalization of the field. The closest he got to legal writing was his participation in the idiosyncratic and little-known legal treatise that was published by Moïse Castelli in his dispute with Hasan al-ʿIdwi in 1872.[24] By contrast, ʿAziz Kahil embarked on a legal education in Europe shortly after the inauguration of the Mixed Courts, and his legal career roughly coincided with the establishment of the National Courts—he was present at their inception as a member of the first cohort of public prosecutors. Shortly after the opening of the National Courts in 1883, he was among the first law-degree holders and professionals to tread the uncharted territory of legal interpretation.[25] During the second half of the 1880s, he published *A Treatise on Taking the Oath* (1886), *A Treatise on the Authority of Civil Rulings* (1889), and *Establishing Evidence in Civil Law* (1889?).[26] These writings held a canonical status in Egyptian legal scholarship and are referenced in later scholarly works, including jurisprudential studies. Given the subject of this book, and as we approach its end, it is worthwhile to turn to his first foray into legal scholarship: *An Interpretation of Egyptian Commercial Law* (1885).

An Interpretation of Egyptian Commercial Law by ʿAziz Kahil is a 439-page tome.[27] It is divided into three parts. The first, "Merchants and Commercial Activities," is the shortest. It addresses conceptual matters such as "who is to be referred to by the term 'merchant' (*lafz tajir*)," which evoke the notions adopted by the mid-nineteenth-century merchant courts. The second and third parts occupy most of the book and offer a detailed treatment of contracts and bankruptcy, respectively. This organization is not surprising given the centrality of the latter two topics to commercial law. As should be clear by now, disputes regarding contracts and bankruptcy were the main issues that the merchant courts heard in the decades preceding the publication of *An Interpretation* in 1885.

Given the consistency of the book's agenda with the practical experience of the merchant courts, which were in operation from the mid-1840s to the mid-1870s, it is astonishing that 'Aziz Kahil, writing less than a decade later, shows virtually no awareness of the recent history of commercial legal practice in Egypt. The only historical context he offers for commercial law revolves around its separation from the larger field of civil law. Reading his own words on the genesis of commercial law highlights his disregard for the rich experience of Egypt's then recently closed merchant courts:

> In the beginning, there was no special law for commercial activities. Instead . . . the rules of civil law applied to all transactions between people, whether it was for the purpose of commerce or otherwise. When the scope of commerce expanded . . . merchants were forced to neglect the stipulations of civil law . . . . They replaced them with customary ways and conventions that allowed them to complete their work . . . . Then, jurists became aware of that [situation] and collected these conventions to enact a law, with clearly articulated expressions . . .[28]

His point is correct in relation to the history of French law. Yet limiting the historical context to this detail ignored the Ottoman and Egyptian recent history. Was this an oversight on the part of the author or a more widely shared attitude of Egypt's new cohort of law-educated professionals? Was it simply a recounting of Euro-centric histories posing as universal ones? Was the rupture between recent history (1870s) and that moment (1880s) so complete that practicing lawyers assumed that it was irrelevant? Was this dismissive attitude political?

To start to consider these questions, it is important to remember that 'Aziz Kahil's first introduction to law as a subject of study occurred in France, to which he traveled in 1877. When he returned to Egypt, the Khedival legal regime was no longer recognizable. The Mixed Courts had been established for several years, and the National Courts were about to start operating. For someone whose legal knowledge was acquired in France and who was entering into a field that was being rearranged, he did not look to the recent past but embraced the present. A fellow judge at the National Courts described ʻAziz years later as a "very intelligent and sharp-witted" man who "spoke and wrote French like a Frenchman, and undoubtedly French was more his native than Arabic, in which he could not claim to be a scholar." To demonstrate his "sometimes abrupt manner," he recounted an anecdote in which ʻAziz shocked a judicial adviser who asked him if he was familiar with certain Ministry of Justice circulars, to which ʻAziz answered in French: "Je ne les lis pas, je les dechire."[29]

When ʻAziz Kahil took on the task of interpreting Egypt's new code of commerce (1883), he needed a translator with a strong command of Arabic, the language in which he was writing. Hence, he reached out to Yusuf Wahba (1852–1934), who served as the head of the translation bureau in the Ministry of Justice at the time. Yusuf Wahba was a career bureaucrat who had studied both French and English at a young age and joined the Egyptian government in the 1870s. He acquired a facility in legal jargon during his work at the Ministry of Justice, his service as the secretary of "the commission of inquiry" that interrogated the ʻUrabists in 1882, and most importantly, when he was tasked with the translation of the laws of the National Courts from French into Arabic.[30] ʻAziz Kahil and Yusuf Wahba completed each other's legal and linguistic expertise, but neither was familiar with the legal landscape of the mid-nineteenth century.

ʻAziz Kahil's lack of interest in the Khedival legal regime was widely shared by his generation of Egyptian lawyers. His contemporary, Ahmad Fathi Zaghlul (1863–1914), who was an influential legal historian of that period, considered the Khedival regime to be "despotic and inefficient . . . [and] essentially characterised by a series of lacks and absences."[31] For example, in his canonical study of the legal profession's history, published in 1900, he noted the absence of lawyers as a professional group in Egypt before the Mixed Courts' establishment in the mid-1870s.[32] Yet neither ʻAziz Kahil nor Ahmad Fathi Zaghlul were completely ignorant of the existence of a previous institutional mechanism for litigating commercial disputes in mid-nineteenth-century Egypt. Rather, they did not understand or appreciate the scope of the commercial-legal infrastructure that was in place since the 1840s, and that resembled their own institutional reality.

To clarify this point, we should look at the infrequent mentions that both authors make of the merchant courts that closed their doors for the last time in 1876. In *An Interpretation*, 'Aziz Kahil mentions the merchant courts once in relation to the subject of brokerage (*samsara*). He does so to explain why commercial law states explicitly that brokerage is a legal activity.

> Article 66 of the Code of Commerce mentions that brokerage is a legally permissible vocation. It is strange that that is mentioned in the law, since the general rule is to grant every person the freedom to engage in commerce, and brokerage is a commercial activity. Therefore, there is no reason to state that it is legally permissible in a specific article. But the legislator did so to negate the brokers' statute (*la'ihat al-samasira*) that was issued [on January 22, 1858] and stated that no one can engage in brokerage except after being affiliated with a known broker for six months, had a sponsor (*kafil*), and received a license from the merchant court.[33]

Reading the preceding paragraph shows that the focus is not on the merchant courts. Rather, it is about the now obsolete commercial regulations that the commercial law of 1883 replaced. In plain language, 'Aziz Kahil is explaining to the reader that the world where brokerage was controlled by a guild and conditioned upon apprenticeship was now a thing of the past. Under the National Courts, commercial law regulated the activities of *individual* merchants—including brokers—directly, without the mediation of an association of practitioners—i.e., a guild.

In his seminal study on the legal profession, Ahmad Fathi Zaghlul mentioned the mid-nineteenth-century merchant courts more frequently and in more detail. However, like 'Aziz Kahil, his interest in these institutions was mainly to highlight a bygone legal regime that was no longer relevant. His documentation of any aspect of the merchant courts' experience was incidental to his effort to document the lineage of the legal profession. Therefore, he included the full text of merchant court statutes because they contained the earliest evidence of the gradual creation of a space for legal representation before judicial bodies. Significantly, however, Ahmad Fathi Zaghlul argued that that space was occupied by unqualified individuals whose knowledge of the law and of technical legal language was faulty at best.[34] In other words, the existence of legal representatives in the years prior to the National Courts was not a sign of continuity but rather of a complete break between the Khedival legal regime that faded away in the mid-1870s and the legal regime that took shape under British rule and that was based on the dual foundations of the Mixed and National court systems.

To conclude this discussion of 'Aziz Kahil's *An Interpretation of Egyptian Commercial Law*, a word is due on the political context that made the Khedival legal regime forgettable in the 1880s. Although the National Courts started their operations months after the British occupation of Egypt, they were a long time coming, as part of the ongoing process of consolidating the legal regime and as an attempt by the surviving 'Urabi sympathizers to establish the rule of law as a substitute for their defeated constitutionalist aspirations. At this juncture, a new nationalist ideal that aimed to preserve the Egyptian elites' material interests and give them an increasing voice within government affairs rose at the expense of the more confrontational approach that characterized the years of the 'Urabist movement.[35] For example, during these years, Muhammad 'Abduh, who had been exiled for his participation in the 'Urabi revolt, grew disillusioned with contentious politics altogether and returned to Egypt after Lord Cromer intervened on his behalf with Khedive Tawfiq in 1888. His first job after his exile was as a judge in the new National Courts, where 'Aziz Kahil served as a prosecutor.[36] *An Interpretation of Egyptian Commercial Law* was also published by the al-Muqatataf Press, the owners of which were best known for their commitment to modern science and their pro-British views. Taken together, this was a moment in Egyptian history when the educated elite, lawyers occupying a central position within it, turned its back on the recent past, which ended in the 'Urabists' defeat and looked instead to itself as the vanguard of a new, modern future in Egypt.

In relation to historical scholarship, the self-centeredness of 'Aziz Kahil's generation is compounded by the contemporary restrictions on accessing state archives in many Middle Eastern countries. Today, the volume of scholarly production on the period of British rule (1882–1922) and years of formal independence under the monarchy (1922–1952) is much larger than the scholarship on the first three-quarters of the nineteenth century. Among the reasons for this uneven interest are the accessibility of British colonial archives and the existence of a large corpus of published materials, including newspapers, which are the legacy of the expansion of modern printing in the late 1800s.[37] By contrast, the interest in Khedival Egypt is the purview of a smaller number of historians who were given limited access to Egypt's impressive state archives, those who had the good fortune of stumbling upon relevant private collections, and those who looked for traces of modern Egyptian history outside of it—for example, in Ottoman imperial state records or in European consular archives. *How Commerce Became Legal* pursued these three paths in order to construct a historical account that is more rigorous and closer to capturing past actuality than the dominant but ultimately inaccurate view that was formulated at the turn of the twentieth century. Both nationalist and colonial voices from that historical moment assumed that much of the nineteenth century was the inverse of the colonial state-building project that they participated in or witnessed. Their assumptions were inherited and popularized by academics, intellectuals, politicians, and school curricula in the postcolonial Egyptian republic.

In light of this background, we can revisit the anecdote that opened this book and understand it better. In the early stages of research for this book, I was puzzled when a senior historian of modern Egypt told me that he had "never heard" of the mid-nineteenth-century merchant courts known as *majalis al-tujjar.* My reaction was that of an inexperienced researcher who assumed that what he found interesting was also objectively so. More significantly, however, that moment was an expression of the state of the field of modern Egyptian history. It is not uncommon for scholars of Egypt under British rule, the monarchy, and even the postcolonial state to understand the preceding Khedival period through the eyes of British colonial administrators and post-'Urabi nationalists. Even if politically opposed, both of these groups justified their own work at the turn of the twentieth century in terms of eradicating what they deemed as the general chaos and failures of the Khedival period and building a new, orderly Egypt in its place. To put it differently, building what Lord Cromer referred to as "Modern Egypt"[38] entailed not only the transcendence but also the erasure of the Khedival legal regime.[39]

Notes

Introduction

1. Jan Goldberg, "On the Origins of *Majalis al-Tujjar* in Mid-Nineteenth Century Egypt," *Islamic Law and Society* 6, no. 2 (1999): 193–223. See also Khalid 'Id al-Naghiya, "Majlis Tujjar Misr (1846–1876): Dirasah Watha'iqiyyah" [Cairo's Merchant Court: A Documentary Study], *al-Ruznamah: The Egyptian Documentary Annals* 2 (2004): 239–405.

2. For two different overviews of these historiographical debates, see Khaled Fahmy, *Mehmed Ali: From Ottoman Governor to Ruler of Egypt* (Oneworld Academic, 2009); Ehud Toledano, "Mehmet Ali Pasa or Muhammad Ali Basha? An Historiographic Appraisal in the Wake of a Recent Book," *Middle Eastern Studies* 21, no. 4 (1985): 141–59.

3. Giancarlo Casale, *The Ottoman Age of Exploration* (Oxford University Press, 2010).

4. Alan Mikhail, *Nature and Empire in Ottoman Egypt: An Environmental History* (Cambridge University Press, 2011), 82–123; Husam 'Abd-al-Mu'ti, *al-'Ilaqat al-Misriyya al-Hijaziyya fil-Qarn al-Thamin 'ashar* [Egyptian-Hijazi Relations in the Eighteenth Century] (al-Hay'a al-Misriyya al-'Amma lil-Kitab, 1999).

5. James E. Baldwin, "The Deposition of Defterdar Ahmed Pasha and the Rule of Law in Seventeenth-Century Egypt," *The Journal of Ottoman Studies* 46 (2015): 131–61.

6. Jane Hathaway, *The Politics of Households in Ottoman Egypt: The Rise of the Qazdaglis* (Cambridge University Press, 1997).

7. James E. Baldwin, *Islamic Law and Empire in Ottoman Cairo* (Edinburgh University Press, 2016); Karen Barkey, *Bandits and Bureaucrats: The Ottoman Route to State Centralization* (Cornell University Press, 1994); Alan Mikhail, *Nature and Empire.*

8. Zoe Griffith, *The Egypt Merchants: Imperial Governance and Economic Life in the Ottoman Mediterranean, 1670–1830* (University of California Press, forthcoming).

9. Abd al-Rahman al-Jabarti, *Napoleon in Egypt: Al-Jabarti's Chronicle of the First Seven Months of the French Occupation, 1798,* trans. Shmuel Moreh (Markus Wiener Publishers, 1993), 24–27. For an explanation of how the outstanding debts of French textile merchants served as a pretext for the French occupation of Egypt, see Griffith, *The Egypt Merchants.*

10. Pascale Ghazaleh, "Trading in Power: Merchants and the State in 19th-Century Egypt," *International Journal of Middle East Studies* 45, no. 1 (2013): 79.

11. Khaled Fahmy, *All the Pasha's Men: Mehmed Ali, His Army and the Making of Modern Egypt* (Cambridge University Press, 1997).

12. Ibrahim Abu-Lughod, "The Transformation of the Egyptian Elite: Prelude to the 'Urabi Revolt," *The Middle East Journal* 21, no. 3 (1967): 325–44; F. Robert Hunter, *Egypt Under the Khedives, 1805–1879: From Household Government to Modern Bureaucracy* (University of Pittsburgh Press, 1984); Ehud R. Toledano, *State and Society in Mid-Nineteenth-Century Egypt* (Cambridge University Press, 1990).

13. See, for example, Aviv Derri's insightful treatment of the Commercial Court of Damascus in the 1880s and 1890s. "Bonds of Obligation, Precarious Fortunes: Empire, Non-Muslim Bankers, and Peasants in Late Ottoman Damascus, 1820s–1890s" (PhD diss., New York University, 2021), 223–85, ProQuest (28715558).

14. Gabriel Baer, "Tanzimat in Egypt —the Penal Code," *Bulletin of the School of Oriental and African Studies* 26, no. 1 (1963): 35.

15. Will Hanley, "When Did Egyptians Stop Being Ottomans? An Imperial Citizenship Case Study," in *Multilevel Citizenship*, ed. Willem Maas (University of Pennsylvania Press, 2013), 90.

16. Rudolph Peters, *Shari'a, Justice and Legal Order: Egyptian and Islamic Law: Selected Essays* (Brill, 2020), especially "Murder on the Nile: Homicide Trials in 19th Century Shari'a Courts" (originally published in 1990); "'For His Correction and as a Deterrent Example for Others:' Mehmed Ali's first Criminal Legislation (1829–1830)" (originally published in 1999).

17. Rudolph Peters, "Administrators and Magistrates: The Development of a Secular Judiciary in Egypt, 1842–1871," *Die Welt des Islams* 39, no. 3 (1999): 378–97.

18. 'Imad Hilal, *al-Falah wal-Sultah wal-Qanun fil-Nisf al-Thani min al-Qarn al-Tasi' 'Ashar* [Peasant, Authority and Law in Egypt in the Second Half of the Nineteenth Century] (Dar al-Kutub wal-Watha'iq al-Qawmiyya, 2007).

19. Khaled Fahmy, *In Quest of Justice: Islamic Law and Forensic Medicine in Modern Egypt* (University of California Press, 2018).

20. Avi Rubin, *Ottoman Nizamiye Courts: Law and Modernity* (Palgrave Macmillan, 2011).

21. Samy Ayoub, *Law, Empire, and the Sultan: Ottoman Imperial Authority and Late Hanafi Jurisprudence* (Oxford University Press, 2020).

22. For example, see Donald Quataert, *Social Disintegration and Popular Resistance in the Ottoman Empire, 1881–1908: Reactions to European Economic Penetration* (New York University Press, 1983); Alexander Schölch, "European Penetration and the Economic Development of Palestine, 1856–82," in *Studies in the Economic and Social History of Palestine in the Nineteenth and Twentieth Centuries*, ed. Roger Owen (The Macmillan Press, 1982), 10–87.

23. J. Wansbrough, Halil İnalcık, A.K.S. Lambton, and G. Baer, "Imtiyazat," in *Encyclopaedia of Islam*, Second Edition.

24. Will Hanley, *Identifying with Nationality: Europeans, Ottomans, and Egyptians in Alexandria* (Columbia University Press, 2017), 11–12.

25. Cihan Artunç and Mohamed Saleh, "The Demand for Extraterritoriality: Religious Minorities in Nineteenth-Century Egypt," *The Economic History Review* 77, no. 3 (2024): 895–927.

26. E. Roger J. Owen, *Cotton and the Egyptian Economy, 1820–1914: A Study in Trade and Development* (The Clarendon Press, 1969), xxiv.

27. Timothy Mitchell, *Rule of Experts: Egypt, Techno- Politics, Modernity* (University of California Press, 2002), 54–79.

28. Aaron G. Jakes, *Egypt's Occupation: Colonial Economism and the Crises of Capitalism* (Stanford University Press, 2020).

29. Pascale Ghazaleh, *Fortunes urbaines et stratégies sociales: généalogies patrimoniales au Caire, 1780–1830*, 2 vols (Institut français d'archéologie orientale du Caire, 2010); Rizq Nuri, *Tujjar al-Qahira fi 'Asr Muhammad 'Ali, 1805–1848* [Cairo's Merchants in the Era of Muhammad Ali, 1805–1848] (al-Hay'a al-Misriyya al-'Amma lil-Kitab, 2018).

30. Ghazaleh, "Trading in Power," 86.

31. Omar Youssef Cheta, "The Economy by Other Means: The Historiography of Capitalism in the Middle East," *History Compass* 16, no. 4 (2018).

32. William H. Sewell, Jr., "A Strange Career: The Historical Study of Economic Life," *History and Theory* 49, no. 4 (2010): 146–66.

33. I use the adjective "Khedival" to refer to the period from the Ottoman recognition of Mehmed Ali's project of hereditary rule in Egypt in 1841 to the British occupation of Egypt in 1882. While Mehmed Ali's grandson, Isma'il (r. 1863–1879), was the first to assume the title "Khedive" formally in 1867 and be officially recognized as such by the Ottoman Empire, the term had already been in use to refer to Egypt's governors earlier in the nineteenth century. The title also continued to be used by Egypt's governors, Tawfiq (r. 1879–1892) and 'Abbas II (r. 1892–1914), under the British occupation until World War I.

34. Michel Foucault, "Afterword: The Subject and Power," in *Michel Foucault: Beyond Structuralism and Hermeneutics*, eds., Hubert L. Dreyfus and Paul Rabinow (The University of Chicago Press, 1983), 221.

35. Ritu Birla, *Stages of Capital: Law, Culture, and Market Governance in Late Colonial India* (Duke University Press, 2009).

36. Aaron Jakes makes a similar point about capitalism. See *Egypt's Occupation*, 10–15.

37. Yoav Di-Capua, *Gatekeepers of the Arab Past: Historians and History Writing in Twentieth-Century Egypt* (University of California Press, 2009).

38. Alan Mikhail, *My Egypt Archive* (Yale University Press, 2023).

39. Lauren Benton, *A Search for Sovereignty: Law and Geography in European Empires, 1400–1900* (Cambridge University Press, 2014).

40. Hanley, *Identifying with Nationality*, 14–15.

Chapter 1

1. DWQ, MTM 3036-000001, *Majlis Tujjar Misr, Sadir* [Cairo Merchant Court, Outgoing Correspondence], 1270 [1853], no. 292, p. 102.

2. The *wirku* was "the key income and professional tax paid by crafts and guilds until its abolition in 1890." John T. Chalcraft, *The Striking Cabbies of Cairo and Other Stories: Crafts and Guilds in Egypt, 1863–1914* (State University of New York Press, 2004), 32.

3. DWQ, MM 2002-008756, *Ifada min Majlis Tujjar wa 'Alayha Sharh min al-Muhafaza* [Statement from the Merchant Court with Commentary from the Governorate], Jumada II 1272 [January/February 1856].

4. Toledano, *State and Society*, 1–36, 108–34.

5. For a useful collection of essays on the transformation of Egypt's administration into a modern bureaucracy, see Nelly Hanna, ed., *The State and Its Servants: Administration in Egypt from Ottoman Times to the Present* (American University in Cairo Press, 1995). To appreciate the scale of this transformation in the Ottoman Empire, and particularly in Egypt, see Rifáat Ali Abou-El-Haj, *Formation of the Modern State: The Ottoman Empire, Sixteenth to Eighteenth Centuries* (Syracuse University Press, 2005); and Stanford Jay Shaw, *The Financial and Administrative Organization and Development of Ottoman Egypt, 1517–1798* (Princeton University Press, 1958).

6. Rudolph Peters, "Administrators and Magistrates."

7. For example, see the merchant councils of Qajar Iran, institutionalized in the mid-1880s under the name "*majalis-i wukala-yi tujjar*," and the deeds, known as "*waraqa*," that carried legal weight across the Indian ocean, despite not being produced by any particular state bureaucracy. Gad G. Gilbar, "The Rise and Fall of the *Tujjar* Councils of Representatives in Iran, 1884–85," *Journal of the Economic and Social History of the Orient* 51, no. 4 (2008): 639–74; Fahad Ahmad Bishara, "Paper Routes: Inscribing Islamic Law Across the Nineteenth-Century Western Indian Ocean," *Law and History Review* 32, no. 4 (2014): 797–820.

8. My colleague Zoe Griffith alerted me to the relevance of the eighteenth-century Diwan of Alexandria to the documentation of merchant activities. For more on this particular institution, see Michael J. Reimer, "Ottoman Alexandria: The Paradox of Decline and the Reconfiguration of Power in Eighteenth-Century Arab Provinces," *Journal of the Economic and Social History of the Orient* 37, no. 2 (1994): 107–46.

9. Nelly Hanna based her study of the seventeenth-century merchant Isma'il Abu-Taqiyya "entirely on court records." *Making Big Money in 1600: The Life and Times of Isma'il Abu Taqiyya, Egyptian Merchant* (Syracuse University Press, 1998), xxi. For an explanation of the content of "the Kadi registers," see Suraiya Faroqhi, *Approaching Ottoman Sources: An Introduction to the Sources* (Cambridge University Press, 2000), 55–57. See also Abraham Marcus, *The Middle East on the Eve of Modernity: Aleppo in the Eighteenth Century* (Columbia University Press, 1989).

10. The *shahbandar* was the chief merchant of the city and served as an intermediary between the merchants and the state authorities. He was usually a merchant of considerable wealth and one who engaged in large-scale commercial ventures. Theoretically, the city's community of merchants elected the *shahbandar*. For a concise explanation of this position, see A. Raymond and M. B. Hooker, "Shah Bandar," *Encyclopedia of Islam, Second Edition* (Brill Online, 2012). http://referenceworks.brillonline.com/.

11. Ghazaleh, "Trading in Power," 79.

12. For an account of the significance of Rashid as a port town and commercial center before being taken over by Alexandria, see Griffith, *The Egypt Merchants*.

13. For more on the government arrangements of eighteenth-century Egypt, especially the proliferation of tax farms such as the *iltizam* or *muqata'a*, see Hathaway, *The Politics of Households*; Mikhail, *Nature and Empire*; Stanford Jay Shaw, *The Financial and Administrative Organization*. For a study of the French occupation's policy toward

these decentralized arrangements, see Nasir Ibrahim, "Al-Faransiyun wa-Nizam al-Iltizam, 1798–1801" [The French and the Iltizam System, 1798–1801], *Annales islamogiques* 37 (2003): 31–54.

14. Pascale Ghazaleh found it "plausible that Napoleon introduced the practice of confirming the head merchant's authority," a practice which continued under Mehmed Ali. "Trading in Power," 79.

15. On the alliance with Copts, see Juan Cole, *Napoleon's Egypt: Invading the Middle East* (Palgrave Macmillan, 2007); Zeinab Abul-Magd, *Imagined Empires: A History of Revolt in Egypt* (University of California Press, 2013), 43–69.

16. Goldberg, "On the Origins of *Majalis Al-Tujjar*"; Michael J. Reimer, *Colonial Bridgehead: Government and Society in Alexandria, 1807–1882* (American University in Cairo Press, 1997), esp. 80–82.

17. Raouf Abbas Hamed, "The *Siyasatname* and the Institutionalization of Central Administration under Muhammad 'Ali," in *The State and Its Servants: Administration in Egypt from Ottoman Times to the Present*, ed. Nelly Hanna (American University in Cairo, 1995), 75–86. It is worth noting that the first instance of extensive legislative activity under Mehmed Ali was in 1829. It focused primarily on crime in the countryside and paid no attention to commerce. See Rudolph Peters, "'For His Correction and as a Deterrent to Others.'"

18. TNA, FO 78/624, Ottoman Empire: Correspondence, 1845.

19. Owen, *Cotton and the Egyptian Economy*, 17–27.

20. According to Nuri, "*majalis al-tujjar*" that existed under Mehmed Ali did not resolve disputes among merchants but rather those between merchants and the state. *Tujjar al-Qahira*, 172.

21. *Siyasatname*, Section 2, Articles 7–8. "Tashkil al-Dawawin wa Qanun al-Siyasatnamah" [The Formation of Government Departments and the *Siyasatname* Law] is published in Ahmad Fathi Zaghlul, *al-Muhamah* [The Legal Profession], (Matba'at al-Ma'arif, 1900), appendix 2, 4–24.

22. *Siyasatname*, Section 2, Article 10.

23. *Siyasatname*, Section 3, Article 8. A similar stipulation could also be found in article 63 of *Bayan ma untukhiba min Qanun al-Siyasa al-Mulkiyya* [Selected Excerpts from the Law of Government Administration], which was promulgated a few months after the issuance of the *Siyasatname* in 1837. For the text of this legislation, see Zaghlul, *al-Muhamah*, appendix 18, 111–19.

24. *Siyasatname*, Section 2, Article 8.

25. *Siyasatname*, Section 2, Article 7.

26. Owen, *Cotton and the Egyptian Economy*, 14–15. For background on the Levant Company, see Despina Vlami, *Trading with the Ottomans: The Levant Company in the Middle East* (I.B. Tauris, 2015).

27. al-Jabarti, *Napoleon in Egypt*, 24–27; Griffith, *The Egypt Merchants*.

28. Owen, *Cotton and the Egyptian Economy*, 21–22.

29. Peters, "Administrators and Magistrates," 381–83.

30. For example, see the petition submitted by three merchants from Madras on behalf of *al-hajj* Khatib Ghulam Muhammad, an indigo merchant from Madras, to the British consul in Cairo. TNA, FO 841/40, British Consulate in Cairo: Consular Court Cases, Miscellanea, 1874. Hanley explains how the "accidental equality" that emerged

from equating the legal status of colonial subjects with that of their colonizers created a heavier work burden for European consulates. See *Identifying with Nationality*, 176–81.

31. Goldberg, "On the Origins of *Majalis Al-Tujjar*," 206–10.

32. For the names of the committee members, see the preamble to *Tartib Majalis al-Tujjar* [The Statute of the Merchant Courts] (1845), published in Zaghlul, *al-Muhamah*, appendix 4, 31–42. The nationalities and functions of the members of the committee are not listed.

33. Italian sources identified ʿAli Bey as the "Colonnello della Guardia Nazionale." Goldberg, "On the Origins of *Majalis Al-Tujjar*," 210, n. 59.

34. Iris Agmon, *Family & Court: Legal Culture and Modernity in Late Ottoman Palestine* (Syracuse University Press, 2006); Avi Rubin, "Was There a Rule of Law in the Late Ottoman Empire?" *British Journal of Middle Eastern Studies* 46, no. 1 (2019): 123–38; Avi Rubin, "The Positivization of Ottoman Law and the Question of Continuity," in *State Law and Legal Positivism: The Global Rise of a New Paradigm*, eds. Badouin Dupret and Jean-Louis Halperin (Brill, 2022), 150–77.

35. *Majlisa Aqalim Bahari wa-Qibli: al-La'iha* [The Statute of the Provincial Councils] (1862) is published in Zaghlul, *al-Muhamah*, appendix 17, 94–99.

36. Arbitration practices were not geographically specific. For example, see Mafalda Ade, "Ottoman Commercial Law and Its Practice in Aleppo Province (1850–1880)," in *Merchants in the Ottoman Empire*, eds. Suraiya Faroqhi and Gilles Veinstein (Peeters Publishers, 2008), 243–58.

37. TNA, FO 841/20, file no. 11, Coen (G) British vs. Sonsino (Haim) Ottoman, 1865.

38. For example, in 1853, the Cairo Merchant Court pleaded with the Austrian consul in order to help collect a debt owed to Yusuf Cohen, an Ottoman merchant, by two subjects of Austria, Yaʿqub and Salamun Menasche. DWQ, MTM 3036-000001, no. 12, 20 Safar 1270 [November 22, 1853].

39. TNA, FO 841/28, file no. 131, Trading Comp[an]y (Egypt[ia]n Com[mercia]l &) British vs. Sharawi (Mohamed) Ottoman, 1867. This position resonates with an earlier British report in which the consulate referred to its own role as "merely the channel of communication for the plaintiff." TNA, FO 78/624, 1845.

40. TNA, FO 78/624, 1845. Negotiations to establish new merchant courts between the European governments on one hand and Mehmed Ali's on the other was motivated by the wish to create an alternative for merchant courts that were closed in 1843.

41. Note that the reference here is to an older forum that preceded the reformed merchant courts that came into existence a year later.

42. TNA, FO 78/624, 1845. Emphasis mine.

43. Interestingly, British consular officials in Syria, another Arabic-speaking Ottoman province, raised a similar question. In that case, the question was resolved without much hesitation. British merchants were not allowed to "native" courts in the urban centers of Beirut and Damascus. In the countryside, British merchants were given the choice to resort to *shariʿa* courts if they thought it to be in their interest. TNA, FO 226/167, Embassy and Consulate, Beirut: Correspondence, 1868.

44. TNA, FO 841/12, file no. 197, Causa In Arbitraggio, 1855.

45. *Tartib Majalis al-Tujjar*, Article 1.

46. Note that even then, the court's president, himself a state representative, could neutralize their vote by siding with the local merchants, thus creating a tie of three against three. In that situation, the case under consideration would be postponed to a future date when all court members were present, thus placing the European merchants in a minority position once more.

47. It is worth noting that this condition gave the European merchants the ability to bring merchant court operations to a halt if two of them did not show up on any given day.

48. See Hunter, *Egypt Under the Khedives*, 115–17; Toledano, *State and Society*, 1–35; Zayn al-'Abidin Shams al-Din Najm, *Misr fi 'Ahdayy 'Abbas wa Sa'id* [Egypt Under 'Abbas and Sa'id] (Dar al-Shuruq, 2007).

49. *Tartib al-Qanasil* is published in Zaghlul, *al-Muhamah*, appendix 5, 43–45.

50. *La'iha* [The Statute of the Merchant Courts] (1861) is published in Zaghlul, *al-Muhamah*, appendix 7, 52–55.

51. *Tartib Majalis al-Tujjar*, Article 1.

52. *La'iha*, Article 1. European consulates restricted the category of "notables" to metropolitan citizens and excluded colonial subjects, such as North Africans and South Asians. However, the methods of this exclusion were not identical across different consulates. Hanley, *Identifying with Nationality*, 179–80.

53. Deputies of the merchants presiding over the court were referred to as *nuwwab* (sing. *na'ib*); the merchant court's vice president was referred to as *mu'awin* (assistant), but that term eventually became replaced with "*wakil*" and "*na'ib*" (deputy).

54. Italian was commonly used to document and communicate about commercial matters. The British consular archives contain many examples of this linguistic choice.

55. *Tartib Majalis al-Tujjar*, Articles 1, 5.

56. In 1853/1854, the non-merchant staff of Cairo's merchant court consisted of four senior government officials (president, deputy, and two unspecified positions), three clerks, two translators, three guards, one coffee maker, and one porter. DWQ, MM 2002-002767, *Muhafazat Misr: Istihqaqat* [Cairo Governorate: Entitlements], 1270 [1853/1854].

57. *La'ihat al-Arba'in Band* [The Forty-Article Statute], Articles 10, 13, 15, 30. Zaghlul, *al-Muhamah*, appendix 6, 45–52. Regarding the importance of speed for recouping outstanding commercial debts, see Ghazaleh, "Trading in Power" and Ade, "Ottoman Commercial Law."

58. *La'ihat al-Arba'in Band*, Article 6.

59. *La'ihat al-Arba'in Band*, Article 21. This method of establishing legal proof was part of a wider bureaucratic practice in the late 1850s and early 1860s. For example, see article 20 of the statute of *Majlis Qumisyun Misr* (1861), a state-organized judicial body concerned with civil disputes. Zaghlul, *al-Muhamah*, appendix 16, 85–94.

60. TNA, FO 841, file no. 100, Corkling (R. & others) British vs. Alfy (A. El & others) Ottoman, 1868.

61. Two years earlier, Egypt's governor Sa'id issued a penal code, which also drew heavily on the Ottoman Penal Code of 1851. Gabriel Baer, "Tanzimat in Egypt."

62. "The Ottoman Commercial Code was completed by the Appendix to the Commercial Code of 1860, the Code of Procedure of 1861 and the Maritime Code of 1863."

Ade, "Ottoman Commercial Law," 1. The text of the Ottoman Commercial Code is published in Gregorius Aristarches, *Législation ottomane, ou Recueil des lois, réglements, ordonnances, traités, capitulations et autres documets officiels de l'Empire ottoman* [Ottoman law, or Collection of Laws, Regulations, Orders, Treaties, Capitulations and Other Official Documents from the Ottoman Empire] (Freres Nicolaïdes, 1873–1888), vol. 1, 275–343.

63. TNA, FO 841/23, file no. 1, Miscellanea, 1866.

64. The 1857 statute, known as *La'ihat al-Arba'in Band*, was to improve and accelerate the operation of the merchant courts. For example, it reasserted the ban on lawyers but allowed representation through attorneys (*wakils*). Additionally, it reiterated the previously established practice of litigants approaching the court in writing through submitting written reports detailing their claims. Omar Youssef Cheta, "A Prehistory of the Modern Legal Profession in Egypt, 1840s–1870s," *International Journal of Middle East Studies* 50, no. 4 (2018): 649–68.

65. *Tartib Majalis al-Tujjar*, Article 19.

66. *Majlisa Aqalim Bahari wa-Qibli: al-La'iha*, Articles 1, 5.

67. *Majlisa Aqalim Bahari wa-Qibli: al-La'iha*, Article 5.

68. *Amr 'Ali Sadir li-Nizarat al-Dakhiliyya, 25 Jumada II 1288* [Khedival Order to the Department of the Interior, 12 August 1871], no. 172 is published in Zaghlul, *al-Muhamah*, appendix 20, 181–206. For more on the Consultative Assembly, see Alexander Schölch, "Constitutional Development in Nineteenth Century Egypt: A Reconsideration," *Middle Eastern Studies* 10, no. 1 (1974): 3–14.

69. Notably, when the jurisdiction of councils in the provincial centers (*al-Majalis al-Markaziyya*) was expanded in 1873, commercial disputes were not mentioned. The jurisdictional expansion covered only criminal and civil offenses. The text of *Thayl li-La'ihat al-Majalis al-Markaziyya* [Appendix to the Statute of the Councils in the Provincial Centers] is published in Zaghlul, *al-Muhamah*, appendix 21, 207–11. See also *Amr 'Ali Sadir li-Nizarat al-Dakhiliyya* (1871), no. 172, Section 4, Article 3.

70. TNA, FO 841/22, file no. 22, Lane (James [illegible] Co.) British vs. Sciammas (Giorgio) Ottoman, 1864.

71. For a similar example that also shows a range of results including Ottoman subjects losing, see TNA, FO 841/23, file no. 27, Naggiar (Felice) British vs. Chalabi (M & A) Ottoman, 1866.

Chapter 2

1. Henry Salt, *A Geometrical Survey of the City of Alexandria* (William Miller, 1806), Bibliothèque nationale de France. https://gallica.bnf.fr/ark:/12148/btv1b10101094s (accessed on March 18, 2025).

2. Charles Muller, *Plan d'Alexandrie, comprenant toutes ses fortifications, rues et édifices publics* (Linassi, 1855), Bibliothèque nationale de France. https://gallica.bnf.fr/ark:/12148/btv1b8440801b (accessed on March 18, 2025).

3. Mahmud Bey al-Falaki, *Kharitat al-Iskandariyya fi Sanat 1282 Hijriyya* [The Map of Alexandria in the Hijri Year 1282] (s.n., 1865), Bibliothèque nationale de France. https://gallica.bnf.fr/ark:/12148/btv1b10104413k (accessed on October 20, 2023).

4. R1, Letter from Butrus Yusuf Tawil to the Consul of Italy in Alexandria, September 10, 1862, 324–25.

5. R1 covers two periods from March 19, 1859 until November 15, 1859 and from June 11, 1862 until December 17, 1862. R2 covers one period from January 4, 1870 until September 27, 1870. R3 also covers one period from December 19, 1862 until September 5, 1863. R4 covers two periods from January 10, 1865 until May 9, 1866 and from May 30, 1869 until January 4, 1870.

6. Especially when compared to the business history of the twentieth century. For example, see Robert Vitalis, *When Capitalists Collide: Business Conflict and the End of Empire in Egypt* (University of California Press, 1995).

7. Terence Walz, "Asyut in the 1260's (1844–53)," *Journal of the American Research Center in Egypt* 15 (1978): 113–26; Terence Walz, "Family Archives in Egypt: New Light on Nineteenth-Century Provincial Trade," in *L'Egypte au XIXe siècle* (Editions du Centre National de la Recherche Scientifique, 1982), 15–33; Terence Walz, *Trade Between Egypt and Bilad as-Sudan, 1700–1820* (Institut français d'archéologie orientale du Caire, 1978). The al-Jawhari family papers include business letters, business ledgers, property deeds, a small number of court documents, as well as family documents.

8. Nelly Hanna, *Making Big Money in 1600*; Nelly Hanna, *In Praise of Books: A Cultural History of Cairo's Middle Class, Sixteenth to the Eighteenth Century* (Syracuse University Press, 2003).

9. Griffith, *The Egypt Merchants.*

10. Dror Ze'evi, "The Use of Ottoman Shari'a Court Records as a Source for Middle Eastern Social History: A Reappraisal," *Islamic Law and Society* 5, no. 1 (1998): 35–56.

11. Carlo Ginzburg, "Microhistory: Two or Three Things That I Know About It," *Critical Inquiry* 20, no. 1 (1993): 33.

12. Syrian immigration to Egypt ensued in two main waves. The first one, in the middle decades of the eighteenth century, brought a few thousands, mainly Greek Catholics from Damascus and Aleppo, to Cairo and Dumyat. The new immigrant community came to dominate commerce between Egypt and Syria through controlling customs administration positions in Egypt and, in parallel, establishing trading networks that spanned coastal and inland cities such as Acre, Beirut, Dumyat, and Damascus. The second wave began with "a limited increase of Egypt's Syrian population in the 1840's and 1850's. Immigration, however, began to grow in earnest only in the 1860's and 1870's and accelerated even more toward the end of the century." Thomas Philipp, *The Syrians in Egypt, 1725–1975* (Ty Aur Press, 2017), 78–95.

13. Akram Khater, *Inventing Home: Emigration, Gender, and the Middle Class in Lebanon, 1870–1920* (University of California Press, 2001); Philipp, *The Syrians in Egypt.*

14. For a thorough account of the autonomous Mount Lebanon Mutasarrifate, which coincided with increased emigration to Egypt and the Americas, see Engin Akarli, *The Long Peace: Ottoman Lebanon, 1861–1920* (University of California Press, 1993).

15. Philipp, *The Syrians in Egypt*, 87.

16. R3, Letter from Qustantin Qattan to Butrus Yusuf Tawil, May 25, 1863, 110.

17. R4, Letter from Butrus Yusuf Tawil to his uncle's wife (*imra'at al-'amm*), July 10, 1869, 333. Note that large parts of the letter are illegible.

18. R3, Letter from Qustantin Qattan to Butrus Yusuf Tawil, June 10, 1863, 87–88.

19. R3, Letter from Qustantin Qattan to Butrus Yusuf Tawil, June 12, 1864, 81.

20. R1, Letter from Butrus Yusuf Tawil to Niqula Tawil, June 21, 1859, 50.

21. R3, Letter from Qustantin Qattan to Butrus Yusuf Tawil, May 21, 1863, 126.

22. For a biographical note on Jirjis Tawil and the text of the *waqf* deed that established the Greek Catholic Cathedral in Alexandria, see *Al-Masarra: Majallat Batriyarkiyat al-Rum al-Kathulik* [Al-Masarra: Magazine of the Greek Catholic Patriarchate], October 15, 1913, 361–68.

23. R3, Letter from Qustantin Qattan to Butrus Yusuf Tawil, June 12, 1864, 81. According to Philipp, the representation of Syrians in certain economic sectors in al-Mansura and Tanta was comparable to Alexandria and Cairo. *The Syrians in Egypt*, 118–20.

24. R2, Letter from Butrus Yusuf Tawil to Ilyas Salhati, August 27, 1870, 74.

25. R4, Letter from Butrus Yusuf Tawil to uncle's wife (*imra'at al-'amm*), July 10, 1869, 333.

26. R4, Letter from Butrus Yusuf Tawil to his brother, February [day illegible] 1866, 370.

27. R4, Letter from Butrus Yusuf Tawil to uncle's wife (*imra'at al-'amm*), July 10, 1869, 333.

28. R4, Letter from Qustantin Qattan to Butrus Yusuf Tawil, March 5, 1865, 447.

29. R4, Letter from Qustantin Qattan to Butrus Yusuf Tawil, February 22, 1865, 467.

30. R4, Letter from Qustantin Qattan to Butrus Yusuf Tawil, February 22, 1865, 467.

31. R3, Letter from Qustantin Qattan to Butrus Yusuf Tawil, June 10, 1863, 87–88.

32. For an ethnographic and historical study of an "*'izba*," albeit one that focuses on the author's own family in the twentieth century, see Mona Abaza, *The Cotton Plantation Remembered: An Egyptian Family Story* (The American University in Cairo Press, 2013). See also Mitchell, *Rule of Experts*, 54–79; Jakes, *Egypt's Occupation*, 66–67, which offer different accounts of what constituted an "*'izba*" in the nineteenth century.

33. Today, sixteen kilometers south of Abu Hummus is a place known as *'Izbat al-Tawil* or *'Izbat al-Tawil al-Kabira*. Nearby are similar estates named after Syrians, such as *'Izbat Qirdahi*.

34. Seventy-eight men and women lived on Butrus's estate in 1885, according to *Recensement Général de l'Égypte*. (Impremerie Nationale, 1885), 76. Fourteen years later, *Qamus Jughrafi lil-Qutr al-Misri* [Geographical Dictionary of Egypt] (al-Matba'a al-Kubra al-Amiriyya, 1899), 132 listed the population of the estate as fifty-two individuals. Note that neither of these sources lists the size of the estate nor the number of children living on it.

35. See *Qamus Jughrafi lil-Qutr al-Misri*.

36. This observation was noted by both Philipp, *The Syrians in Egypt* and Mas'ud Dahir, *Hijrat al-Shawam: Al-Hijra al-Lubnaniyya ila Misr* [The Emigration of the Shawam: The Lebanese Emigration to Egypt] (Dar al-Shuruq, 2009).

37. For example, from May 20, 1863 to June 22, 1863 and from February 20, 1865 to March 25, 1865.

38. R3, Letter from Qustantin Qattan to Butrus Yusuf Tawil, May [day illegible] 1863, 117.

39. R4, Letter from Qustantin Qattan to Butrus Yusuf Tawil, March 16, 1865, 438–39.

40. R3, Several letters from Qustantin Qattan to Butrus Yusuf Tawil, May 21–June 12, 1863, 81–126.

41. R4, Letter from Qustantin Qattan to Butrus Yusuf Tawil, February 20, 1865, 468.

42. R3, Letter from Qustantin Qattan to Butrus Yusuf Tawil, June 10, 1863, 87–88.

43. R4, Letter from Qustantin Qattan to Butrus Yusuf Tawil, March 3, 1865, 450.

44. Owen, *Cotton and the Egyptian Economy*; Ahmad Ahmad al-Hitta, *Tarikh al-Zira'a al-Misriyya fi 'Ahd Muhammad 'Ali al-Kabir* [The History of Egyptian Agricultural in the Era of Muhammad Ali] (Al-Hay'a al-Misriyya al-'Amma lil-Kitab, 2012); Ra'uf 'Abbas Hamid, *Al-Milkiyyat al-Zira'iyya al-Misriyya wa Dawruha fi al-Mujtama' al-Misri, 1837–1914* [The History of Egyptian Agricultural Landownership and Its Role in Egyptian Society, 1837–1914] (Al-Majlis al-A'la lil-Thaqafa, 2011).

45. Owen, *Cotton and the Egyptian Economy*, xxiv.

46. Owen, *Cotton and the Egyptian Economy*, 58.

47. Owen, *Cotton and the Egyptian Economy*, xxiv.

48. To put Butrus's focus on cotton in perspective, consider the al-Jawhari commercial firm which, starting in the 1840s, "suppl[ied] European merchants with wheat, lentils, beans, and barley, a market that boomed for at least 15 years." Whereas Butrus exported cotton grown in the Nile Delta region to Europe through Alexandria, the Asyut-based al-Jawhari's were "located between two anxious markets," Europe and Sudan. Terence Walz, email exchange with the author, August 28, 2015; Walz, "Asyut in the 1260's," 119.

49. R3, Unsigned letter to Bishara Qattan, July 9, 1863, 42.

50. R1, Letter from Butrus Yusuf Tawil to 'Awad Rizq, June 11, 1862, 489; R1, Letter from Butrus Yusuf Tawil to 'Abd-al-Masih Rizq, June 11, 1862, 488.

51. R2, Letter from Qustantin Qattan to Jirjis Zughayb, February 3, 1870, 394.

52. R1, Letter from Butrus Yusuf Tawil to *al-sadat* Muhammad and Mahmud al-Faraqawi, June 14, 1862, 484.

53. R3, Unsigned letter to Jubran Ishaq, March 8, 1863, 311.

54. R3, Unsigned letter to *ikhwan* Samnah, January 23, 1863, 380.

55. R3, Unsigned letter to *ikhwan* Samnah, February 13, 1863, 340.

56. R4, Several letters from Butrus Yusuf Tawil to Qustantin Najjar and Co. of Marseilles, December 3, 1865; January 12, 1866; April 17, 1866; May 9, 1866, 338, 341, 375, 386.

57. R3, Letter from Butrus Yusuf Tawil to *ikhwan* 'Ubayd & Company, April 23, 1863, 211.

58. Ziad Fahmy, *Ordinary Egyptians: Creating the Modern Nation Through Popular Culture* (Stanford University Press, 2011), 26–27.

59. For a discussion of the history and politics of the nineteenth-century railroads in Egypt, see On Barak, *On Time: Technology and Temporality in Modern Egypt* (University of California Press, 2013), 22–44; Helen Anne B. Rivlin, "The Railway Question in the Ottoman-Egyptian Crisis of 1850–1852," *Middle East Journal* 15, no. 4 (1961): 365–85.

60. Barak, *On Time*, 44–52.

61. R3, Unsigned letter to Bishara Qattan, July 13, 1863, 31.

62. R3, Unsigned letter to *ikhwan* Samnah, February 21, 1863, 325.

63. The construction of a railroad line in Egypt that connected the Mediterranean and the Red Sea was linked to British plans to shorten the time for travel between

Britain and India. When the British government explored the possibility of achieving this goal through building steamers on the Euphrates in Ottoman Iraq in 1833, Mehmed Ali attempted to frustrate it. Khaled Fahmy, *All the Pasha's Men*, 298–300.

64. R3, Letter from Qustantin Qattan to Butrus Yusuf Tawil, June 2, 1863, 98.

65. R1, Letter from Butrus Yusuf Tawil to Surur Afandi *wakil mahattat* Samannud, December 10, 1862, 105. The following month, Butrus was still complaining to a Mansura-based associate that shipments were still being delayed in Samannud. See R3, Letter from Butrus Yusuf Tawil to As'ad Qalush, January 15, 1863, 402.

66. In his unpublished dissertation, On Barak argues that the regular public display of these telegrams was equivalent to publishing "the first Egyptian daily newspaper." "Egyptian Times: Temporality, Personhood, and the Technopolitical Making of Modern Egypt, 1830–1930" (PhD diss., New York University, 2009), 306–27, ProQuest (3380301).

67. R3, Telegram, July 26, 1863, 19.

68. R3, Unsigned letter to Jubran Ishaq, May 4, 1863, 186.

69. Koray Çalışkan, *Market Threads: How Cotton Farmers and Traders Create a Global Commodity* (Princeton University Press, 2010).

70. Brian Schoen, *The Fragile Fabric of Union: Cotton, Federal Politics, and the Global Origins of the Civil War* (Johns Hopkins University Press, 2009).

71. Havas is the predecessor of the contemporary Agence France-Presse. Ami Ayalon, *The Press in the Arab Middle East: A History* (Oxford University Press, 1995), 18–19.

72. R3, Telegram, May 22, 1863, p. 122. Notably, Butrus based his appraisal of the situation on British public opinion. If British merchants were not responding to an impending watershed moment, it was likely that the war was not coming to an end. Indeed, on that same day, Butrus wrote a letter to *al-sayyid* 'Ali al-Haki' to update him on the transactions he undertook in his (i.e., *al-sayyid* 'Ali's) name over the past week. He ended his letter with a confirmation that nothing has happened since he sent him the telegram. "Egyptian cotton sales were low in general in Liverpool for the reasons that I mentioned to you in the midday's communiqué. May God improve the situation." Before mailing the letter, fresh news had come to his attention, so he added the following postscript in pencil: "Correction. Private telegrams received this evening contain information about the calmness of the market but mention nothing about the end of the war in America. From that it becomes clear that the news that we have sent to you earlier have no basis." R3, Letter from Butrus Yusuf Tawil to *al-sayyid* 'Ali al-Haki', May 22, 1863, 121.

73. R3, Letter from Qustantin Qattan to Butrus Yusuf Tawil, May 28, 1863, 104.

74. R1, Unsigned letter to *ikhwan* Samnah, November 12, 1862, 166.

75. For example, R3, Letter from Butrus Yusuf Tawil [no specified recipient], April 24, 1863, 206.

76. R2, Letter from Butrus Yusuf Tawil to Qustantin Qattan, September 26, 1870, 27.

77. R2, Letter from Qustantin Qattan to Butrus Yusuf Tawil, July 15, 1870, 133. France declared war on Prussia four days later, on July 19.

78. R2, Letter from Qustantin Qattan to Butrus Yusuf Tawil, (noon) July 18, 1870, 126.

79. R2, Letter from Qustantin Qattan to Butrus Yusuf Tawil, (evening) July 18, 1870, 125.

80. R2, Letter from Butrus Yusuf Tawil to Butrus Sayigh, September 24, 1870, 31.

81. R4, Letter from Qustantin Qattan to Butrus Yusuf Tawil, March 5, 1865, 447.

82. R4, Letter from Qustantin Qattan to Butrus Yusuf Tawil, March 16, 1865, 438–39.

83. R1, Letter from Butrus Yusuf Tawil to Hasanayn Muhammad al-Sarraj, November 22, 1862, 136.

84. R3, Letter from Butrus Yusuf Tawil to Yusuf Hanna Kahil, January 13, 1863, 415. In an earlier letter, Yusuf Kahil's work plans are described as "commercial work (*ashghal al-tijara*)." R3, Letter from Butrus Yusuf Tawil to Yusuf Kahil, January 8, 1863, 429.

85. Separating residence and workspace was not only a Mediterranean phenomenon. Thomas Bender documents a similar trend in New York City as early as 1819. Thomas Bender, *The Unfinished City: New York and the Metropolitan Idea* (New York University Press, 2007).

86. David S. Landes, *Bankers and Pashas: International Finance and Economic Imperialism in Egypt* (Harvard University Press, 1958), 61–62.

87. The reference is likely to E. Landau and Co. of Alexandria, which merged two months later with the Continental Bank Corp. of London to form the London and Mediterranean Bank. Landes, *Bankers and Pashas*, 244, n. 3.

88. R4, Letter from Qustantin Qattan to Butrus Yusuf Tawil, February 28, 1865, 451.

89. R2, Letter from Qustantin Qattan to Butrus Yusuf Tawil, June 18, 1870, 126.

90. R3, Letter from Qustantin Qattan to Bishara Qattan, March 28, 1863, 288.

91. R1, Unsigned letter to Bishara Qattan, June 23, 1862, 464.

92. R1, Letter from Qustantin Qattan to Bishara Qattan, June 26, 1862, 455.

93. R3, Letter from Butrus Yusuf Tawil to Bishara Qattan, May 26, 1863, 293.

94. R4, Letter from Qustantin Qattan to *al-sayyid* 'Ali al-Haki', February 12, 1865, 474.

95. R4, Letter from Qustantin Qattan to *al-sayyid* 'Ali al-Haki', February 14, 1865, 470.

96. R4, Letter from Qustantin Qattan to *al-sayyid* 'Ali al-Haki', February 24, 1865, 458.

97. In conducting the research for this book, I did not come across any references to him. However, it is difficult to say with certainty that no references exist because of the absence of a searchable database for merchant court cases.

98. For example, see Leslie Peirce, *Morality Tales: Law and Gender in the Ottoman Court of Aintab* (University of California Press, 2003), 129–42, 251–75, 351–74, where she used the records of what happened inside the courthouse to construct plausible scenarios of what might have unfolded outside. See also Ze'evi, "The Use of Ottoman Shari'a Court Records," 42–50. Even though the article focuses on *shari'a* courts, its main idea applies to any official forum for dispute resolution.

99. R3, Unsigned letter to *khawaja* As'ad Qalush, January 15, 1863, 402.

100. R4, Unsigned letter to al-*sayyid* 'Ali al-Haki', March 29, 1865, 435.

101. Mafalda Ade has observed a similar approach in her study of Fratelli Poche & Cie during the same period. The Aleppo-based commercial house tried every possible

way to collect an outstanding debt before resorting to the courts, which, in this case, only took place a full decade after the debt was due. Ade, "Ottoman Commercial Law."

102. R2, Letter from Butrus Yusuf Tawil to *khawaja* Ishaq Jubran, April 21, 1870, 245.

103. R2, Letter from Butrus Yusuf Tawil to *khawaja* Faransis Tadrus, April 13, 1870, 253.

104. R3, Letter from Butrus Yusuf Tawil to Khuri, Tasu and Co., March 29, 1863, 282; R3, Letter from Butrus Yusuf Tawil to Khuri, Tasu and Co., July 12, 1863, 34; R3, Letter from Butrus Yusuf Tawil to Khuri, Tasu and Co., August 9, 1863, 13.

105. R3, Letter from Yusuf Butrus Tawil to the Deputy Governor of al-Buhayra, no date, 2; R3, Letter from Yusuf Butrus Tawil to the Governor of al-Buhayra, date illegible, 3; R2, Letter from Yusuf Butrus Tawil to Monsieur Di Martino Consul General of Italy in Alexandria, July 13, 1870, 137.

106. "Mohamed el Sawah (Av. Manusardi) contre Pierre Tawil (Av. Gilly), Cour d'Appel, Alexandrie, le 9 Mars 1882," *Jurisprudence des tribunaux de la réforme en Égypte: recueil officiel* 7 (1881–1882): 124–26.

107. "Pierre Tawil contre Mohamed Emin Bey es-qualite, Alexandrie, le 6 Juin 1889," *Bulletin de législation et de jurisprudence égyptiennes* (V. Pennason, 1889–1890): 222–24.

108. "Gouvernement Egyptien contre Pierre Tawil, Alexandrie, le 22 Janvier 1890," *Bulletin de législation*: 386–87.

109. "Pierre Tawil (Av. Colucci) contre Gouvernement Egyptien (Av. Schiarabati Bey), Cour d'Appel, Alexandrie, le 10 Mai 1906," *Jurisprudence des tribunaux de la réforme en Égypte: recueil officiel* 31 (1908): 512–15.

Chapter 3

1. For example, see DWQ, MTM 3036-000503: *Daftar Qayd Madhbatat al-Ahkam al-Sadira min Majlis Tujjar Misriyya* [Register of the Rulings Issued by the Cairo Merchant Court], "*Ibtida al-sanna bil-nisba li-tartib al-'a'da'*" [The beginning of the year with respect to the election of members], 18 Dhul-Hijja 1288 [February 27, 1872], 29.

2. Richard Hill, *A Biographical Dictionary of the Sudan* (Routledge, 1967), 283.

3. P. M. Holt and M. W. Daly, *The History of the Sudan: From the Coming of Islam to the Present Day* (Routledge, 1979), 67, 78–79.

4. Holt and Daly, *The History of the Sudan*, 51.

5. "Fi 10 Rajab 1275 Amr 'Ali li-Mudiriyat Asyut" [On February 12, 1859, Khedival Order to the Governorate of Asyut], Amin Sami, *Taqwim al-Nil*, vol. 3 (Matba'at Dar al-Kutub wal-Watha'iq al-Qawmiyya, 2003), 312–13.

6. "Fi 12 Rajab 1275 Amr 'Ali li-Diwan al-Dakhiliyya" [On February 14, 1859, Khedival Order to the Department of the Interior], Sami, *Taqwim al-Nil*, vol. 3, 313–14.

7. "Fi 12 Rajab 1275 Amr 'Ali li-Diwan al-Dakhiliyya," Sami, *Taqwim al-Nil*, vol. 3, 313–14. This road along the Nile would replace an older caravan route to its east that cut across the Nubian desert connecting Korosko to Abu-Hamad.

8. Ilyas al-Ayubi, *Tarikh Misr fi 'Ahd al-Khidiwi Isma'il Basha* [Egypt's History During the Reign of Isma'il Basha] (Hindawi Foundation, 2012), 460. https://www.hindawi.org/books/24697404/.

9. Hill, *A Biographical Dictionary*, 274–75.

10. See the case of "Muhammad 'Uthman abu Qarja," who was "a pilot of a river boat belonging to Hamad al-'Aqqad of the trading house of 'Aqqad & Co" but eventually joined the Mahdist revolt. Hill, *A Biographical Dictionary*, 279.

11. Hill, *A Biographical Dictionary*, 110–11.

12. Terence Walz, "Libya, the Trans-Saharan Trade of Egypt, and 'Abdallah al-Kahhal, 1880–1914," *Islamic Africa* 1, no. 1 (2010): 85–107.

13. TNA, FO 841/29, file no. 1, Miscellanea, 1868.

14. "Ma'iyya Saniyya, 1282 [1864], 1:3–2 Sadir Awamir, Mudiriyat Bani Swaif and Fayum," qtd. in Amira El-Azhary Sonbol, *The New Mamluks: Egyptian Society and Modern Feudalism* (Syracuse University Press, 2000), 98–99.

15. Nabil al-Sayyid al-Tukhi, *Tawa'if al-Hiraf fi-Madinat al-Qahira fil-Nisf al-Thani min al-Qarn al-Tasi' 'Ashar* [The Trade Guilds in Cairo During the Second Half of the Nineteenth Century] (al-Hay'a al-Misriyya al-'Amma lil-Kitab, 2009), 184–86.

16. Ali Mubarak, *al-Khitat al-Tawfiqiyya al-Jadida*, vol. 2 (al-Matba'a al-Amiriyya al-Kubra, 1886–1889), 30.

17. Ali Mubarak, *al-Khitat al-Tawfiqiyya*, vol. 6, 31.

18. Ali Barakat, *Tatwwur al-Milkiyya al-Zira'iyya fi Misr wa-Atharuhu 'ala al-Haraka al-Siyasiyya, 1813–1914* [The Development of Landownership in Egypt and Its Effect on the Political Movement, 1813–1914] (Dar al-Thaqafa al-Jadida, 1977), 219. In a noteworthy parallel development, Bedouin leaders in the Syrian interior established a system of land rights even prior to Ottoman-sanctioned polices came into effect in the 1860s. Thus, land rights enabled the generation of the capital that fueled commercial activities. Nora Elizabeth Barakat, *Bedouin Bureaucrats: Mobility and Property in the Ottoman Empire* (Stanford University Press, 2023), 75–115.

19. 'Abbas Mahmud al-'Aqqad, *Rijal 'Ariftuhum* [Men Whom I Knew] (Hindawi Foundation, 2013), 25, 59. https://www.hindawi.org/books/95950851/.

20. Jens Hanssen and Max Weiss, "Introduction: Language, Mind, Freedom and Time: The Modern Arab Intellectual Tradition in Four Words," in *Arabic Thought Beyond the Liberal Age: Towards an Intellectual History of the Nahda*, eds. Jens Hanssen and Max Weiss (Cambridge University Press, 2016), 1–38; Elizabeth M. Holt, *Fictitious Capital: Silk, Cotton, and the Rise of the Arabic Novel* (Fordham University Press, 2017).

21. Yusuf Ramitsh, *Usrat al-Muwaylhi wa Atharuha fil-Adab al-'Arabi* [The Muwaylhi Family and Their Influence on Arabic Literature] (Dar al-Ma'arif, 1980), 144; Mahmud Muhammad Kasbar, *al-Tarikh Bayna al-Siyasa wal-Ijtima': Ru'yah Susyulujiyah* [History Between Politics and Sociology: A Sociological View] (Dar al-Ma'rifa al-Jami'iya, 1987), 192.

22. AbdelAziz EzzelArab, *European Control and Egypt's Traditional Elites: A Case Study in Elite Economic Nationalism* (The Edwin Mellen Press, 2002), 23–41.

23. Sonbol, *The New Mamluks*, xxiv.

24. Richard Hill, *A Biographical Dictionary*, 274–75; al-Ayubi, *Tarikh Misr*, 461.

25. Husam Muhammad 'Abd-al-Mu'ti and Sa'ida Muhammad Husni, ed., *Mahadir Majlis Shura al-Nuwwab: Al-Hay'a al-Niyabiyya al-Thaniyya, 1870–1873* [The Minutes of the Consultative Council: The Second Parliamentary Convention, 1870–1873] (Matba'at Dar al-Kutub wal-Watha'iq al-Qawmiyya, 2006), 29.

26. 'Abd-al-Mun'im Ibrahim al-Dusuqi al-Jumay'i, *al-Thawra al-'Urabiyya: Buhuth wa Dirasat Watha'iqiyya* [The 'Urabist Revolution: Research and Documentary Studies]

(Markaz al-Dirasat al-Siyasiyya wal-Istratijiyya bil-Ahram, 1982), 133–34. Nikki Keddie argued that Afghani's influence emerged later. See *An Islamic Response to Imperialism: Political and Religious Writings of Sayyid Jamal ad-Din "al-Afghani"* (University of California Press, 1983), 20.

27. Keddie, *An Islamic Response*, 19.

28. EzzelArab, *European Control*, 34.

29. Sa'ida Muhammad Husni, "Analytical Introduction," in *Mahadir Majlis Shura al-Nuwwab*, vol. 2, ed. Husam Muhammad 'Abd-al-Mu'ti and Sa'ida Muhammad Husni, 22.

30. 'Abd-al-Mu'ti and Husni, ed., *Mahadir Majlis Shura al-Nuwwab*, vol. 2, 29.

31. The document is reproduced in al-Jumay'i, *al-Thawra al-'Urabiyya*, 257.

32. For more on Edouard Dervieu's career, see Landes, *Bankers and Pashas*.

33. EzzelArab, *European Control*, 159. It is worth noting that other merchants were engaged in the same economic activity.

34. EzzelArab, *European Control*, 81.

35. AbdelAziz EzzelArab, "The Experiment of Sharif Pasha's Cabinet (1879): An Inquiry into the Historiography of Egypt's Elite Movement," *International Journal of Middle East Studies* 36, no. 4 (2004): 561–89.

36. EzzelArab, *European Control*, 160.

37. al-Jumay'i, *al-Thawra al-'Urabiyya*, 134–36.

38. Hasan Musa al-'Aqqad's name was listed as a creditor in "Qanun Lajnat al-Tasfiya al-Dawliya." The text of the "Qanun" is reproduced in Salim Khalil al-Naqqash, *Misr lil-Misryyin* [Egypt for the Egyptians], vol. 4 (Matba'at Jaridat al-Mahrusa, 1884), 78; Filib Jallad, *Qamus al-Idara wal-Qaqa'* [General Encyclopedia of the Administration and the Judiciary], vol. 2 (al-Matba'a al-Bukhariyya, Yanni Lagudakis, 1890–1892), 221.

39. Abu-al-Su'ud died shortly after the campaign.

40. Jacob M. Landau, "Prolegomena to a Study of Secret Societies in Modern Egypt," *Middle Eastern Studies* 1, no. 2 (1965): no. 200, 184.

41. Wilfrid Scawen Blunt and Ahmad Urabi, *Secret History of the English Occupation of Egypt* (Alfred A Knopf, 1922), 373. https://www.gutenberg.org/ebooks/41373.

42. The idea was for the different interests within society to be represented by one person each. Hasan Musa al-'Aqqad would have represented the merchant class. See Blunt, *Secret History*, 66.

43. A. M. Broadley, *How We Defended Arabi and His Friends: A Story of Egypt and the Egyptians* (Chapman and Hall Ltd, 1884), 362–63. Broadley's account of his first encounter with Hasan Musa al-'Aqqad, in which the latter insisted that "I, too, like Ahmed Arabi, demand the services of the English lawyer," is also of relevance. Broadley, *How We Defended*, 357–58. For a concise biography of 'Abduh, see Mark Sedgwick, *Muhammad Abduh* (Oneworld, 2009).

44. Jonathan Miran, "Endowing Property and Edifying Power in a Red Sea Port: Waqf, Arab Migrant Entrepreneurs, and Urban Authority in Massawa, 1860s–1880s," *International Journal of African Historical Studies* 42, no. 2 (2009): 156–59.

45. Miran, "Endowing Property," 161–62.

46. Miran, "Endowing Property," 176.

47. Jonathan Miran, "From Bondage to Freedom on the Red Sea Coast: Manumitted Slaves in Egyptian Massawa, 1873–1885," *Slavery & Abolition: A Journal of*

Slave and Post-Slave Studies 34, no. 1 (2013): 151. For more on Hasan Musa al-'Aqqad's status, including a reference to his agent, see also Jonathan Miran, "Red Sea Translocals: Hadrami Migration, Entrepreneurship, and Strategies of Integration in Eritrea, 1840s–1970s," *Northeast African Studies* 12, no. 1 (2012): 129–67.

48. It is important to note that Hasan al-'Aqqad's involvement in the administration of *waqfs* could not have been unknown to Cairo's state officials, who, for example, oversaw other religious appointments, most importantly that of the "Mufti of Massawa." One such *mufti*, Ahmad Khalil al-Qusi, may have been dismissed from his position because of his 'Urabist sympathies. 'Imad Ahmad Hilal, *al-Ifta' al-Misri,* vol. 5 (Matba'at Dar al-Kutub wal-Watha'iq al-Qawmiyya, 2010–2015), 3145.

49. Stephen C. Bruner, *Late Nineteenth-Century Italy in Africa: The Livraghi Affair and the Waning of Civilizing Aspirations* (Cambridge Scholars Publishing, 2017), 38.

50. An Egyptian obelisk became the "Dogali Monument" in Rome.

51. Bruner, *Late Nineteenth-Century Italy in Africa*, 39–41.

52. Bruner, *Late Nineteenth-Century Italy in Africa*, 37–88.

53. Muhammad Farid, *Mudhakkirat Muhammad Farid* [The Memoirs of Muhammad Farid], ed. Ra'uf 'Abbas Hamid, vol. 1 ('Alam al-Kutub, 1975), 151; al-Jumay'i, *al-Thawra al-'Urabiyya*, 148. Khedive Abbas II pardoned many leaders of the 'Urabi movement, including, for example, 'Abdallah al-Nadim (1843–1896).

54. For example, Ahmad 'Urabi, *Mudhakkirat al-Za'im Ahmad 'Urabi* [The Memoirs of Ahmad 'Urabi], ed. 'Abd-al-Mun'im Ibrahim al-Jumay'i, vol. 3 (Matba'at Dar al-Kutub wal-Watha'iq al-Qawmiyya, 2005), 1237–79.

55. "Dame Fatma Épouse El Ezabi contre Hassan Moosa El Akkad, Cour d'Appel Mixte, Alexandrie, le 1 Fevrier 1893," *Bulletin de législation et de jurisprudence égyptiennes*, 95–96.

56. "51. Adjudications," *Gazette des Tribunaux mixtes d'Égypte: revue judiciaire mensuelle* 43, no. 87 (January 10, 1918): 27–28.

57. *Recensement Général de l'Égypte*, 250, lists two *'izba*s owned by "Moussa-el-'Akkad" in "Hossafah . . . Kalioub" and "Matarieh . . . Choubra."

58. Isma'il Muhammad Zayn al-Din, *Al-Zira'a al-Misriyya fi 'Ahd al-Ihtilal al-Britani, 1882–1914* [Egyptian Agriculture Under the British Occupation] (Al-Hay'a al-Misriyya al-'Amma lil-Kitab, 1995), 120–27.

59. "State Representative v. Hassan Moussa El Akkad and Others, Tribunal of Cairo, Judgement on Appeal, 12 May 1900," *Al-Majmu'a al-Rasmiyya lil-Mahakim al-Ahliyya* [Official Bulletin of the Native Tribunals] 2, no. 2 (February 1901): 54–61.

60. "Ma Hiya al-Harb allati Nushhiruha 'Ala al-Inkliz?" [What Is the War That We Are Declaring Against the English?], *Al-Qutr al-Misri* 1, no. 2 (May 22, 1908): 145–149; al-Jumay'i, *al-Thawra al-'Urabiyya*, 153.

61. DWQ, MTM 3036-000125, *Majlis Tujjar Misr: Khulasat wa-Qararat wa-Ifadat* [Cairo Merchant Court: Summaries, Decisions and Statements], "Khulasat Da'wa *khawaja* Umil Bashuh ma'a Mahmud 'Abd-al-Mu'ti wa Musa al-'Aqqad," 27 Muharram 1272 [October 8, 1855], 10–11.

62. DWQ, MTM 3036-000409, *Majlis Tujjar Misr: Qayd al-Qararat al-Intiha'iyya* [Cairo Merchant Court: Register of Final Decisions], case #92, June 3, 1862, 33–34.

63. DWQ, MTM 3036-000409, case #149, July 19, 1862, 57–58.

64. DWQ, MTM 3036-000409, February 17, 1862, 1.

65. DWQ, MTM 3036-000409, case #117, June 30, 1862, 44–45.

66. The Cairo Governorate was also the institutional home of the Cairo Merchant Court.

67. DWQ, MTM 3036-000409, case #60, May 10, 1862, 22–23.

68. TNA, FO 841/21, "Argi (Mussa) (British) vs. El Akkad (Mussa) (Ottoman)," 1865; FO 841/23, "Argi (Mussa) (British) vs. El Akkad (Mussa) (Ottoman)," 1866.

69. DWQ, MTM 3036-000503, 14 Dhul-Qi'da 1288 [January 25, 1872], 26.

70. DWQ, MTM 3036-000503, 19 Dhul-Hijja 1288 [February 28, 1872], 30.

71. DWQ, MTM 3036-000503, 19 Dhul-Hijja 1288 [February 28, 1872], 30.

72. DWQ, MTM 3036-000503, 26 Dhul-Hijja 1288 [March 6, 1872], 33.

73. DWQ, MTM 3036-000503, 23 Rabi' I 1289 [May 30, 1872], 50.

74. DWQ, MTM 3036-000503, 21 Rabi' II 1289 [June 27, 1872], 55.

75. Cheta, "A Prehistory of the Modern Legal Profession in Egypt."

76. al-Jumay'i, *al-Thawra al-'Urabiyya*, 1061–1963.

77. DWQ, MTM 3036-000503, 25 Sha'ban 1288 [October 26, 1871], 15.

78. DWQ, MTM 3036-000206, *Majlis Tujjar Misriyya: Khulasat wa-Qararat wa-Ifadat* [Cairo Merchant Court: Summaries, Decisions and Statements], case #25, 29 Shaaban 1290 [October 21, 1873], 17–19.

79. DWQ, MTM 3036-000503, 4 Muharram 1289 [March 13, 1872], 35.

80. DWQ, MTM 3036-000503, 17 Muharram 1289 [March 26, 1872], 36.

81. DWQ, MTM 3036-000503, 26 Muharram 1289 [April 4, 1872], 37.

82. DWQ, MTM 3036-000503, 21 Shawwal 1288 [January 2, 1872], 21.

83. DWQ, MTM 3036-000503, 14 Dhul-Qi'da 1288 [January 24, 1872], 26.

84. DWQ, MTM 3036-000503, 22 Dhul-Qi'da 1288 [February 1, 1872], 28–29.

85. DWQ, MTM 3036-000503, 4 Jumada I 1289 [July 9, 1872], 59.

86. "Conte Menandro Zizinia (Avv. Mathieu et De Régusse) contro Il Governo Egiziano (Avv. A. Colucci e C. Ara), Alessandria, 2 Dicembre 1878," *Jurisprudence des tribunaux de la réforme en Égypte: recueil officiel* 3 (1878–79): 224–31. For more on Zizinia, see Alexander Kitroeff, *The Greeks and the Making of Modern Egypt* (The American University in Cairo Press, 2019).

87. For a copy of the original list of signatures, see Muhammad Khalil Subhi, *Tarikh al-Haya al-Niyabiyya fi Misr* [History of Parliamentary Life in Egypt], vol. 5 (Matba'at Dar al-Kutub al-Misriyya, 1939), 100–103. For a helpful classification of this long list, see EzzelArab, *European Control*.

88. See AbdelAziz EzzelArab's discussion of "National Mercantile Interests" in *European Control*, 156–59.

89. "Dame Fatma Épouse El Ezabi contre Hassan Moosa El Akkad."

90. Ibrahim Jammal, ed., *Kitab al-Qada' al-Misri al-Ahli* [The Book of the National Egyptian Judiciary] (Matba'at al-Akhbar, 1909), 109–10, 172, 278, 433.

91. "Mustaqbal al-'Amil wal-Fallah fi Misr," *Al-Jami'a*, vol. 7, no. 2 (January 1910), 108–11.

92. Jammal, *Kitab al-Qada'*, i.

93. Jammal, *Kitab al-Qada'*, 109.

Chapter 4

1. "Séance du 5 Novembre 1897," *Bulletin de l'Institut égyptien*, 182.

2. "Séance du 5 Novembre 1897," *Bulletin de l'Institut égyptien*, 182–83.

3. "Séance du 5 Novembre 1897," *Bulletin de l'Institut égyptien*, 184.

4. "Séance du 18 Decembre 1897," *Bulletin de la Société de Géographie d'Égypte*, 355–57.

5. *Bollettino della Società africana d'Italia periodico mensile*, Gennaio-Febbraio 1898, 31.

6. *Transactions of the Supreme Council 33d for the Southern Jurisdiction of the United States of America* (House of the Temple, October 1903), 411.

7. For a recent study of this dynamic, see Shana Minkin, *Imperial Bodies: Empire and Death in Alexandria, Egypt* (Stanford University Press, 2019).

8. Owen, *Cotton and the Egyptian Economy.*

9. Carter Vaughn Findley, "The Tanzimat," in *The Cambridge History of Turkey*, vol. 4, ed. Resat Kasaba (Cambridge University Press, 2008), 11–37.

10. For more on the political transition from Mehmed Ali's rule to that of his descendants see Hunter, *Egypt Under the Khedives*; Toledano, *State and Society in Mid-Nineteenth-Century Egypt.*

11. James Heyworth-Dunne, *An Introduction to the History of Education in Modern Egypt* (Cass, 1968), 324.

12. *Bulletin de la Société de Géographie d'Égypte*, V Série, numéro 5, Septembre 1899, 320.

13. *Bollettino della Società africana d'Italia periodico mensile*, Gennaio-Febbraio 1898, 31; "Séance du 5 Novembre 1897," *Bulletin de l'Institut égyptien*, 182.

14. Heyworth-Dunne, *An Introduction*, 157–80.

15. Heyworth-Dunne, *An Introduction*, 243–63.

16. Heyworth-Dunne, *An Introduction*, 323–30.

17. Cheta, "A Prehistory of the Modern Legal Profession in Egypt."

18. Pascale Ghazaleh, "Heirs and Debtors: Blood Relatives, Qur'anic Heirs and Business Associates in Cairo, 1800–50," in *Society and Economy in Egypt and the Eastern Mediterranean, 1600–1900: Essays in Honor of Andre Raymond*, eds. Nelly Hanna and Raouf Abbas (American University in Cairo Press, 2005), 141–56.

19. "In the 1830s and 1840s, Britain and France first codified the laws and procedures to be used at their consulates." Hanley, *Identifying with Nationality*, 13.

20. DWQ, MTM 3036-000420: *Qayd al-Qararat al-Ibtida'iyya bi-Majlis Tujjar Misriyya* [Register of First Instance Decisions at the Cairo Merchant Court], case #273, 25 Safar 1280 [August 10, 1863], 93–94.

21. Stefano G. Poffandi, *Indicateur égyptien administratif et commercial* (Imprimerie Générale, 1896), 115.

22. *Bolletino del Grande Oriente della Massoneria in Italia*, vol. II, year III, issues IV, V, VI (June, July, August 1867), 186–88.

23. *Il Libero pensiero: giornale dei razionalisti*, 19 Novembre 1868, 328–31.

24. Statistica generale del regno d'Italia, *Censimento degli italiani all'estero, 31 Dicembre 1871* (Rome: Stamperia Reale, 1874), li.

25. *Bollettino della Società geografica italiana*, January–February 1877, no page number.

26. *Memorie della Società geografica italiana* (Stabilimento Giuseppe Civelli, 1878), ix.

27. *Livre d'or de l'Institut égyptien* (Imprimerie de l'Institut de Bibliographie, 1899), 62.

28. *Compte Rendu Des Travaux de la Commission de la Dette Publique d'Egypte* (n.p., 1876), 24.

29. Philippe Gelat Bey, *Répertoire général annoté de la législation et de l'administration egyptiennes, 1840–1908* (Imprimerie J. Lagoudakis, 1908), 312–21.

30. Poffandi, *Indicateur égyptien administratif et commercial*, 107, 115, 147; Yusuf Asaf and Qaysar Nasr, *Dalil Misr* [The Egypt Directory] (Al-Matba'a al-'Umumiyya, 1889).

31. F. Garcin, "Un notable français du Caire à la fin du XIXe siècle," *Revue des mondes musulmans et de la Méditerranée* 30 (1980), n. 119–20, 94–95.

32. *Sharp & Alleman's Lawyers and Bankers Directory for 1901* (John R. McFetridge & Sons, 1901), 210.

33. The school was renamed after Vittorio Emanuele II upon his death in 1878.

34. *L'Italia evangelica giornale delle chiese, delle scuole e delle famiglie*, year II, issue 26, July 1, 1882, 202–203.

35. *Proceedings of the Supreme Council of Sovereign Grand Inspectors-General of the Thirty-Third and Last Degree, Ancient Accepted Scottish Rite* (1892), 102–103.

36. P. Panceri and F. Gasco, *Viaggio in Egitto dei socii P. Panceri e F. Gasco nell'anno 1873–1874* (Stabilimento Tipografico A. Trani, 1876), 109.

37. *Bollettino della Società africana d'Italia* (Stabilimento Tipografico dell'Unione, 1884).

38. Poffandi, *Indicateur égyptien administratif et commercial*, 79.

39. *Il corriere israelitico: periodico mensile per la storia e la letteratura israelitica*, year III, issue 8, 1894, 178–79. The bride, Gabriella, was the daughter of Abramino Tilche, an Italian banker based in Alexandria and, like Tito, a prominent freemason. See *Transactions of the Supreme Council* (1903), 411.

40. See *Transactions of the Supreme Council* (1903), 411.

41. *Bollettino della Società africana d'Italia*, Gennaio-Febbraio 1898, 31.

42. *Tartib Majalis al-Tujjar*, Article 6.

43. For example, Mikha'il al-Musili representing Faraj-Allah al-Musili in DWQ, MTM 3036-000125, unspecified date between September and November 1855, 28–30.

44. Amalia D. Kessler, *A Revolution in Commerce: The Parisian Merchant Court and the Rise of Commercial Society in Eighteenth-Century France* (Yale University Press, 2007), 28.

45. *La'ihat al-Arba'in Band*, Articles 1, 8.

46. DWQ, MTM 3036-000420, case #273, 25 Safar 1280 [August 10, 1863], 93–94.

47. *Tartib Majalis al-Tujjar*, Articles 1, 5.

48. Sven Beckert, *Empire of Cotton: A Global History* (Vintage Books, 2015), 312–39, esp. 334–35.

49. The number is based on counting the cases in DWQ, MTM 3036-000503, 26 Jumada II 1288 [September 12, 1871]–2 Rajab 1289 [September 5, 1872].

50. Tito translated 'Urabi's speech on this occasion. *L'Italia evangelica*, July 1, 1882, 202.

51. *L'Exploration: revue des conquetes de la civilisation sur tous les points du globe*, vol. 8, year 6, September 1882 (Librarie de la Société Bibliographique), 210–11.

52. DWQ, MTM 3036-000206, case #54, 8 Shawwal 1290 [November 29, 1873]. See also DWQ 3036-000419, *Majlis Tujjar Misriyya Qayd al-Qararat al-Intiha'iyya* [Register of Final Decisions at the Cairo Merchant Court], case #3, 22 Sha'ban 1292 [September 23, 1875], and case #12, 12 Shawwal 1292 [November 11, 1875].

53. DWQ, MTM 3036-000419, case #27, 4 Dhul-Qi'da 1292 [December 2, 1875].

54. DWQ, MTM 3036-000419, case #37, 29 Dhul-Qi'da 1292 [December 27, 1875]. The terms "*rasmiyya / ghayr rasmiyya*" and "*shar'iyya / ghayr shar'iyya*" are used interchangeably.

55. Al-'Idwi was also the chief Maliki *mufti*. For a brief biography, see Hilal, *Al-Ifta' al-Misri*, vol. 3, 1511.

56. For an overview of the dispute, see Kathryn A. Schwartz, "The Political Economy of Private Printing in Cairo as Told from a Commissioning Deal Turned Sour, 1871," *International Journal of Middle East Studies* 49, no. 1 (2017): 25–45.

57. For an analysis of the legal treatise that al-Kabis translated, see Omar Youssef Cheta and Kathryn A. Schwartz, "A Printer's Odd Plea to Reform Legal Pluralism in Khedival Egypt," *Past & Present* 252, no. 1 (2021): 179–211.

58. DWQ, MTM 3036-000503, no case number, 4 Muharram 1289 [March 14, 1872], 35; no case number, 10 Muharram 1289 [March 27, 1872], 36; no case number, 26 Muharram 1289 [March 28, 1872], 37.

59. DWQ, MTM 3036-000206, case #179, 24 Jumada I 1291 [July 8, 1874], 113.

60. DWQ, MTM 3036-000419, case #8, 8 Ramadan 1292 [October 7, 1875], 5.

61. Eve M. Troutt Powell, *A Different Shade of Colonialism: Egypt, Great Britain, and the Mastery of the Sudan* (University of California Press, 2003), 149–56.

62. DWQ, MTM 3036-000503, no case number, 28 Jumada II 1288 [September 14, 1871], 1, and no case number, 13 Rajab 1288 [September 28, 1871], 5.

63. DWQ, MTM 3036-000206, case #156, 18 Rabi' I 1291 [June 3, 1874], 94.

64. DWQ, MTM 3036-000503, no case number, 23 Sha'ban 1288 [November 7, 1871], 13.

65. DWQ, MTM 3036-000503, no case number, 24 Sha'ban 1288 [November 8, 1871], 14.

66. DWQ, MTM 3036-000503, no case number, 9 Ramadan 1288 [November 19, 1871], 16.

67. DWQ, MTM 3036-000503, no case number, 4 Jumada I 1289 [July 10, 1872], 59.

68. DWQ, MTM 3036-000206, case #13, 9 Sha'ban 1290 [October 2, 1873], 10.

69. DWQ, MTM 3036-000419, case #6, 24 Sha'ban 1292 [September 25, 1875], 4.

70. DWQ, MTM 3036-000419, case #37, 29 Dhul-Qi'da 1292 [December 27, 1875], 17-18.

71. DWQ, MTM 3036-000206, case #75, 11 Dhul-Qi'da 1290 [December 31, 1873], 44-45.

72. Farhat J. Ziadeh, *Lawyers, the Rule of Law and Liberalism in Modern Egypt* (Hoover Institution Publications, 1968), vii, 29.

73. ". . . its membership consisted of European lawyers and *mandataires*. The Egyptian *wukala'* who had practiced before the provincial councils did not figure among the early membership, perhaps because of their ignorance of foreign languages." Ziadeh, *Lawyers*, 29.

74. DWQ, MTM 3036-000419, case #1, 16 Sha'ban 1292 [September 17, 1875], 1.

75. DWQ, MTM 3036-000206, case #178, 23 Jumada I 1291 [July 7, 1874], 111–13. Note that arbitrators were chosen and they made the decision, which was then ratified by the merchant court.

76. Gelat Bey, *Répertoire général*, 312–21.

77. Roger Owen, *Lord Cromer: Victorian Imperialist, Edwardian Proconsul* (Oxford University Press, 2005), 207–10.

78. *Raccolta degli atti stampati per ordine della Camera documenti*, vol. 2 (Tipografia della Camera dei deputati, 1886), 161–93.

79. *Parliamentary Papers: Accounts and Papers, Session 9 February 1888–24 December 1888,* vol. 46 (Harrison and Sons, 1888), 24–25, 32–33.

80. Gelat Bey, *Répertoire général*, 674–76.

81. Guiseppe Cuzzi published his memoires in 1900, one year after his liberation and the defeat of the Mahdists. See Guiseppe Cuzzi, *Fifteen Years Prisoner of the False Prophet*, trans. Hans Resener (University of Khartoum, 1968).

82. An influential study on the complex political and cultural dynamic among Egypt, Sudan, and Great Britain is Troutt Powell, *A Different Shade of Colonialism.*

83. *Jurisprudence des tribunaux de la réforme en Égypte: recueil officiel* 26 (Imprimerie Générale A. Mourès & c, 1902), 432–35.

84. "Le Testament de Gessi," *La gazette géographique et l'exploration* 12, 2 Septembre 1881, 40–42.

85. Romolo Gessi Pasha, *Seven Years in the Soudan: Being a Record of Explorations, Adventures, and Campaigns Against the Arab Slave Hunters,* trans. Lily Wolffsohn and Bettina Woodward (S. Low, Marston & Co., 1892).

86. *Raccolta degli atti stampati*, 124.

87. *Raccolta degli atti stampati*, 124.

88. Wilfrid Scawen Blunt, *The Land War in Ireland: Being a Personal Narrative of Events, in Continuation of "A Secret History of the English Occupation of Egypt"* (Stephen Swift and Co. Ltd, 1912), 207.

89. Blunt, *The Land War*, 221.

90. Blunt, *The Land War*, 218.

91. Blunt, *The Land War*, 236.

92. Blunt, *The Land War*, 211, 213.

93. Blunt, *The Land War*, 239.

Chapter 5

1. TNA, FO 841/14, Miscellaneous Petitions Filed in 1863, "Petition filed by Cristidas on behalf of Spiridione Zangarus, 30 March 1863."

2. Guy Burak, *The Second Formation of Islamic Law: The Hanafi School in the Early Modern Ottoman Empire* (Cambridge University Press, 2015).

3. Rudolph Peters, "What Does It Mean to Be an Official Madhhab? Hanafism and the Ottoman Empire," in *The Islamic School of Law: Evolution, Devolution, and Progress*, eds. Peri Bearman, Rudolph Peters, and Frank E. Vogel (Harvard University Press, 2006), 157.

4. Peters, "What Does It Mean," 158.

5. Ahmed Fekry Ibrahim, *Pragmatism in Islamic Law: A Social and Intellectual History* (Syracuse University Press, 2015).

6. Fahmy, *In Quest of Justice*, 124–27.

7. Hilal, *al-Ifta' al-Misri*, vol. 3, 1691–734.

8. The closest we can get to a faint Islamic legal connection to the merchant courts was the 1857 statute that was issued by *Majlis al-Ahkam*, which included a *mufti* among its members.

9. Ze'evi, "The Use of Ottoman Shari'a Court Records."

10. Ibrahim, *Pragmatism in Islamic Law*, 1–28.

11. Hilal, *al-Ifta' al-Misri*, vol. 3.

12. Guy Burak, "Mufti," in *The Oxford Encyclopedia of the Islamic World: Digital Collection*, ed. John L. Esposito (Oxford University Press, 2022).

13. For more on the circumstances of al-'Abbasi al-Mahdi's rise despite his youth and lack of experience, see Hilal, *al-Ifta' al-Misri*, vol. 3, 1391–1414. Also note that al-'Abbasi al-Mahdi was briefly dismissed from his position during the 'Urabi revolt, most probably because of his loyalty to Khedive Tawfiq.

14. Rudolph Peters, "Muhammad Al-'Abbasi al-Mahdi (d. 1897), Grand Mufti of Egypt, and His 'al-Fatawa al-Mahdiyya,'" *Islamic Law and Society* 1, no. 1 (1994): 75–78.

15. See Hilal, *al-Ifta' al-Misri,* vol. 3, 1500–11.

16. Occasionally, European consulates accommodated *shari'a*-related demands when dealing with their Muslim subjects. Hanley, *Identifying with Nationality*, 186.

17. For "an overview of the contents and range of subjects treated in legal works," see Wael B. Hallaq, *An Introduction to Islamic Law* (Cambridge University Press, 2009), 28–30.

18. Note that a few years earlier, Marqus al-Kabis had collaborated with Tito Figari in the case that pit Moïse Castelli against Hasan al-'Idwi. He was also employed in Tito's office at one point in his career.

19. DWQ, MTM 3036-000419, case #3, 22 Sha'ban 1292 [September 22, 1875], 2. Emphasis mine.

20. For example, Ehud Toledano takes on the difficult task of rehabilitating the legacy of Abbas Pasha but not that of his successor, Sa'id. Toledano, *State and Society in Mid-Nineteenth-Century Egypt.*

21. Avi Rubin, *Nizamiye*, 73–78. Rubin explains that the Ottoman state found the rule difficult to apply into the twentieth century due to the conflicting demands of the *shari'a* courts and the European consuls.

22. DWQ, MTM 3036-000420, case #278, 27 Safar 1280 [August 12, 1863], 95.

23. See article 19 of the Ottoman Reform Edict of 1856. Musa Gümüş, "Anayasal Meşrûtî Yönetime Medhal: 1856 Islahat Fermanı'nın Tam Metin İncelemesi" [An Introduction to Constitutional Government: A Full Text Analysis of the 1856 Reform Edict], *Bilig: Türk Dünyası Sosyal Bilimler Dergisi* 47, no. 3 (2008): 215–40.

24. Jessica M. Marglin, "Extraterritoriality Meets Islamic Law: Legal Pluralism and Elements of Proof in the International Mixed Court of Morocco, 1871–1872," *Quaderni Storici* 51, no. 153 (2016): 673–700.

25. DWQ, MTM 3036-000409, case #125, 6 Muharram 1279 [July 3, 1862], 47–48.

26. DWQ, MTM 3036-000206, case #32, 14 Ramadan 1290 [November 5, 1873], 23.

27. DWQ, MTM 3036-000206, case #18, 17 Sha'ban 1290 [October 8, 1873], 13–14.

28. Terence Walz, "Sudanese, Habasha, Takarna, and Barabira: Trans-Saharan Africans in Cairo as Shown in the 1848 Census," in *Race and Slavery in the Middle East: Histories of Trans-Saharan Africans in Nineteenth-Century Egypt, Sudan, and the Ottoman Mediterranean*, eds. Terence Walz and Kenneth M. Cuno (American University in Cairo Press, 2010), 43–76; Al-Jabarti wrote about the corruption that marred the process of building al-Silahdar's *waqf.* Nuri, *Tujjar al-Qahira*, 83.

29. Muhammad al-'Abbasi al-Mahdi, *Al-Fatawa al-Mahdiyya* (Henceforth, FM), vol. 3 (al-Matba'a al-Azhariyya, 1883–1884), 15 Rabi' I 1279 [September 9, 1862], 427.

30. DWQ, MTM 3036-000206, case #20, 17 Sha'ban 1290 [October 8, 1873], 14–15.

31. Peters, "Administrators and Magistrates"; Findley, "The Tanzimat."

32. Khaled Fahmy, *In Quest of Justice*; Rudolph Peters, "Controlled Suffering: Mortality and Living Conditions in 19th-Century Egyptian Prisons," *International Journal of Middle East Studies* 36, no. 3 (2004): 387–407; Rudolph Peters, "Egypt and the Age of the Triumphant Prison: Legal Punishment in Nineteenth-Century Egypt," *Annales Islamologiques* 36 (2002): 132–67; Rudolph Peters, "Prisons and Marginalisation in Nineteenth-Century Egypt," in *Outside In: On the Margins of the Modern Middle East*, ed. Eugene Rogan (I.B. Tauris, 2002), 31–53; Kent F. Schull, *Prisons in the Late Ottoman Empire: Microcosms of Modernity* (Edinburgh University Press, 2014).

33. Wael B. Hallaq, *Shari'a: Theory, Practice, Transformations* (Cambridge University Press, 2009), 200–208; Rudolph Peters, *Crime and Punishment in Islamic Law: Theory and Practice from the Sixteenth to the Twenty-First Century* (Cambridge University Press, 2005), 69–102, 125–41.

34. On the banishment of women, see various examples in Leslie Peirce, *Morality Tales: Law and Gender in the Ottoman Court of Aintab* (University of California Press, 2003); Elyse Semerdjian, *"Off the Straight Path": Illicit Sex, Law, and Community in Ottoman Aleppo* (Syracuse University Press, 2008).

35. Fahmy, *In Quest of Justice*, 226–70.

36. Najwa Al-Qattan, "Dhimmis in the Muslim Court: Legal Autonomy and Religious Discrimination," *International Journal of Middle East Studies* 31, no. 3 (1999): 429–44.

37. Hanna, *Making Big Money*.

38. Ghazaleh, *Fortune urbaines et stratégies sociales*.

39. Fahad Ahmad Bishara, *A Sea of Debt: Law and Economic Life in the Western Indian Ocean, 1780–1950* (Cambridge University Press, 2017).

40. Ghazaleh, "Trading in Power."

41. For example, see FM, vol. 4, 2 Jumada II 1266 [April 14, 1850], and 19 Muharram 1268 [November 13, 1851], 58, 111–12.

42. DWQ, MTM 3036-000419, case #26, 4 Dhul-Qi'da 1292 [December 2, 1875], 13.

43. DWQ, MTM 3036-000206, case #21, 17 Sha'ban 1290 [October 10, 1873], 15.

44. For another example where the ledger was used to prove money owed, see DWQ, MTM 3036-000409, case #205, 29 Safar 1279 [August 25, 1862], 75.

45. DWQ, MTM 3036-000419, case #2, 16 Sha'ban 1292 [September 17, 1875], 1–2.

46. DWQ, MTM 3036-000206, case #93, 20 Muharram 1291 [March 9, 1874], 54.

47. DWQ, MTM 3036-000206, case #75, 11 Dhul-Qi'da 1290 [December 31, 1873], 44–45.

48. FM, vol. 3, 19 Safar 1276 [September 17, 1859], 249.

49. For more on late *Hanafi* jurists, referred to as "*al-muta'akhirun*," see Ayoub, *Law, Empire, and the Sultan*.

50. FM, vol. 4, 19 Muharram 1268 [November 13, 1851], 111–12.

51. FM, vol. 4, 19 Muharram 1268 [November 13, 1851], 111–12.

52. DWQ, MTM 3036-000125, 24 Safar 1272 [November 4, 1855], 30.

53. FM, vol. 3, 8 Safar 1269 [November 20, 1852] and 21 Rabi' I 1265 [February 13, 1849], 332–33, 12.

54. FM, vol. 4, 2 Jumada II 1266 [April 14, 1850], 58.

55. FM, vol. 4, 23 Jumada II 1266 [May 5, 1850], 60.

56. FM, vol. 4, 29 Jumada II 1267 [April 30, 1851], 94.

57. FM, vol. 3, 15 Dhul-Qi'da 1273 [July 6, 1857], 134.

58. FM, vol. 4, 17 Muharram 1267 [November 21, 1850], 392.

59. FM, vol. 3, 7 Safar 1267 [December 11, 1850], 44–45.

60. FM, vol. 2, 1 Dhul-Hijja 1283 [April 5, 1867] and 18 Dhul-Hijja 1283 [April 22, 1867], 425; FM, vol. 4, 14 Safar 1266 [December 29, 1849], 48–49.

61. DWQ, MTM 3036-000419, case #1, 16 Sha'ban 1292 [September 17, 1875], 1.

62. DWQ, MTM 3036-000206, case #81, 29 Dhul-Qi'da 1290 [January 18, 1874], 47–48.

63. DWQ, MTM 3036-000206, case #168, 11 Jumada I 1291 [June 25, 1874], 105–106.

64. DWQ, MTM 3036-000420, case #19, 20 Rabi' I 1279 [September 15, 1862], 6.

65. DWQ, MTM 3036-000409, case #11, 10 Ramadan 1278 [March 10, 1862], 6.

66. DWQ, MTM 3036-000206, case #23, 22 Sha'ban 1290 [October 15, 1873], 16.

67. FM, vol. 4, 19 Muharram 1270 [October 22, 1853] and 30 Jumada I 1270 [February 28, 1854], 181, 191–92.

68. DWQ, MTM 3036-000409, case #13, 20 Ramadan 1278 [March 20, 1862], 7.

69. DWQ, MTM 3036-000420, case #269, 7 Safar 1280 [July 23, 1863], 92.

70. Chalcraft, *The Striking Cabbies of Cairo and Other Stories*; Pascale Ghazaleh, "Masters of the Trade: Crafts and Craftspeople in Cairo, 1750–1850," *Cairo Papers in Social Science* 22, no. 3 (Fall 1999).

71. DWQ, MTM 3036-000125, 12 Rabi' II 1272 [March 9, 1856], 42–45. *Bayt al-Mal* is not mentioned explicitly in the records. The court contacted "*Mulla Afandi* [*sic*]." Based on similar cases, however, it is most likely that the records were in *Bayt al-Mal* and that *Mulla Afandi* was contacted in his capacity as overseer of *Bayt al-Mal*.

72. FM, vol. 4, 10 Sha'ban 1265 [July 1, 1849], 28.

73. FM, vol. 3, 21 Rabi' II 1272 [December 30, 1855], 374.

74. Kenneth M. Cuno, *The Pasha's Peasants: Land, Society, and Economy in Lower Egypt, 1740–1858* (Cambridge University Press, 1992), 189–97.

75. Denise Jorgens, "A Comparative Examination of the Provisions of the Ottoman Land Code and Khedive Sa'id's Law of 1858," in *New Perspectives on Property and Land in the Middle East*, ed. Roger Owen (Harvard University Press, 2000), 93–120.

76. Cuno, *The Pasha's Peasants*, 203–204.

77. Mitchell, *Rule of Experts*.

78. Jakes, *Egypt's Occupation*.

79. DWQ, MTM 3036-000206, case #190, 29 Jumada II 1291 [August 11, 1874], 118–19.

80. The exact language is: "*al-amr al-'ali al-sadir li-majlis al-tijara bil-qutr al-misri*."

81. Jallad, *Qamus al-Idara*, vol. 2, 60.

82. Jammal, *Kitab al-Qada'*, 109–10.

83. DWQ, MTM 3036-000206, case #100, 27 Muharram 1291 [March 16, 1874], 59.

84. DWQ, MTM 3036-000419, case #11, 22 Ramadan 1292 [October 22, 1875], 6–7; DWQ, MTM 3036-000206, case #77, 13 Dhul-Qi'da 1290 [January 2, 1874], 46. Land and properties are often treated similarly in merchant court documents. About two years before Sophocle and 'Ali's dispute was heard in court, Mus'ad al-Jamal, an indebted merchant from Dumyat, faced a similar situation. In that case, the merchant court made a similar decision, only this time it ordered the sequestration of Mus'ad's properties (*'aqarat*).

85. DWQ, MTM 3036-000206, case #62, 20 Shawwal 1290 [December 11, 1873], 36–38.

86. DWQ, MTM 3036-000206, case #7, 26 Rajab 1290 [September 17, 1873], 4–5.

87. DWQ, MTM 3036-000206, case #35, 21 Ramadan 1290 [November 7, 1873], 25.

88. FM, vol. 2, 25 Rabi' I 1268 [January 17, 1852], 327–28.

89. FM, vol. 4, 30 Dhul-Hijja 1272 [August 31, 1856], 510–11.

Epilogue

1. Evelyn Baring became the 1st Earl of Cromer in 1892.

2. Owen, *Lord Cromer*, 215–35.

3. Already in the 1860s, at least two decades before the British occupation of Egypt, British officials were complaining about the ineffectiveness of the merchant courts, an opinion that was shared by Nubar Pasha (1825–1899), the Khedival state official who would oversee the phasing out of the merchant courts in the mid-1870s. David Todd, "Beneath Sovereignty: Extraterritoriality and Imperial Internationalism in Nineteenth-Century Egypt," *Law and History Review* 36, no. 1 (2018): 123–24. Nubar Pasha is best remembered for his leading role in establishing the Mixed Courts in Egypt, a lengthy and difficult process that entailed negotiating with various European powers as well as the Ottoman Empire for over a decade. Nubar Pasha, *Mudhakkirat Nubar Pasha* [The Memoirs of Nubar Pasha], trans. Garo Robert Tabakian (Dar al-Shuruq, 2009).

4. At their inception in 1883, *Al-Mahakim al-Ahliyya* were referred to as "*tribunaux indigènes*" in French and "Native Courts" in English. In the late 1930s, "the translation shifted to 'National Courts.'" Hanley, *Identifying with Nationality*, 61.

5. Latifa Muhammad Salim, *Al-Nizam al-Qada'i al-Misri al-Hadith* [The Modern Egyptian Judicial System], vol. 1 (Dar al-Shuruq, 2010), 378–413.

6. 'Amr al-Shalaqani, *Izdihar wa-Inhiyar al-Nukhba al-Qanuniyya al-Misriyya, 1805–2005* [The Rise and Fall of the Egyptian Legal Elite, 1805–2005] (Dar al-Shuruq, 2013), 92–101.

7. *Qanun al-Tijara* [Commercial Law of Egypt] (al-Matba'a al-Miriyya bi-Bulaq, 1883). https://www.loc.gov/item/2021666259 (accessed on March 13, 2024).

8. In official documents, his name also appears as "'Abd-al-'Aziz Kahil." I opted for the name used most commonly in narrative sources, "'Aziz Kahil," for simplicity.

9. I approximated Kahil's year of birth based on the fact that he reached the age of retirement from the National Courts in 1920. For the list of students who traveled on scholarship in 1877, see Amin Sami, *Taqwim al-Nil*, vol. 3, 1517.

10. Ilyas Zakhura, *Kitab Mir'at al-'Asr fi Tarikh wa-Rusum Akabir al-Rijal bi-Misr* [The Mirror of the Times], vol. 2 (Matba'at Ilyas Zakhura, 1916), 283.

11. *Al-Muqtataf*, vol. 10, no. 10, July 1886, 640.

12. For a summary of a court case that he heard in that capacity, see "The Prosecutor vs. Muhammad Mahmud Mahmud," *al-Huquq*, vol. 13, no. 11, March 19, 1898, 82–85.

13. For a brief entry that refers to him in that capacity, see "Ruling number 39," *al-Istiqlal*, vol. 2, February 28, 1903, 44.

14. For a summary of a court case that he heard in that capacity, see "[Case number] 4, 17 February 1920," *al-Majmu'a al-Rasmiyya lil-Mahakim al-Ahliyya* [Official Bulletin of the Native Tribunals], vol. 22 (al-Matba'a al-Amiriyya, 1921), 5–7.

15. For a summary of a court case that he heard in that capacity, see "108. Cassation: The Interest of the Accused," *al-Huquq*, vol. 20, no. 34, October 14, 1905, 261–62.

16. "Reports by his Majesty's High Commissioner on the Finances, Administration, and Condition of Egypt and the Soudan for the Year 1920," in *Parliamentary Papers*, vol. 42 (Session February 15, 1921–November 10, 1921), 95.

17. Philipp, *The Syrians*, 123–26.

18. Sa'd Zaghlul, *Mudhakkirat Sa'd Zaghlul* [The Memoirs of Sa'd Zaghlul], ed. 'Abd-al-'Azim Ramadan (al-Hay'a al-Misriyya al-'Amma lil-Kitab, 1987).

19. Ibrahim al-Hilbawi, *Mudhakkirat Ibrahim al-Hilbawi* [The Memoirs of Ibrahim al-Hilbawi] (al-Hay'a al-Misriyya al-'Amma lil-Kitab, 1995).

20. Muhammad Rashid Rida, *Tarikh al-Ustadh al-Imam al-Shaykh Muhammad 'Abduh*, vol. 3 (Matba'at al-Manar, 1906), 173.

21. Zakhura, *Kitab Mir'at*, 78.

22. "Nashat 25 Sana," *Sarkis Magazine*, vol. 9, no. 7–8, April/May 1916, 246–47.

23. Philipp, *The Syrians*, 154.

24. This example was discussed briefly in Chapter Four, and in more detail in Cheta and Schwartz, "A Printer's Odd Plea."

25. A slightly earlier attempt that is relevant to this point is Muhammad Qadri Pasha's unpublished book manuscript on the application of the parts of French Civil Law that are consistent with the *Hanafi* school of Islamic law. See al-Shalaqani, *Izdihar wa-Inhiyar*, 101. For more on Qadri, see Hans-Georg Ebert, "Muhammad Qadri Pasha," *Encyclopaedia of Islam, Three.* http://dx.doi.org/10.1163/1573-3912_ei3_COM_40619 (accessed on March 13, 2024).

26. Jurji Zaydan, *Kitab Tarikh Adab al-Lugha al-'Arabiyya* [The History of Arabic Literature], vol. 4 (Matba'at al-Hilal, 1914), 302–303.

27. 'Abd-al-'Aziz Kahil, *Sharh al-Qanun al-Tijari al-Misri* [An Interpretation of Egyptian Commercial Law] (Matba'at al-Muqtataf, 1885). https://catalog.hathitrust.org/Record/102752256 (accessed on March 13, 2024).

28. Kahil, *Sharh al-Qanun al-Tijari al-Misri*, 4–5.

29. J. E. Marshall, *The Egyptian Enigma: 1890–1928* (John Murray, 1928), 54–57.

30. For more on Yusuf Wahba, who would later serve as prime minister, see Asaf and Nasr, *Dalil Misr*, 303–304; Zakhura, *Kitab Mir'at*, 93–94.

31. Khaled Fahmy, "Law and Pain in Khedival Egypt," in *Outside In: On the Margins of the Modern Middle East*, ed. Eugene Rogan (I.B. Tauris, 2002), 86–87.

32. Cheta, "A Prehistory of the Modern Legal Profession in Egypt," 651–55.

33. Kahil, *Sharh al-Qanun al-Tijari al-Misri*, 61.

34. Zaghlul, *al-Muhamah*, especially the section entitled "The State of the Legal Profession in That Time," 248–66.

35. Al-Shalaqani, *Izdihar*, 92–101; Tariq al-Bishri, *al-Wad' al-Qanuni al-Mu'asir bayna al-Shari'a al-Islamiyya w-al-Qanun al-Wad'i* [The Contemporary Legal Situation Between Islamic Law and Positive Law] (Dar al-Shuruq, 2005).

36. Sedgwick, *Muhammad Abduh*, 31–36, 71–74.

37. For more on the history of modern printing in the Middle East, see Kathryn A. Schwartz, "Meaningful Mediums: A Material and Intellectual History of Manuscript and Print Production in Nineteenth-Century Ottoman Cairo" (PhD diss., Harvard University, 2015), ProQuest (10591599).

38. The Earl of Cromer, *Modern Egypt*, 2 vols. (The Macmillan Company, 1916).

39. The use of the term "erasure" was applied most recently by Emad Helal in relation to criminal law. See "An Erased Experiment: Penal Legislation Between 1823 and 1883," in *The Oxford Handbook of Modern Egyptian History,* eds. Beth Baron and Jeffrey Culang (Oxford University Press, 2024), 240–61.

Bibliography

Archival Sources

DWQ: Dar al-Watha'iq al-Qawmiyya (The Egyptian National Archives), Cairo, Egypt

MTM (3036)—Majlis Tujjar Misr (The Merchant Court of Cairo)
MM (2002)—Muhafazat Misr (Cairo Governorate)

Rare Books and Special Collections Library, American University in Cairo, Egypt

Tawil Papers:

R1 (Business correspondence from March 19, 1859 to November 15, 1859 and from June 11, 1862 to December 17, 1862)
R2 (Business correspondence from January 4, 1870 to September 27, 1870)
R3 (Business correspondence from December 19, 1862 to September 5, 1863)
R4 (Business correspondence from January 10, 1865 to May 9, 1866 and from May 30, 1869 to January 4, 1870)

TNA: The National Archives, London, United Kingdom

Foreign Office Papers:

FO 78: Ottoman Empire
FO 841: British Consulate in Cairo
FO 226: Embassy and Consulate, Beirut

Selected Periodicals

Arabic Periodicals

Al-Huquq
Al-Istiqlal
Al-Jami'a
Al-Majmu'a al-Rasmiyya lil-Mahakim al-Ahliyya [Official Bulletin of the Native Tribunals]
Al-Masarra
Al-Muqtataf

Al-Qutr al-Misri
Sarkis

Other Periodicals
Bollettino del Grande Oriente della Massoneria in Italia
Bollettino della Società africana d'Italia periodico mensile
Bollettino della Società geografica italiana
Bulletin de l'Institut égyptien
Bulletin de législation et de jurisprudence égyptiennes
Bulletin de la Société de Géographie d'Égypte
Il corriere israelitico: periodico mensile per la storia e la letteratura israelitica
L'Exploration: revue des conquetes de la civilisation sur tous les points du globe
Gazette des Tribunaux mixtes d'Égypte: revue judiciaire mensuelle
La gazette géographique et l'exploration
L'Italia evangelica giornale delle chiese, delle scuole e delle famiglie
Jurisprudence des tribunaux de la réforme en Égypte: recueil officiel
Il Libero pensiero: giornale dei razionalisti

Other Published Sources Cited

Abaza, Mona. *The Cotton Plantation Remembered: An Egyptian Family Story*. The American University in Cairo Press, 2013.

'Abd-al-Mu'ti, Husam. *Al-'Ilaqat al-Misriyya al-Hijaziyya fil-Qarn al-Thamin 'ashar* [Egyptian-Hijazi Relations in the Eighteenth Century]. Al-Hay'a al-Misriyya al-'Amma lil-Kitab, 1999.

'Abd-al-Mu'ti, Husam, and Sa'ida Muhammad Husni, eds. *Mahadir Majlis Shura al-Nuwwab: Al-Hay'a al-Niyabiyya al-Thaniyya, 1870–1873* [The Minutes of the Consultative Council: The Second Parliamentary Convention, 1870–1873]. Vol. 2. Matba'at Dar al-Kutub wal-Watha'iq al-Qawmiyya, 2006.

Abou-El-Haj, Rifáat Ali. *Formation of the Modern State: The Ottoman Empire, Sixteenth to Eighteenth Centuries*. Syracuse University Press, 2005.

Abu-Lughod, Ibrahim. "The Transformation of the Egyptian Elite: Prelude to the 'Urabi Revolt." *Middle East Journal* 21, no. 3 (1967): 325–44.

Abul-Magd, Zeinab. *Imagined Empires: A History of Revolt in Egypt*. University of California Press, 2013.

Ade, Mafalda. "Ottoman Commercial Law and Its Practice in Aleppo Province (1850–1880)." In *Merchants in the Ottoman Empire*, edited by Suraiya Faroqhi and Gilles Veinstein. Peeters Publishers, 2008.

Agmon, Iris. *Family & Court: Legal Culture and Modernity in Late Ottoman Palestine*. Syracuse University Press, 2006.

Akarli, Engin. *The Long Peace: Ottoman Lebanon, 1861–1920*. University of California Press, 1993.

Al-'Aqqad, 'Abbas Mahmud. *Rijal 'Ariftuhum* [Men Whom I Knew]. Hindawi Foundation, 2013. https://www.hindawi.org/books/95950851.

Aristarches, Gregorius. *Législation ottomane, ou Recueil des lois, réglements, ordonnances, traités, capitulations et autres documets officiels de l'Empire ottoman* [Ottoman law, or

Collection of Laws, Regulations, Orders, Treaties, Capitulations and Other Official Documents from the Ottoman Empire]. 7 vols. Freres Nicolaïdes, 1873–1888.

Artunç, Cihan, and Mohamed Saleh. "The Demand for Extraterritoriality: Religious Minorities in Nineteenth-Century Egypt." *The Economic History Review* 77, no. 3 (2024): 895–927.

Asaf, Yusuf, and Qaysar Nasr. *Dalil Misr* [The Egypt Directory]. Al-Matba'a al-'Umumiyya, 1889.

Ayalon, Ami. *The Press in the Arab Middle East: A History.* Oxford University Press, 1995.

Ayoub, Samy. *Law, Empire, and the Sultan: Ottoman Imperial Authority and Late Hanafi Jurisprudence.* Oxford University Press, 2020.

Al-Ayubi, Ilyas. *Tarikh Misr fi 'Ahd al-Khidiwi Isma'il Basha* [Egypt's History During the Reign of Isma'il Pasha]. Hindawi Foundation, 2012. https://www.hindawi.org/books/24697404.

Baer, Gabriel. "Tanzimat in Egypt—the Penal Code." *Bulletin of the School of Oriental and African Studies* 26, no. 1 (1963): 29–49.

Baldwin, James E. "The Deposition of Defterdar Ahmed Pasha and the Rule of Law in Seventeenth-Century Egypt." *The Journal of Ottoman Studies* 46 (2015): 131–61.

Baldwin, James E. *Islamic Law and Empire in Ottoman* Cairo. Edinburgh University Press, 2016.

Barak, On. "Egyptian Times: Temporality, Personhood, and the Technopolitical Making of Modern Egypt, 1830–1930." PhD diss., New York University, 2009. ProQuest (3380301).

Barak, On. *On Time: Technology and Temporality in Modern Egypt.* University of California Press, 2013.

Barakat, Ali. *Tatwwur al-Milkiyya al-Zira'iyya fi Misr wa-Atharuhu 'ala al-Haraka al-Siyasiyya, 1813–1914* [The Development of Landownership in Egypt and Its Effect on the Political Movement, 1813–1914]. Dar al-Thaqafa al-Jadida, 1977.

Barakat, Nora Elizabeth. *Bedouin Bureaucrats: Mobility and Property in the Ottoman Empire.* Stanford University Press, 2023.

Barkey, Karen. *Bandits and Bureaucrats: The Ottoman Route to State Centralization.* Cornell University Press, 1994.

Beckert, Sven. *Empire of Cotton: A Global History.* Vintage Books, 2015.

Bender, Thomas. *The Unfinished City: New York and the Metropolitan Idea.* New York University Press, 2007.

Benton, Lauren. *A Search for Sovereignty: Law and Geography in European Empires, 1400–1900.* Cambridge University Press, 2014.

Birla, Ritu. *Stages of Capital: Law, Culture, and Market Governance in Late Colonial India.* Duke University Press, 2009.

Bishara, Fahad Ahmad. "Paper Routes: Inscribing Islamic Law Across the Nineteenth-Century Western Indian Ocean." *Law and History Review* 32, no. 4 (2014): 797–820.

Bishara, Fahad Ahmad. *A Sea of Debt: Law and Economic Life in the Western Indian Ocean, 1780–1950.* Cambridge University Press, 2017.

Al-Bishri, Tariq. *Al-Wad' al-Qanuni al-Mu'asir bayna al-Shari'a al-Islamiyya w-al-Qanun al-Wad'i* [The Contemporary Legal Situation Between Islamic Law and Positive Law]. Dar al-Shuruq, 2005.

Blunt, Wilfrid Scawen. *The Land War in Ireland: Being a Personal Narrative of Events, in Continuation of "A Secret History of the English Occupation of Egypt."* Stephen Swift and Co. Ltd, 1912.

Blunt, Wilfrid Scawen, and Ahmad Urabi. *Secret History of the English Occupation of Egypt*. Alfred A Knopf, 1922. https://www.gutenberg.org/ebooks/41373.

Broadley, A. M. *How We Defended Arabi and His Friends: A Story of Egypt and the Egyptians*. Chapman and Hall Ltd, 1884.

Burak, Guy. *The Second Formation of Islamic Law: The Hanafi School in the Early Modern Ottoman Empire*. Cambridge University Press, 2015.

Burak, Guy. "Mufti." In *The Oxford Encyclopedia of the Islamic World: Digital Collection*, edited by John L. Esposito. Oxford University Press, 2022.

Bruner, Stephen C. *Late Nineteenth-Century Italy in Africa: The Livraghi Affair and the Waning of Civilizing Aspirations*. Cambridge Scholars Publishing, 2017.

Çalışkan, Koray. *Market Threads: How Cotton Farmers and Traders Create a Global Commodity*. Princeton University Press, 2010.

Casale, Giancarlo. *The Ottoman Age of Exploration*. Oxford University Press, 2010.

Chalcraft, John T. *The Striking Cabbies of Cairo and Other Stories: Crafts and Guilds in Egypt, 1863–1914*. State University of New York Press, 2004.

Cheta, Omar Youssef. "The Economy by Other Means: The Historiography of Capitalism in the Middle East." *History Compass* 16, no. 4 (2018).

Cheta, Omar Youssef. "A Prehistory of the Modern Legal Profession in Egypt, 1840s–1870s." *International Journal of Middle East Studies* 50, no. 4 (2018): 649–68.

Cheta, Omar Youssef, and Kathryn A. Schwartz. "A Printer's Odd Plea to Reform Legal Pluralism in Khedival Egypt." *Past & Present* 252, no. 1 (2021): 179–211.

Cole, Juan. *Napoleon's Egypt: Invading the Middle East*. Palgrave Macmillan, 2007.

Compte Rendu Des Travaux de la Commission de la Dette Publique d'Egypte. n.p., 1876.

Cromer, The Earl of. *Modern Egypt*. 2 vols. The Macmillan Company, 1916.

Cuno, Kenneth M. *The Pasha's Peasants: Land, Society, and Economy in Lower Egypt, 1740–1858*. Cambridge University Press, 1992.

Cuzzi, Guiseppe. *Fifteen Years Prisoner of the False Prophet*. Translated by Hans Resener. University of Khartoum, 1968.

Dahir, Mas'ud. *Hijrat al-Shawam: Al-Hijra al-Lubnaniyya ila Misr* [The Emigration of the Shawam: The Lebanese Emigration to Egypt]. Dar al-Shuruq, 2009.

Derri, Aviv. "Bonds of Obligation, Precarious Fortunes: Empire, Non-Muslim Bankers, and Peasants in Late Ottoman Damascus, 1820s–1890s." PhD diss., New York University, 2021. ProQuest (28715558).

Di-Capua, Yoav. *Gatekeepers of the Arab Past: Historians and History Writing in Twentieth-Century Egypt*. University of California Press, 2009.

Ebert, Hans-Georg. "Muhammad Qadri Pasha." In *Encyclopaedia of Islam Three Online*, edited by K. Fleet, G. Krämer, D. Matringe, J. Nawas, and D. J. Stewart. Brill, 2021. doi: https://doi.org/10.1163/1573-3912_ei3_COM_40619.

EzzelArab, AbdelAziz. *European Control and Egypt's Traditional Elites: A Case Study in Elite Economic Nationalism*. The Edwin Mellen Press, 2002.

EzzelArab, AbdelAziz. "The Experiment of Sharif Pasha's Cabinet (1879): An Inquiry into the Historiography of Egypt's Elite Movement." *International Journal of Middle East Studies* 36, no. 4 (2004): 561–89.

Fahmy, Khaled. *All the Pasha's Men: Mehmed Ali, His Army and the Making of Modern Egypt.* Cambridge University Press, 1997.

Fahmy, Khaled. "Law and Pain in Khedival Egypt." In *Outside In: On the Margins of the Modern Middle East*, edited by Eugene Rogan. I.B. Tauris, 2002.

Fahmy, Khaled. *Mehmed Ali: From Ottoman Governor to Ruler of Egypt.* Oneworld Academic, 2009.

Fahmy, Khaled. *In Quest of Justice: Islamic Law and Forensic Medicine in Modern Egypt.* University of California Press, 2018.

Fahmy, Ziad. *Ordinary Egyptians: Creating the Modern Nation Through Popular Culture.* Stanford University Press, 2011.

Al-Falaki, Mahmud Bey. *Kharitat al-Iskandariyya fi Sanat 1282 Hijriyya* [The Map of Alexandria in the Hijri Year 1282]. s.n., 1865. Bibliothèque nationale de France. https://gallica.bnf.fr/ark:/12148/btv1b10104413k.

Farid, Muhammad. *Mudhakkirat Muhammad Farid* [The Memoirs of Muhammad Farid], edited by Ra'uf 'Abbas Hamid. 'Alam al-Kutub, 1975.

Faroqhi, Suraiya. *Approaching Ottoman Sources: An Introduction to the Sources.* Cambridge University Press, 2000.

Findley, Carter Vaughn. "The Tanzimat." In *The Cambridge History of Turkey*, vol. 4, edited by Resat Kasaba. Cambridge University Press, 2008.

Foucault, Michel. "Afterword: The Subject and Power." In *Michel Foucault: Beyond Structuralism and Hermeneutics*, edited by Hubert L. Dreyfus and Paul Rabinow. The University of Chicago Press, 1983.

Garcin, F. "Un notable français du Caire à la fin du XIXe siècle." *Revue des mondes musulmans et de la Méditerranée* 30 (1980): 71–99.

Gelat Bey, Philippe. *Répertoire général annoté de la législation et de l'administration egyptiennes, 1840–1908.* Imprimerie J. Lagoudakis, 1908.

Gessi Pasha, Romolo. *Seven Years in the Soudan: Being a Record of Explorations, Adventures, and Campaigns against the Arab Slave Hunters.* Translated by Lily Wolffsohn and Bettina Woodward. S. Low, Marston & Co., 1892.

Ghazaleh, Pascale. "Masters of the Trade: Crafts and Craftspeople in Cairo, 1750–1850." *Cairo Papers in Social Science* 22, no. 3 (Fall 1999).

Ghazaleh, Pascale. "Heirs and Debtors: Blood Relatives, Qur'anic Heirs and Business Associates in Cairo, 1800–50." In *Society and Economy in Egypt and the Eastern Mediterranean, 1600–1900: Essays in Honor of Andre Raymond*, edited by Nelly Hanna and Raouf Abbas. American University in Cairo Press, 2005.

Ghazaleh, Pascale. *Fortunes urbaines et stratégies sociales: généalogies patrimoniales au Caire, 1780–1830.* Institut français d'archéologie orientale du Caire, 2010.

Ghazaleh, Pascale. "Trading in Power: Merchants and the State in 19th-Century Egypt." *International Journal of the Middle East Studies* 45, no. 1 (2013): 71–91.

Gilbar, Gad G. "The Rise and Fall of the *Tujjar* Councils of Representatives in Iran, 1884–85." *Journal of the Economic and Social History of the Orient* 51, no. 4 (2008): 639–74.

Ginzburg, Carlo. "Microhistory: Two or Three Things That I Know About It." *Critical Inquiry* 20, no. 1 (1993): 10–35.

Goldberg, Jan. "On the Origins of *Majalis al-Tujjar* in Mid-Nineteenth Century Egypt." *Islamic Law and Society* 6, no. 2 (1999): 193–223.

Griffith, Zoe. *The Egypt Merchants: Imperial Governance and Economic Life in the Ottoman Mediterranean, 1670–1830.* University of California Press, forthcoming.

Gümüş, Musa. "Anayasal Meşrûtî Yönetime Medhal: 1856 Islahat Fermanı'nın Tam Metin İncelemesi" [An Introduction to Constitutional Government: A Full Text Analysis of the 1856 Reform Edict]. *Bilig: Türk Dünyası Sosyal Bilimler Dergisi* 47, no. 3 (2008): 215–40.

Hallaq, Wael B. *An Introduction to Islamic Law.* Cambridge University Press, 2009.

Hallaq, Wael B. *Shari'a: Theory, Practice, Transformations.* Cambridge University Press, 2009.

Hamed, Raouf Abbas. "The *Siyasatname* and the Institutionalization of Central Administration under Muhammad 'Ali." In *The State and Its Servants: Administration in Egypt from Ottoman Times to the Present*, edited by Nelly Hanna. American University in Cairo Press, 1995.

Hamed, Raouf Abbas [Hamid, Ra'uf 'Abbas]. *Al-Milkiyyat al-Zira'iyya al-Misriyya wa Dawruha fi al-Mujtama' al-Misri, 1837–1914* [The History of Egyptian Agricultural Landownership and Its Role in Egyptian Society, 1837–1914]. Al-Majlis al-A'la lil-Thaqafa, 2011.

Hanley, Will. "When Did Egyptians Stop Being Ottomans? An Imperial Citizenship Case Study." In *Multilevel Citizenship*, edited by Willem Maas. University of Pennsylvania Press, 2013.

Hanley, Will. *Identifying with Nationality: Europeans, Ottomans, and Egyptians in Alexandria.* Columbia University Press, 2017.

Hanna, Nelly. *Making Big Money in 1600: The Life and Times of Isma'il Abu Taqiyya, Egyptian Merchant.* Syracuse University Press, 1998.

Hanna, Nelly. *In Praise of Books: A Cultural History of Cairo's Middle Class, Sixteenth to the Eighteenth Century.* Syracuse University Press, 2003.

Hanna, Nelly, ed. *The State and Its Servants: Administration in Egypt from Ottoman Times to the Present.* American University in Cairo Press, 1995.

Hanssen, Jens, and Max Weiss. "Introduction: Language, Mind, Freedom and Time: The Modern Arab Intellectual Tradition in Four Words." In *Arabic Thought Beyond the Liberal Age: Towards an Intellectual History of the Nahda*, edited by Jens Hanssen and Max Weiss. Cambridge University Press, 2016.

Hathaway, Jane. *The Politics of Households in Ottoman Egypt: The Rise of the Qazdaglis.* Cambridge University Press, 1997.

Helal, Emad [Hilal, 'Imad]. *Al-Falah wal-Sultah wal-Qanun fil-Nisf al-Thani min al-Qarn al-Tasi' 'Ashar* [Peasant, Authority and Law in Egypt in the Second Half of the Nineteenth Century]. Dar al-Kutub wal-Watha'iq al-Qawmiyya, 2007.

Helal Emad [Hilal, 'Imad]. *Al-Ifta' al-Misri.* Vols. 3–5. Matba'at Dar al-Kutub wal-Watha'iq al-Qawmiyya, 2010–2015.

Helal, Emad. "An Erased Experiment: Penal Legislation Between 1823 and 1883." In *The Oxford Handbook of Modern Egyptian History*, edited by Beth Baron and Jeffrey Culang. Oxford University Press, 2024.

Heyworth-Dunne, James. *An Introduction to the History of Education in Modern Egypt.* Cass, 1968.

Al-Hilbawi, Ibrahim. *Mudhakkirat Ibrahim al-Hilbawi* [The Memoirs of Ibrahim al-Hilbawi]. Al-Hay'a al-Misriyya al-'Amma lil-Kitab, 1995.

Hill, Richard. *A Biographical Dictionary of the Sudan.* Routledge, 1967.

Al-Hitta, Ahmad Ahmad. *Tarikh al-Zira'a al-Misriyya fi 'Ahd Muhammad 'Ali al-Kabir* [The History of Egyptian Agricultural in the Era of Muhammad Ali]. Al-Hay'a al-Misriyya al-'Amma lil-Kitab, 2012.

Holt, Elizabeth M. *Fictitious Capital: Silk, Cotton, and the Rise of the Arabic Novel.* Fordham University Press, 2017.

Holt, P. M., and M. W. Daly. *The History of the Sudan: From the Coming of Islam to the Present Day.* Routledge, 1979.

Hunter, F. Robert. *Egypt Under the Khedives, 1805–1879: From Household Government to Modern Bureaucracy.* University of Pittsburgh Press, 1984.

Husni, Sa'ida Muhammad. "Analytical Introduction." In *Mahadir Majlis Shura al-Nuwwab: Al-Hay'a al-Niyabiyya al-Thaniyya, 1870–1873* [The Minutes of the Consultative Council: The Second Parliamentary Convention, 1870–1873], vol. 2, edited by Husam 'Abd-al-Mu'ti, and Sa'ida Muhammad Husni. Matba'at Dar al-Kutub wal-Watha'iq al-Qawmiyya, 2006.

Ibrahim, Ahmed Fekry. *Pragmatism in Islamic Law: A Social and Intellectual History.* Syracuse University Press, 2015.

Ibrahim, Nasir. "Al-Faransiyun wa Nizam al-Iltizam, 1798–1801" [The French and the Iltizam System, 1798–1801], *Annales islamogiques* 37 (2003): 31–54.

Al-Jabarti, Abd al-Rahman. *Napoleon in Egypt: Al-Jabarti's Chronicle of the First Seven Months of the French Occupation, 1798.* Translated by Shmuel Moreh. Markus Wiener Publishers, 1993.

Jakes, Aaron G. *Egypt's Occupation: Colonial Economism and the Crises of Capitalism.* Stanford University Press, 2020.

Jallad, Filib. *Qamus al-Idara wal-Qaqa'* [General Encyclopedia of the Administration and the Judiciary]. 7 vols. Al-Matba'a al-Bukhariyya, Yanni Lagudakis, 1890–1892.

Jammal, Ibrahim, ed. *Kitab al-Qada' al-Misri al-Ahli* [The Book of the National Egyptian Judiciary]. Matba'at al-Akhbar, 1909.

Jorgens, Denise. "A Comparative Examination of the Provisions of the Ottoman Land Code and Khedive Sa'id's Law of 1858." In *New Perspectives on Property and Land in the Middle East,* edited by Roger Owen. Harvard University Press, 2000.

Al-Jumay'i, 'Abd-al-Mun'im Ibrahim al-Dusuqi. *Al-Thawra al-'Urabiyya: Buhuth wa Dirasat Watha'iqiyya* [The 'Urabist Revolution: Research and Documentary Studies]. Markaz al-Dirasat al-Siyasiyya wal-Istratijiyya bil-Ahram, 1982.

Kahil, 'Abd-al-'Aziz. *Sharh al-Qanun al-Tijari al-Misri* [An Interpretation of Egyptian Commercial Law]. Matba'at al-Muqtataf, 1885.

Kasbar, Mahmud Muhammad. *Al-Tarikh Bayna al-Siyasa wal-Ijtima': Ru'yah Susyulujiyah* [History Between Politics and Sociology: A Sociological View]. Dar al-Ma'rifa al-Jami'iyya, 1987.

Keddie, Nikki. *An Islamic Response to Imperialism: Political and Religious Writings of Sayyid Jamal ad-Din "al-Afghani."* University of California Press, 1983.

Kessler, Amalia D. *A Revolution in Commerce: The Parisian Merchant Court and the Rise of Commercial Society in Eighteenth-Century France.* Yale University Press, 2007.

Khater, Akram. *Inventing Home: Emigration, Gender, and the Middle Class in Lebanon, 1870–1920.* University of California Press, 2001.

Kitroeff, Alexander. *The Greeks and the Making of Modern Egypt.* American University in Cairo Press, 2019.

Landau, Jacob M. "Prolegomena to a Study of Secret Societies in Modern Egypt." *Middle Eastern* Studies 1, no. 2 (1965): 135–86.

Landes, David S. *Bankers and Pashas: International Finance and Economic Imperialism in Egypt.* Harvard University Press, 1958.

Livre d'or de l'Institut égyptien. Imprimerie de l'Institut de Bibliographie, 1899.

Al-Mahdi, Muhammad al-'Abbasi. *Al-Fatawa al-Mahdiyya.* 7 vols. Al-Matba'a al-Azhariyya, 1883–1884.

Marcus, Abraham. *The Middle East on the Eve of Modernity: Aleppo in the Eighteenth Century.* Columbia University Press, 1989.

Marglin, Jessica M. "Extraterritoriality Meets Islamic Law: Legal Pluralism and Elements of Proof in the International Mixed Court of Morocco, 1871–1872." *Quaderni Storici* 51, no. 153 (2016): 673–700.

Marshall, J. E. *The Egyptian Enigma: 1890–1928.* John Murray, 1928.

Memorie della Società geografica italiana. Stabilimento Giuseppe Civelli, 1878.

Mikhail, Alan. *Nature and Empire in Ottoman Egypt: An Environmental History.* Cambridge University Press, 2011.

Mikhail, Alan. *My Egypt Archive.* Yale University Press, 2023.

Minkin, Shana. *Imperial Bodies: Empire and Death in Alexandria, Egypt.* Stanford University Press, 2019.

Miran, Jonathan. "Endowing Property and Edifying Power in a Red Sea Port: Waqf, Arab Migrant Entrepreneurs, and Urban Authority in Massawa, 1860s–1880s." *International Journal of African Historical Studies* 42, no. 2 (2009): 156–59.

Miran, Jonathan. "Red Sea Translocals: Hadrami Migration, Entrepreneurship, and Strategies of Integration in Eritrea, 1840s–1970s." *Northeast African Studies* 12, no. 1 (2012): 129–67.

Miran, Jonathan. "From Bondage to Freedom on the Red Sea Coast: Manumitted Slaves in Egyptian Massawa, 1873–1885." *Slavery & Abolition: A Journal of Slave and Post-Slave Studies* 34, no. 1 (2013): 135–57.

Mitchell, Timothy. *Rule of Experts: Egypt, Techno-Politics, Modernity.* University of California Press, 2002.

Mubarak, 'Ali. *Al-Khitat al-Tawfiqiyya al-Jadida.* 20 vols. Al-Matba'a al-Amiriyya al-Kubra, 1886–1889.

Muller, Charles. *Plan d'Alexandrie, comprenant toutes ses fortifications, rues et édifices publics.* Linassi, 1855. Bibliothèque nationale de France. https://gallica.bnf.fr/ark:/12148/btv1b8440801b.

Al-Naghiya, Khalid 'Id. "Majlis Tujjar Misr (1846–1876): Dirasah Watha'iqiyyah" [Cairo's Merchant Court: A Documentary Study]. *Al-Ruznamah: The Egyptian Documentary Annals* 2 (2004): 239–405.

Najm, Zayn al-'Abidin Shams al-Din. *Misr fi 'Ahdayy 'Abbas wa Sa'id* [Egypt Under 'Abbas and Sa'id]. Dar al-Shuruq, 2007.

Al-Naqqash, Salim Khalil. *Misr lil-Misryyin* [Egypt for the Egyptians]. 9 vols. Matba'at Jaridat al-Mahrusa, 1884.

Nuri, Rizq. *Tujjar al-Qahira fi 'Asr Muhammad 'Ali, 1805–1848* [Cairo's Merchants in the Era of Muhammad Ali, 1805–1848]. Al-Hay'a al-Misriyya al-'Amma lil-Kitab, 2018.

Owen, E. Roger J. *Cotton and the Egyptian Economy, 1820–1914: A Study in Trade and Development*. The Clarendon Press, 1969.

Owen, Roger. *Lord Cromer: Victorian Imperialist, Edwardian Proconsul*. Oxford University Press, 2005.

Panceri, P., and F. Gasco. *Viaggio in Egitto dei socii P. Panceri e F. Gasco nell'anno 1873–1874*. Stabilimento Tipografico A. Trani, 1876.

Parliamentary Papers: Accounts and Papers, Session 9 February 1888–24 December 1888. Vol. 46. Harrison and Sons, 1888.

Pasha, Nubar. *Mudhakkirat Nubar Pasha* [The Memoirs of Nubar Pasha]. Translated by Garo Robert Tabakian. Dar al-Shuruq, 2009.

Peirce, Leslie. *Morality Tales: Law and Gender in the Ottoman Court of Aintab*. University of California Press, 2003.

Peters, Rudolph. "Muhammad Al-'Abbasi al-Mahdi (d. 1897), Grand Mufti of Egypt, and His 'al-Fatawa al-Mahdiyya'." *Islamic Law and Society* 1, no. 1 (1994): 75–78.

Peters, Rudolph. "Administrators and Magistrates: The Development of a Secular Judiciary in Egypt, 1842–1871." *Die Welt des Islams* 39, no. 3 (1999): 378–97.

Peters, Rudolph. "Egypt and the Age of the Triumphant Prison: Legal Punishment in Nineteenth-Century Egypt." *Annales Islamogiques* 36 (2002): 132–67.

Peters, Rudolph. "'For His Correction and as a Deterrent Example for Others': Mehmed Ali's First Criminal Legislation (1829–1830)." *Islamic Law and Society* 6, no. 2 (1999): 164–92.

Peters, Rudolph. "Prisons and Marginalisation in Nineteenth-Century Egypt." In *Outside In: On the Margins of the Modern Middle East*, edited by Eugene Rogan. I.B. Tauris, 2002.

Peters, Rudolph. "Controlled Suffering: Mortality and Living Conditions in 19th-Century Egyptian Prisons." *International Journal of Middle East Studies* 36, no. 3 (2004): 387–407.

Peters, Rudolph. *Crime and Punishment in Islamic Law: Theory and Practice from the Sixteenth to the Twenty-First Century*. Cambridge University Press, 2005.

Peters, Rudolph. "What Does It Mean to Be an Official Madhhab? Hanafism and the Ottoman Empire." In *The Islamic School of Law: Evolution, Devolution, and Progress*, edited by Peri Bearman, Rudolph Peters, and Frank E. Vogel. Harvard University Press, 2006.

Peters, Rudolph. *Shari'a, Justice and Legal Order: Egyptian and Islamic Law: Selected Essays*. Brill, 2020.

Philipp, Thomas. *The Syrians in Egypt, 1725–1975*. Ty Aur Press, 2017.

Poffandi, Stefano G. *Indicateur égyptien administratif et commercial*. Imprimerie Générale, 1896.

Proceedings of the Supreme Council of Sovereign Grand Inspectors-General of the Thirty-Third and Last Degree, Ancient Accepted Scottish Rite. n.p., 1892.

Qamus Jughrafi lil-Qutr al-Misri [Geographical Dictionary of Egypt]. Al-Matbaʿa al-Kubra al-Amiriyya, 1899.

Qanun al-Tijara [Commercial Law of Egypt]. Al-Matbaʿa al-Miriyya bi-Bulaq, 1883.

Al-Qattan, Najwa. "Dhimmis in the Muslim Court: Legal Autonomy and Religious Discrimination." *International Journal of Middle East Studies* 31, no. 3 (1999): 429–44.

Quataert, Donald. *Social Disintegration and Popular Resistance in the Ottoman Empire, 1881–1908: Reactions to European Economic Penetration*. New York University Press, 1983.

Raccolta degli atti stampati per ordine della Camera documenti. Vol. 2. Tipografia della Camera dei deputati, 1886.

Ramitsh, Yusuf. *Usrat al-Muwaylhi wa Atharuha fil-Adab al-ʿArabi* [The Muwaylhi Family and Their Influence on Arabic Literature]. Dar al-Maʿarif, 1980.

Raymond, A., and M. B. Hooker. "Shah Bandar." In *Encyclopaedia of Islam New Edition Online (EI-2 English)*, edited by P. J. Bearman. Brill, 2012. doi: https://doi.org/10.1163/1573-3912_islam_COM_1023.

Reimer, Michael J. "Ottoman Alexandria: The Paradox of Decline and the Reconfiguration of Power in Eighteenth-Century Arab Provinces." *Journal of the Economic and Social History of the Orient* 37, no. 2 (1994): 107–46.

Reimer, Michael J. *Colonial Bridgehead: Government and Society in Alexandria, 1807–1882*. American University in Cairo Press, 1997.

Recensement Général de l'Égypte. Impremerie Nationale, 1885.

Rida, Muhammad Rashid. *Tarikh al-Ustadh al-Imam al-Shaykh Muhammad ʿAbduh*. Vol. 3. Matbaʿat al-Manar, 1906.

Rivlin, Helen Anne B. "The Railway Question in the Ottoman-Egyptian Crisis of 1850–1852." *Middle East Journal* 15, no. 4 (1961): 365–85.

Rubin, Avi. *Ottoman Nizamiye Courts: Law and Modernity*. Palgrave Macmillan, 2011.

Rubin, Avi. "Was There a Rule of Law in the Late Ottoman Empire?" *British Journal of Middle Eastern Studies* 46, no. 1 (2019): 123–38.

Rubin, Avi. "The Positivization of Ottoman Law and the Question of Continuity." In *State Law and Legal Positivism: The Global Rise of a New Paradigm*, edited by Badouin Dupret and Jean-Louis Halperin. Brill, 2022.

Salim, Latifa Muhammad. *Al-Nizam al-Qada'i al-Misri al-Hadith* [The Modern Egyptian Judicial System]. 2 vols. Dar al-Shuruq, 2010.

Salt, Henry. *A Geometrical Survey of the City of Alexandria*. William Miller, 1806. Bibliothèque nationale de France. https://gallica.bnf.fr/ark:/12148/btv1b10101094s.

Sami, Amin. *Taqwim al-Nil*. 3 vols. Matbaʿat Dar al-Kutub wal-Watha'iq al-Qawmiyya, 2003.

Schoen, Brian. *The Fragile Fabric of Union: Cotton, Federal Politics, and the Global Origins of the Civil War*. Johns Hopkins University Press, 2009.

Schölch, Alexander. "Constitutional Development in Nineteenth Century Egypt: A Reconsideration." *Middle Eastern Studies* 10, no. 1 (1974): 3–14.

Schölch, Alexander. "European Penetration and the Economic Development of Palestine, 1856–82." In *Studies in the Economic and Social History of Palestine in the Nineteenth and Twentieth Centuries*, edited by Roger Owen. The Macmillan Press, 1982.

Schull, Kent F. *Prisons in the Late Ottoman Empire: Microcosms of Modernity*. Edinburgh University Press, 2014.

Schwartz, Kathryn A. "Meaningful Mediums: A Material and Intellectual History of Manuscript and Print Production in Nineteenth-Century Ottoman Cairo." PhD diss., Harvard University, 2015. ProQuest (10591599).

Schwartz, Kathryn A. "The Political Economy of Private Printing in Cairo as Told from a Commissioning Deal Turned Sour, 1871." *International Journal of Middle East Studies* 49, no. 1 (2017): 25–45.

Sedgwick, Mark. *Muhammad Abduh.* Oneworld, 2009.

Semerdjian, Elyse. *"Off the Straight Path": Illicit Sex, Law, and Community in Ottoman Aleppo.* Syracuse University Press, 2008.

Sewell, Jr., William H. "A Strange Career: The Historical Study of Economic Life." *History and Theory* 49, no. 4 (2010): 146–66.

Al-Shalaqani, 'Amr. *Izdihar wa-Inhiyar al-Nukhba al-Qanuniyya al-Misriyya, 1805–2005* [The Rise and Fall of the Egyptian Legal Elite, 1805–2005]. Dar al-Shuruq, 2013.

Sharp & Alleman's Lawyers and Bankers Directory for 1901. John R. McFetridge & Sons, 1901.

Shaw, Stanford Jay. *The Financial and Administrative Organization and Development of Ottoman Egypt, 1517–1798.* Princeton University Press, 1958.

Sonbol, Amira El-Azhary. *The New Mamluks: Egyptian Society and Modern Feudalism.* Syracuse University Press, 2000.

Statistica generale del regno d'Italia. *Censimento degli italiani all'estero, 31 Dicembre 1871.* Rome: Stamperia Reale, 1874.

Subhi, Muhammad Khalil. *Tarikh al-Haya al-Niyabiyya fi Misr* [History of Parliamentary Life in Egypt]. Vol. 5. Matba'at Dar al-Kutub al-Misriyya, 1939.

Todd, David. "Beneath Sovereignty: Extraterritoriality and Imperial Internationalism in Nineteenth-Century Egypt." *Law and History Review* 36, no. 1 (2018): 105–37.

Toledano, Ehud. "Mehmet Ali Pasa or Muhammad Ali Basha? An Historiographic Appraisal in the Wake of a Recent Book." *Middle Eastern Studies* 21, no. 4 (1985): 141–59.

Toledano, Ehud R. *State and Society in Mid-Nineteenth-Century Egypt.* Cambridge University Press, 1990.

Transactions of the Supreme Council 33d for the Southern Jurisdiction of the United States of America. House of the Temple, October 1903.

Troutt Powell, Eve M. *A Different Shade of Colonialism: Egypt, Great Britain, and the Mastery of the Sudan.* University of California Press, 2003.

Al-Tukhi, Nabil al-Sayyid. *Tawa'if al-Hiraf fi-Madinat al-Qahira fil-Nisf al-Thani min al-Qarn al-Tasi' 'Ashar* [The Trade Guilds in Cairo During the Second Half of the Nineteenth Century]. Al-Hay'a al-Misriyya al-'Amma lil-Kitab, 2009.

'Urabi, Ahmad. *Mudhakkirat al-Za'im Ahmad 'Urabi* [The Memoirs of Ahmad 'Urabi], edited by 'Abd-al-Mun'im Ibrahim al-Jumay'i. Vol. 3. Matba'at Dar al-Kutub wal-Watha'iq al-Qawmiyya, 2005.

Vitalis, Robert. *When Capitalists Collide: Business Conflict and the End of Empire in Egypt.* University of California Press, 1995.

Vlami, Despina. *Trading with the Ottomans: The Levant Company in the Middle East.* I.B. Tauris, 2015.

Walz, Terence. "Asyut in the 1260's (1844–53)." *Journal of the American Research Center in Egypt* 15 (1978): 113–26.

Walz, Terence. *Trade Between Egypt and Bilad as-Sudan, 1700–1820.* Institut français d'archéologie orientale du Caire, 1978.

Walz, Terence. "Family Archives in Egypt: New Light on Nineteenth-Century Provincial Trade." In *L'Egypte au XIXe siècle.* Editions du Centre National de la Recherche Scientifique, 1982.

Walz, Terence. "Libya, the Trans-Saharan Trade of Egypt, and 'Abdallah al-Kahhal, 1880–1914." *Islamic Africa* 1, no. 1 (2010): 85–107.

Walz, Terence. "Sudanese, Habasha, Takarna, and Barabira: Trans-Saharan Africans in Cairo as Shown in the 1848 Census." In *Race and Slavery in the Middle East: Histories of Trans-Saharan Africans in Nineteenth-Century Egypt, Sudan, and the Ottoman Mediterranean*, edited by Terence Walz and Kenneth M. Cuno. American University in Cairo Press, 2010.

Wansbrough, J., Halil İnalcık, A.K.S. Lambton, and G. Baer. "Imtiyazat." In *Encyclopaedia of Islam New Edition Online (EI-2 English)*, edited by P.J. Bearman. Brill, 2012. doi: https://doi.org/10.1163/1573-3912_islam_COM_0371.

Zaghlul, Ahmad Fathi. *Al-Muhamah* [The Legal Profession]. Matba'at al-Ma'arif, 1900.

Zaghlul, Sa'd. *Mudhakkirat Sa'd Zaghlul* [The Memoirs of Sa'd Zaghlul], edited by 'Abd-al-'Azim Ramadan. Al-Hay'a al-Misriyya al-'Amma lil-Kitab, 1987.

Zakhura, Ilyas. *Kitab Mir'at al-'Asr fi Tarikh wa Rusum Akabir al-Rijal bi-Misr* [The Mirror of the Times]. Vol. 2. Matba'at Ilyas Zakhura, 1916.

Zaydan, Jurji. *Kitab Tarikh Adab al-Lugha al-'Arabiyya* [The History of Arabic Literature]. Vol. 4. Matba'at al-Hilal, 1914.

Zayn al-Din, Isma'il Muhammad. *Al-Zira'a al-Misriyya fi 'Ahd al-Ihtilal al-Britani, 1882–1914* [Egyptian Agriculture Under the British Occupation]. Al-Hay'a al-Misriyya al-'Amma lil-Kitab, 1995.

Ze'evi, Dror. "The Use of Ottoman Shari'a Court Records as a Source for Middle Eastern Social History: A Reappraisal." *Islamic Law and Society* 5, no. 1 (1998): 35–56.

Ziadeh, Farhat J. *Lawyers, the Rule of Law and Liberalism in Modern Egypt.* Hoover Institution Publications, 1968.

Index

Page numbers with an *f* refer to a figure or a caption; an *n* indicates a note.

www.ingramcontent.com/pod-product-compliance
Lightning Source LLC
Jackson TN
JSHW020946060825
88512JS00002B/4
9781503643390